CORNELL STUDIES IN CLASSICAL PHILOLOGY

EDITED BY

FREDERICK M. AHL * KEVIN C. CLINTON
JOHN E. COLEMAN * GREGSON DAVIS
JUDITH R. GINSBURG * G. M. KIRKWOOD
GORDON M. MESSING * PHILIP MITSIS
ALAN NUSSBAUM * PIETRO PUCCI
JEFFREY S. RUSTEN * DANUTA SHANZER
WINTHROP WETHERBEE

VOLUME XXXI

A Study of Sophoclean Drama

By G. M. KIRKWOOD

D1087761

A Study of Sophoclean Drama

With a New Preface and Enlarged
Bibliographical Note

G. M. KIRKWOOD

Cornell University Press

ITHACA AND LONDON

THE PENNSYLVANIA STATE UNIVERSITY
COMMONWEALTH CAMPUS LIBRARIES
DELAWARE COUNTY

Copyright © 1958 by Cornell University

Preface and Bibliographical Note to Paperback Edition copyright
© 1994 by Cornell University

All rights reserved. Except for brief quotations in a review, this book,
or parts thereof, must not be reproduced in any form without
permission in writing from the publisher. For information address
Cornell University Press, Sage House, 512 East State Street, Ithaca,
New York 14850.

First published 1958 by Cornell University Press.
First printing, Cornell Paperbacks, 1994.
Second printing 1996.

Printed in the United States of America

♾ The paper in this book meets the minimum requirements of the
American National Standard for Information Sciences—Permanence of
Paper for Printed Library Materials, ANSI Z39.48-1984.

Library of Congress Cataloging-in-Publication Data

Kirkwood, Gordon MacDonald, 1916–
    A Study of Sophoclean drama : with a new preface and enlarged
bibliographical note / G.M. Kirkwood.
        p.   cm.—(Cornell studies in classical philology ; v. 31)
    Includes bibliographical references (p.) and index.
    ISBN 0-8014-8241-0 (pbk.)
    1. Sophocles—Criticism and interpretation. 2. Mythology, Greek,
in literature. 3. Tragedy. I. Title. II. Series.
PA4417.K48   1994
882'.01—dc20
                                                    94-22808

To PATRICIA

Contents

Stasimon Two—*Antigone* Stasimon Two—Evidence of separate passages inconclusive—Deity in *Oedipus at Colonus* and *Philoctetes*—In *Electra*—In *Ajax* and *Antigone*—In *Oedipus Tyrannus*—In *The Trachinian Women*—Deity allied with moral rectitude, but impersonal and remote—Individual deities chosen for dramatic propriety—Impersonal fate in Sophocles—The *daimon* in Sophocles as source of irony of situation—Suffering and tragedy in Sophocles.

Preface to the
Paperback Edition

SOPHOCLEAN criticism, like criticism of Greek tragedy generally, has since 1958, when this book was published, taken new directions. Two factors have had an especially strong influence: increased attention to the social and religious history of fifth-century Athens and the impact of structuralist and post-structuralist criticism. Because this book is virtually unchanged in contents from the original edition (with the exception of this new preface and a brief account of recent publications added to the Bibliographical Note), it stands apart from more recent writing on Sophocles. But perhaps it is useful to reintroduce a critical approach that concentrates on aspects of the poet's own dramatic art.

Two parts of Chapter 1 may no longer seem relevant to the understanding of the plays. The first is the review of earlier studies of Sophocles' dramatic art. Most of these works have been largely forgotten, whatever their merits were, though the influence of Tycho Wilamowitz, reinforced by John Jones's *Aristotle and Greek Tragedy*, flourishes and deserves respect. (The place of Jones's book in Sophoclean criticism is briefly assessed in the Bibliographical Note.)

The second part concerns issues that were of immediate concern in 1958 and need some clarification here: that is, my comments about the element of ritual in relation to Sophoclean criticism. My rejection of Gilbert Murray's theory that the adventures of Jane Harrison's *eniautos daimon* were the core, the *Urform*, of tragedy was timely in 1958, when that theory was still influential. Few critics now would quarrel with the position I took. But of course my view as expressed then, which I still hold, goes beyond the rejection of that specific theory and maintains that the poet's own, conscious dramaturgical art is the primary and controlling force in the form and meaning of his plays. Nevertheless, I recognize the importance of recent scholarly work concerning the significant presence of ritual elements in the plays of Sophocles. For example, Walter Burkert's observations in "Opferritual bei Sophokles," *Der Altsprachliches Unterricht*, 28 (1985), 5–20, on the dramatic relevance of rituals in three plays of Sophocles have clear interpretative value. The analogy he draws between the famous offering to the Eumenides, *Oedipus at Colonus* 461–509, and the ultimate joining of Oedipus to the earth of Colonus enriches our understanding of the play and brings us closer to the impact of its enactment in 401 B.C. Though I recognize the value of such observations, I continue to have reservations about more inclusive claims of ritual dominance, such as the categorizing of *Oedipus Tyrannus* as an embodiment of a scapegoat ritual and the interpretation of the part of Neoptolemus in *Philoctetes* as representing the Athenian ephebic initiation experience. I continue to believe that Sophocles' creative genius is paramount; even where ritual elements are present, the respects in which the dramatic whole differs from them are very important. Observation of ritual elements is valuable, but these elements by no means explain the plays in which they are observed. (Some references and comments pertaining to this aspect of recent criticism are made in the Bibliographical Note.)

Although it is necessary, when discussing our only substantial evidence for ancient critical attitudes toward tragedy, namely, Aristotle's *Poetics*, to keep in mind Aristotle's insistence on the priority of *muthos*, it does not follow that study of dramatic characterization is anachronistic. Character subserves action, but it is a very important part of action, and Aristotle recognizes its role in his analysis, in Chapter 6 of the *Poetics*, of the constituent elements of tragedy. The Bibliographical Note contains some comments on this aspect of Sophoclean criticism, especially in relation to John Jones's influential book.

Some critics have disliked my use of the term *diptych* to describe three of the plays. I sympathize with their point of view; categorization by the introduction of technical terms seldom clarifies anything. Nevertheless, three of the plays share a double focus that separates them structurally from the four others, and the word *diptych*, already in use in the criticism of Greek tragedy, provides a brief way of indicating this difference. But I do not ascribe to the word any intrinsic technical value.

Determination of what is relevant and important in the criticism of Greek tragedy is bound to be matter for disagreement. At its initial appearance this book was judged favorably by most reviewers, and I can only hope that what it offers is still useful. I think I can fairly claim that the observations made in it have sufficient grounding in the plays themselves to merit attention.

To the colleagues whose help is acknowledged in the original preface I add Phillip Mitsis for his advice and encouragement during the preparation of this edition.

G. M. K.

Ithaca, New York

Preface

THE reader will find in Chapter I a description of the organization and purpose of this book. Here I need only say a few words of explanation and discharge the pleasant and important duty of acknowledging help.

The book is mainly a philological study of certain aspects of Sophocles' plays and is meant for the attention of those who are themselves engaged in the study of the plays. But since, apart from the chapter on diction, I have usually given quotations in translation, the book should be usable by those who read Sophocles in translation only. My line references and quotations follow the Oxford Classical Text of A. C. Pearson.

This study has taken shape over the course of many years, and it would be impossible to acknowledge the help of all those who have had a share in it—teachers, colleagues, students, and authors. I must restrict myself to my most obvious debts. Some basic parts of the book, now mainly incorporated in Chapter III, formed a doctoral dissertation written at Johns Hopkins University under the scholarly and sympathetic guidance of Professor Harold Cherniss. Professor H. D. F. Kitto kindly read part of my manuscript and discussed with me many things about Sophocles, to my great benefit, during his stay at Cornell as visiting professor in the spring term of 1954. The anonymous reader for the Cornell University Press made numerous valuable criticisms. The co-operation and expert advice of the Cornell University Press staff must not go unmentioned. My three colleagues in Classics at Cornell and fellow editors of this series, Professors Harry Caplan, James Hutton, and Friedrich Solmsen, have helped me at every stage; to their learning and good judgment I owe more than I can say, both for the suggestion of ideas and for the correction of many mistakes. The book is dedicated to my wife not only as a mark of affection but as a recognition of devoted and invaluable assistance.

G. M. KIRKWOOD

Ithaca, New York
April 3, 1958

CHAPTER I

Introduction

i. A Statement of Purpose

THIS book is primarily an examination of Sophocles' methods of procedure in dramatic composition, written with a view to determining as accurately as possible how his plays are constructed and why they are constructed as they are. The point is not so much to present a new or a complete interpretation of Sophoclean tragedy or of the individual plays as to observe and, if possible, to explain such matters as the portrayal of character, the place of the chorus, and the different kinds of organization that are found in the several plays.

Structure and technique in Sophocles' plays have, of course, been talked about and admired very often. Sophocles has been the acknowledged craftsman of the theater from Aristotle on; everybody knows him as the skilled portrayer of character, the dramatist of striking contrasts, the master of construction. A book largely devoted to just these matters may seem open to criticism for laboring the obvious. But it is quite apparent that the venerable tradition of Sophocles' mastery of dramatic form is accepted with casual and superficial deference rather than fully and clearly understood. That is why disagreements of the most crucial sort continue to flourish in the interpretation of all seven extant plays of this master of form—disagreements that arise from the very matters of structure that ought to be most clear, if only the understanding of Sophoclean form were as firm as the tradition of its perfectness is long. In one play after another these problems of structure appear: in *Ajax* critics differ as to the connection of the part of the play after Ajax's death to the part before; in *Antigone* the dramatic relationship between Antigone and Creon is variously explained, and so is that between Deianeira and Heracles in *The Trachinian Women;* indeed the whole ending of *The Trachinian Women* with its strange and violent picture of Heracles remains, to judge by the almost equally violent disagreement of interpreters, a provocative riddle; the epiphany of Heracles at the end of *Philoctetes* and the sudden *volte-face* of Philoctetes raise thorough critical discord; the question of unity or lack of unity of themes in *Oedipus at Colonus* is quite unsettled. All these problems (and there are more like them) are to a large degree problems of structure. Does an examination of Sophoclean dramatic structure need any more justification?

The truth is that while these aspects of Sophoclean dramaturgy have indeed been mentioned in many books about Sophocles they are usually mentioned in passing, and they are all too often disregarded in the interpretation of the plays. Perhaps the very fact that Sophocles' perfection of form has been so readily acknowledged has deterred critics from exploring that mastery as thoroughly as it deserves. The plot of *Oedipus Tyrannus,* for example, is developed, we all know, "in accordance with probability or necessity," but the play does not have its extraordinary effectiveness of form only, or principally, because it exemplifies the Aristotelian dictum. Far more significant than Sophocles' ability to impart to a dramatic action a measure of naturalness and logic is his remarkable power—of which *Oedipus Tyrannus* is a prime example—of maintaining a unique and excellent kind of dramatic vitality throughout the play. Only when we inquire into the means by which Sophocles invests his plays with their constant air not only of relevance but of immediacy do we begin to understand Sophoclean form. The present study has been made in the conviction that for a better understanding of Sophocles' plays there must be a fuller comprehension of how they are built.

Most books on Sophocles are designed to interpret the meaning of the plays rather than to analyze their composition. Of the numerous major works on Sophoclean drama since 1900, only five that I know of have been devoted to dramatic method, and all five have been tendentious or special in their approach; we shall presently return to these books. The great majority of critics are primarily in search of the philosophical, moral, or religious meaning of Sophoclean tragedy, and such criticism is certainly valuable, provided it is done with philological soundness and literary taste. But books of this sort are necessarily subjective, for a critic must interpret, basically, in the light of his own understanding of the wide questions he is discussing, and he therefore tends to range rather far from the playwright's pages, or to concentrate on certain pages at the expense of others. And so there is need, too, for criticism that recalls attention to the *ipsissima verba* and keeps in view the whole text, not what someone may decide to be the essence of the text. If it does no more than provide a means whereby the student of Sophocles can more readily discriminate between admissible and inadmissible interpretation, such a book will have served its purpose. Although interpretation is not shunned in the present study, nor is complete objectivity sought (to be altogether objective in literary criticism is probably impossible and almost certainly undesirable), my first purpose is to offer a basis for the interpretation of Sophocles.

But perhaps it is a mirage, this picture of a "dramatic technique" that will account for the excellence and the special nature of a playwright's work? There is some point to this suspicion. It is folly to attempt to reduce the tragic drama of

Sophocles to a set of procedures, and it was no doubt in a spirit of impatience with such mechanical criticism of drama that G. B. Shaw, with typical unrestraint, made the spirited comment that "there is not a pennyworth of difference between the methods of Sophocles or Shakespeare and those of the maker of the most ephemeral farce." Let these words of Shaw stand as a reminder, which I shall try to heed, that rigorous categorization and reliance on mechanical analysis are the course of unwisdom in criticism. But Shaw's comment is not the whole truth; and in the same short article [1]—typically again—he himself refutes it. He tells us that when a play was taking shape in his mind the first components of it were persons in conversation, at first only vaguely existing but gradually assuming more definite and individual form. Shaw's way of beginning was, then, with the characters. This is not the only way. Ibsen is said to have made a practice of beginning a dramatic composition by writing a short lyric poem embodying the essence of what he would state more expansively in the finished drama. Shaw began with characters, Ibsen with a lyrically conceived essential thought; here is a very real difference in dramatic method. We have no firsthand access to the mental procedures of the ancient dramatists; perhaps Sophocles set his down in his work *On the Chorus,* but that precious document has, if not entirely, then almost entirely perished. A well-known sentence preserved in Plutarch's *De profectibus in virtute,* in which Sophocles describes three stages of his dramatic art, may possibly be from it; in any case, the sentence is a proof that Sophocles had evolved something that could reasonably be called a dramatic technique that he regarded as peculiarly his own, one that was "the most expressive of character and the best." [2]

[1] The article is in Barrett H. Clark, *European Theories of the Drama* (New York, 1947), 475.

[2] *Moralia* 79 B. The statement refers to dramatic style, not only to dic-

There have not been wanting critics of Sophoclean drama to take Shaw's position; in fact, the attitude of two of the five works on dramatic method that were alluded to above is very much like Shaw's. Forty years ago Tycho Wilamowitz declared, in his *Die Dramatische Technik des Sophokles* (1917), that it is wasted time to search for unity of plot or consistency of characterization in Sophoclean drama, for Sophocles neither cared nor knew about such unity; his whole aim was to render each scene individually as moving and as stageworthy as possible. His book came at a point when some critics had pressed too far in the psychological interpretation of Sophoclean characters and was therefore timely; but it had the unfortunate result, in Germany especially, of inducing critics to close their eyes to what is obvious to any unprejudiced mind, the infinite care that Sophocles uses in the depiction of character, above all in his management of character relationships. Writing a decade later and in sharp disagreement with Wilamowitz's approach, Wolfgang Schadewaldt nevertheless considered it necessary to limit his assessment of Sophoclean characterization by refusing to see, for example, that the sententiousness of Creon, in *Antigone*, is an indication of his character.[3] (And yet it remains a fact that, to a marked degree, Creon does speak in maxims, while Antigone just as markedly keeps to simplicity of speech. Are we to suppose that this is accidental? "Sophocles did not allow accidents," H. D. F. Kitto warns; he is speaking of the meters,[4] but the warning applies to every aspect of the art of this subtle and careful artist.) Other writers were more deeply influenced by the attitude of Tycho Wilamowitz; and

tion. The context in Plutarch is decisive on this point. For a discussion of the passage see C. M. Bowra, "Sophocles on His Own Development," *AJP*, 61 (1940), 385–401, reprinted as Chapter VII of *Problems in Greek Poetry* (Oxford, 1953).

[3] "Sophokles, Aias und Antigone," *Neue Wege zur Antike*, 8 (1929), 65.

[4] "Sophocles, Statistics, and the *Trachiniae*," *AJP*, 60 (1939), 179.

even Karl Reinhardt's masterly *Sophokles*, though perhaps not directly influenced by Wilamowitz, is marred, as a comprehensive study of Sophoclean drama, by inadequate attention to the portrayal of character.

Wilamowitz's excesses no longer exercise an influence, but he has had a successor. In a lively and readable book that is thoroughly iconoclastic, takes to task virtually every critic of Sophocles since Wilamowitz, and yet is free of malice or heat, A. J. A. Waldock, in *Sophocles the Dramatist* (1951), reasserted, in his own way, the thesis that elaborate study of Sophoclean structure and painful search for the poet's moral and theological message are out of order: Sophocles was writing *plays*, and that is that. We shall have occasion to come back to Waldock's book, but one general instance of its approach may be worth mentioning here. In his chapter on *Philoctetes* Waldock writes throughout as if the play were virtually an extempore invention. We can almost imagine, as we read Waldock's account, Sophocles backstage during the first episode frantically scribbling down Episode Two; there is no premeditated purpose, no architectonic control. Such an interpretation of Sophocles' art runs counter to the plain evidence of the play. It is impossible to read *Philoctetes* through and accept Waldock's helter-skelter account of it; the very balance—not to go into details at this point—that is maintained, and used, among the three leading characters is proof enough of Sophocles' purposefulness and thoroughness in planning the structure of his play. Waldock's book, like that of Wilamowitz, has served a useful purpose in disposing of a good deal of wrong criticism, but its failure to offer anything tenable in place of the rejected critical attitudes makes it inadequate as an account of Sophoclean dramatic method.

Of the other books devoted primarily to dramatic technique, two are works of the first years of the present century. W. Dopheide's *De Arte Sophoclis Dramatica* (1910) is a precursor of Wilamowitz's longer and more influential work and suffers from the same defects. F. Allègre's *Sophocle, étude sur les ressorts dramatiques de son théâtre et la composition de ses tragédies* (1905) has many incidental comments of value but is afflicted by a strange basic idea. Allègre believes that two conflicting motive forces lie behind Sophoclean dramatic action—the power of fate (or whatever we call the forces lying beyond human control) and the power of human character—and that a good deal of the composition of a Sophoclean drama is aimed at alleviating or masking this basic conflict. Sophoclean studies since Allègre's book have shown, I think conclusively, that these two motive forces need by no means be in irreconcilable conflict as constituents of a dramatic action; in fact, there are excellent grounds for believing that Sophocles, far from being embarrassed by the presence of the two, deliberately and successfully exploited them together as underlying causes of the action of his plays. Allègre insists also that the plays regularly have an ending enforced by fate in direct opposition to the ending which the characters would naturally produce. Some scholars would agree with this judgment in the case of *Philoctetes,* but no one would now be willing to call this discrepancy a regular feature of Sophoclean drama. The fifth study is C. R. Post's essay, "The Dramatic Art of Sophocles" (*Harvard Studies in Classical Philology,* 1912). It is Post's idea that a Sophoclean drama consists essentially of a series of tests of the central figure; out of each test the hero emerges newly revealed with added strength. This is a fruitful approach to Sophoclean drama, though Post magnifies somewhat unduly the place of such incidents in the structure of each play and does not take any serious account of other aspects of structure—the place of the chorus, for example. The essay may be described as a useful study but too specialized to justify its title.

We cannot pretend that the five studies have been seriously reviewed in these brief remarks; all of them certainly have values for the understanding of Sophocles that are not fairly accounted for in a cursory description. But they have been fairly characterized with regard to their general approach to Sophoclean dramatic method: three are tendentious, one is limited in scope, the fifth is iconoclastic beyond acceptability. The present study owes something to most of them, but it ought to be able, profiting by their shortcomings, to present a more balanced and inclusive description of the subject. It need hardly be added that many other books on Sophocles have been very helpful; most of my specific debts will be mentioned where they occur, but a few words concerning some of the books which have been drawn on most heavily are in order here.

T. B. L. Webster's *Introduction to Sophocles* (1936) is the work that the present study most resembles in form, and though I differ *toto caelo* from Webster on many points of interpretation I have found valuable help in his book on many aspects of Sophoclean drama, especially in matters of structure and characterization. The present study does not attempt so wide a range as Webster's essays, which deal with many subjects, some of which lie outside or on the periphery of dramatic method. Reinhardt's *Sophokles* (1933; 3rd ed. 1947) is particularly illuminating on the structure of the plays, and on structure there are also valuable comments in Sir Maurice Bowra's *Sophoclean Tragedy* (1944). For the characters Heinrich Weinstock's *Sophokles* (1931), Kitto's *Greek Tragedy* (1939; 2nd ed. 1950), and Gennaro Perrotta's *Sofocle* (1935) are especially helpful. J. C. Opstelten's *Sophocles and Greek Pessimism* (1952) and Cedric Whitman's *Sophocles* (1951) both contain ideas that I have found valuable, though I cannot subscribe to the basic outlook of either book.

The form of this book is determined by its aim. It would have been more conventional and more attractive to combine all that is said about each play in a single chapter. And if our first aim were to study in full the meaning of each play, this would also be the most useful method of arrangement. But for the purpose of examining aspects of Sophocles' dramatic method, it seems better to put examples drawn from all the plays together in each chapter. To proceed by individual plays would mean either abandoning the advantage of close comparison or indulging in much repetition.

ii. A Preliminary Definition

Since "drama" and "tragedy" are words that will be used often in the following chapters, it seems only fair to give the reader some preliminary notion of what these elastic terms will mean in this study. Defining tragedy and drama in the absolute is a pleasant but frustrating game. A generous sampling of such definitions can be found in Barrett H. Clark's *European Theories of the Drama*, a perusal of which is likely to suggest that what critics have spent so much labor to define is not a definable literary genre, but a matter of effect: "tragedy" is what a great playwright can make us feel, in a serious play, about human character and its destiny, about deity or fate, and about the circumstances in which man lives. Each playwright's type of "tragedy," in this meaning of the word, is likely to be unique; and even within the work of a single dramatist more than one kind of tragic effect is often found; Euripides' *Medea* and *The Trojan Women*, for example, are different in kind, and so are Shakespeare's *Hamlet* and *Antony and Cleopatra*, and Ibsen's *Brand* and *A Doll's House*. Strict definition of the effect of tragedy is impossible, except in statements so broad as to be critically useless. To define the dramatic form which achieves tragic effect is at least difficult. Even so modest and general a statement as Ashley Thorndike's, that a typical tragedy is concerned with "a great personality engaged in a struggle that ends disastrously," [5] though it describes succinctly some aspects of Sophoclean tragedy, where great personality and struggle are

[5] *Tragedy* (Boston and New York, 1908), 9.

always present, is nevertheless not fully adequate for Sophocles in view of his last two plays, if no others. Indeed, can we assert beyond fear of contradiction that any play of Sophocles really ends in disaster?

To the ancient Greeks, δρᾶμα, as applied to the theater, had no more significance than our word "play," [6] and tragedy meant a drama other than comedy and satyr play. The *Oresteia* is tragedy, *Philoctetes* is tragedy, though probably neither, and certainly not the latter, would be called tragedy if written to-day. There is no descriptive definition of Greek tragedy that will embrace all members of the species and satisfy all critics other than the statement that a tragedy is a serious play; even here some difficulty may be felt concerning *Helen* and one or two other plays of Euripides. Even when we restrict our definition to Sophocles we must be cautious; perhaps, using Thorn-dike's definition as a guide, we might say that a Sophoclean tragedy is a serious play in which a person of strong and noble character is confronted with a crucial situation and responds to it in his special way. Can we add anything to make this statement more specific? "Suffering is the essence of Greek tragedy," says Weinstock.[7] The assertion is doubtful, but suffering is one constant and essential element of all our Sophoclean plays; and it can therefore be properly said that the "crucial situation" must involve suffering on the part of the principal character. If we add that Sophoclean drama is concerned with moral and, sometimes, religious problems, we have specified as much as we safely can.

As a definition, that is still vague; most of its terms need, and will in the course of this study receive, clarification. But it is more meaningful and useful than at first glance may appear, because it eliminates or subordinates certain conceptions about the nature of Sophoclean tragedy that are not essential: that it has to do primarily with the all-controlling power of

[6] Cf., e.g., Aristophanes *Frogs* 920.   [7] *Sophokles*, 227.

fate; that it demonstrates the power of deity over against the weakness of man or the knowledge of deity over against the ignorance of man; that it is character tragedy; that it shows punishment for moral delinquencies. All these themes are important with Sophocles—fate, divine power and knowledge, human character and its ignorance and shortcomings, as well as its wisdom and magnificence. But the mainspring is none of these; at the heart of every play of Sophocles there lies the life-giving combination of strong character and revealing situation. We are not here attempting to outline the meaning or the purpose of Sophoclean tragedy, or Sophocles' view of life, but rather the special dramatic form through which he achieves his purpose and reveals his view.

We have left out one consideration which has begun to loom large in contemporary criticism of Greek tragedy, the element of ritual. Everyone knows that the performance of Greek tragedy in the fifth century B.C. was part of a religious ritual in honor of Dionysus and that the plots of Greek tragedy are nearly all drawn from myth. To some literary critics of our time the proximity of myth and ritual to a literary form constitutes an irresistible lure; it has even been maintained that all literary forms can be derived from patterns of myth and ritual. In view of the recent trend among mythologists to find the origin of all myth—or nearly all—in ritual, the temptation to ally ritual myth to the form of Greek tragedy, where we have in the background not only myth but an undeniable context of ritual, becomes powerful. Can this background be usefully exploited in the criticism of Greek tragedy?

That the element of ritual had an effect on the reception of Greek tragedy by its original audience is certain. The atmosphere of a religious celebration, however attenuated or secularized the actual worship has become, is different from that of an evening of theater, and more intense and personal. The very fact that it was a communal affair in which audience

as well as playwright and actors participated removes the ancient
Greek theater to a special realm.[8] But what about the plays
themselves? Can we say that by their very nature they form a
significant ritual entity? It may be that in the act of composition and in the act of performance playwright and actors were
affected by the religious circumstances of the performance, but
this is not the kind of influence that can be used in criticism.
What is needed is evidence of the influence of ritual upon the
form of the drama, and it is this kind of influence that has been
stressed by critics who wish to make ritual a meaningful factor
in the criticism of Greek drama. Is there such evidence?

We must carefully distinguish between a ritual origin, which
no one would deny to Greek tragedy or to some of its plots,
and ritual qualities in the actual plays. Ritual origin is a matter
of cultural and literary history, with only a general and critically intangible effect on any one concrete play; ritual elements,
if they exist in substantial form, come within the province of
the critic in his estimate of an individual play. A recent critic
states that "the Cambridge School of Classical Anthropology
has shown in great detail that the form of Greek tragedy follows
the form of a very ancient ritual" [9]—that of the *eniautos-daimon*,
Jane Harrison's seasonal god. We need to distinguish between
the theories of the anthropologists and the evidence of the

[8] Opstelten, *Pessimism*, goes at least as far as one can safely go in describing the effect of ritual on the play's reception. In discussing *OT* he
has the following: "We should never forget that it was a play staged in
honour of Dionysus. . . . While experiencing an inescapable tragic
feeling with his eyes and ears, [the spectator] at the same time shared,
as the highest climax in the interesting communion of poet, players, and
the public, . . . the paradoxical and tremendous experience of the
Absolute, by the power of which all sensations of littleness and greatness,
of death and resurrection, were inextricably combined into one mighty
emotion which filled him with a magical transcendence" (p. 63).

[9] Francis Fergusson, *The Idea of a Theater* (Princeton, 1949), 26. All
my further quotations from Fergusson are from the chapter in this book
on *OT*.

plays; there is no better aid for this distinction than the searching criticism of the anthropologists' theories in A. W. Pickard-
Cambridge's *Dithyramb, Tragedy and Comedy*, where the
author makes abundantly clear that the gap between theory
and evidence is deplorably broad. Gilbert Murray has elabo-
rated, on the basis of anthropological theory, an archetype of
tragedy in which the six steps of the ritual of the *eniautos-
daimon* exist in proper order; but both the ritual and the daimon
are hypothetical, and, above all, Murray's attempt to relate
his fictitious archetype to extant plays is a complete and obvious
failure. There is no evidence that allows us to suppose that
Greek playwrights were consciously or unconsciously adhering
to a ritual pattern in the construction, or the spirit, of their
plays. They adhered, of course, to the general form of the
myths they dramatized; but even supposing that we could assert
that all these myths originated in rites, there is no reason to believe that the myths, with one or two possible exceptions, were
concerned with the adventures of a year spirit.[10]

[10] Thirty years or so ago, when the influence of Frazer's *The Golden
Bough* was at its zenith, it was usual to ascribe the origin of nearly all
religious rituals to the worship of year spirits. Since then the situation
among anthropologists and comparative religionists has changed; the
influence of Arnold van Gennep's *Les rites de passage* (Paris, 1909) and
of later similar theories has outstripped the Frazerian view, and it is now
fashionable to ascribe the origin of nearly all religious rituals to initiation ceremonies. Even the worship of such a favorite *eniautos-daimon* as
Dionysus has recently been declared to contain substantial elements of
initiation ceremonies. (Cf. H. Jeanmaire, *Dionysus* [Paris, 1951]). In a
general survey of the present state of research in Greek mythology
Fernand Chapouthier ("De l'avenir des études sur la mythologie
grecque," *Actes du Premier Congrès de la Fédération Internationale des
Associations d'Etudes Classiques* [Paris, 1951], 259–267) observes that
the interpretation of myth has in the course of the past century made its
way from heaven (the solar mythology of Max Müller) to earth (the
year spirits and earth mothers), and now to what lies between—man
(initiation rites). The notion that ritual underlies myth has also been
questioned, and excellent evidence has been produced to show that

This kind of ritual influence we must discard as critically unusable. No doubt it is valuable to have a background of knowledge about the origin—the possible origin—of Greek tragedy, but that is all. It will not help in the least to call the Teiresias scene of *Oedipus Tyrannus* an *agon;* we have not the slightest grounds for supposing that it was such in any ritual way.

There is further reason for caution in assessing the importance of ritual in the performance of Greek tragedy. One of the basic elements of ritual is repetition; a ritual formula is sacred and moving precisely because it is unchangeable, because every word, every gesture, has to be just so; performer and audience alike are keenly conscious in advance of every detail that must come. Even assuming what we have no right to' suppose, that every Greek tragedy is a repetition of one "Ur-myth," the effect of the repetition would not be the effect of ritual, because the story is told so differently each time. We must therefore disagree with Fergusson when he says of Greek tragedy that "the element which distinguishes this theater, giving it its unique directness and depth, is the *ritual expectancy.* . . . The nearest thing we have to this ritual sense of theater . . . [is] an Easter performance of the *Mattias Passion.*" It need hardly be pointed out that the ritual element, that which permits "ritual

---

either myth or ritual may give rise to the other, or either may develop and flourish without the other. (Cf. Clyde Kluckhohn, "Myths and Rituals: A General Theory," *HTR*, 35 [1942], 45–79.)

It follows that in making assumptions about the nature of myth and ritual literary critics would do well to proceed with extreme caution and to be wary about accepting any theory as the final and incontrovertible word. In the case of Greek tragedy the ritual origin and nature of the occasion of performance, the Dionysia, are not open to doubt. (For the ancient evidence, see Pickard-Cambridge, *Dithyramb, Tragedy and Comedy, passim.*) But the connection between these matters and the origin and nature of the form of individual dramas and their myths is wholly uncertain. For Murray's theory, see Jane Harrison, *Themis* (Cambridge, 1912), Ch. viii, Appendix.

expectancy" in an Easter performance of the *Mattias Passion*, lies in the fact that it is a performance of the same religious work at the same festival time and again; if Greek tragedy consisted of an annual performance, at the Dionysia, of Euripides' *Bacchae*, this analogy of Fergusson's would hold good.[11] But Greek tragic performances consisted of the presentation of a large number of very different plays at the Dionysia. All we can salvage of ritual in Greek tragedy is (*a*) that the occasion of performance was a ritual, which made its mark on the atmosphere of the performance, and (*b*) that, probably, some of the myths dramatized were ultimately of ritual origin; but of the nature and meaning of the original rites we know virtually nothing—not even what aspects of life the rites were concerned with.

I have labored this point for two reasons: first, because the study of myth and ritual in relation to literary form and meaning has lately become a subject of deep and growing interest to many critics, and therefore it is well, in discussing a Greek dramatist, to assess at the outset the value of such an approach to Greek tragedy; secondly, the question of myth (and thus implicitly though very indirectly of ritual) has a special signifi-

[11] The same objection obtains, far more strongly, in the case of Fergusson's further "analogy": "We can also observe something similar in the dances and ritual mummery of the Pueblo Indians" (p. 28). According to Ruth Benedict (*Patterns of Culture*, 55), the Pueblo Indians are zealously devoted to the exact reproductions of traditional rites. Therefore in spirit they are almost directly opposite to the Athenians of the fifth century B.C. In our excitement at finding that the ancient Greeks had rites and traditions in their religious and social life for which parallels can be found in other cultures, we must not forget that one great and historically important distinguishing mark of ancient Greek artists was their capacity to transcend tradition without at once abandoning it.

A closer analogy would be the performance of various works, written by different composers, at Easter. This analogy would of course minimize the effect of ritual on any single work, and even it would not be quite on the mark, because the celebration of the Dionysia had no such religious pre-eminence as the celebration of Easter.

cance for Sophocles among the Greek dramatists. Since I have hitherto quoted Fergusson's book only to disagree with it, let me conclude this matter with a sentence of his that has my approval. He speaks of "the prerational image of human nature and destiny which the ritual conveyed; which Sophocles felt as still alive and significant for his generation." Here is a matter that is real in Sophocles, and significant for the criticism of his plays. I am not sure about the notion of prerationality and would substitute "myth" for "ritual"; with these provisos, I believe that this sentence describes an important element in Sophocles' dramatic method and helps to distinguish him from his two great compeers: Sophocles, in his plays, "thinks mythically," that is, he keeps himself within the confines of the traditional mythological setting in a way that is foreign to Aeschylus with his creative use of myth and to Euripides with his critical use of myth. In the next section we shall briefly consider the importance of this attitude toward myth for Sophoclean drama.

In defining Sophoclean drama, we must reject the ritual element as a thing intangible. Returning to the preliminary statement made above, we may say that Sophoclean tragedy is an action in which admirable character and crucial situation are combined; the situation involves religious and moral issues and entails suffering for the leading figure. This definition stresses two related factors which, as I shall attempt to show in the following two chapters, are fundamental in Sophocles' plays: emphasis on the behavior of noble character [12] and em-

---

[12] In general I shall avoid using the term "hero" in describing the leading persons in Sophocles' plays. They are, of course, "tragic heroes" if we use the term, as it often is used, to mean simply the principal person of a tragedy. Thus Medea, Macbeth, and Willy Loman (in Arthur Miller's *Death of a Salesman*) are tragic heroes, the words implying nothing about the kind of person but something about his position in the play. There is, moreover, a large degree of heroism, in its less technical sense of human greatness, in all Sophocles' tragic heroes. But to what extent

phasis on the sphere of human action and interaction—not dissociated from the divine but separate from it.

iii. Myth and Plot

In all but a very few of the Greek tragedies that we know of the raw material of the drama is myth; neither Sophocles nor Euripides, as we can tell almost certainly from the titles and from other scraps of information that we have about their lost plays, ever drew on any other source. This is the most immediately apparent general feature of the tragic drama of the second half of the fifth century as we know it or are ever likely to know it, and it may be worth while to inquire into the motives for this striking conservatism. We cannot dismiss the matter by supposing that the dramatists were tied to myth through the religious origins of the theater and that it was therefore "the function of tragedy to interpret myths." [13] If Aeschylus and Phrynichus could leave the confines of myth to dramatize historical subjects, it is incredible that in an age of increasingly secular spirit the same liberty would have been denied to the later poets. A comment of Aristotle's has a bearing on our question: "At first the poets accepted any stories that came their way, but now the best tragedies composed have to do with only a few families." [14] Aristotle is referring, in the second part of his sentence, to the playwrights of his day, not to those of the fifth century. But the restriction that he speaks of, to "a

---

they are to be called heroes in this wider sense is a question that must await discussion in Chapter III. In the present context it would be difficult to call these persons heroes without suggesting to the reader that they are not only tragic heroes but moral heroes, a suggestion that would be out of place. It is advisable, moreover, to avoid confusion between "hero" in the modern (and Homeric) sense and ἥρως in its usual ancient Greek sense (a man worshiped after his death, or a city founder, or a local deity). Ajax and Oedipus were ἥρωες. It does not automatically follow that they were heroes.

[13] As the editor of the Loeb *Poetics* states.   [14] *Poetics* 1453 a 17–19.

few families" (the context of the statement shows clearly that
he means families of mythology), was to a large extent observed also in the fifth century.[15] In view of the hundreds of
myths available, it is rather surprising to find that of our thirty-
two extant tragedies twenty-four deal with just four "houses"
or groups of mythical figures: the heroes of the Trojan war,
Heracles and related figures, the house of Atreus, and the house
of Thebes. The reason for this voluntary restriction, Aristotle
goes on to say, is that the stories of these families have, to a
pre-eminent degree, the essential ingredients of tragedy.

Aristotle's explanation leads to a new question: Why should
it be that certain mythological stories have this special tragic
force? This question, in its ramifications, is far beyond our
scope, for it involves the whole nature of myth and its relation
to literature. We can only touch on the subject. Of recent
years some literary critics have given ear to what the anthropologists and the psychologists have to say about the nature
and source of myth; among psychological theories the most
influential on literary criticism has been C. G. Jung's theory of
"archetypes," primal imaginative entities or metaphors which
are inherent in the subconscious mind and which, being a part
of the "collective unconscious," are the common possession of
the human imagination.[16] The theory of a common inheritance
of mythological patterns is not without substantial basis; students of comparative religion and mythology are as near to
agreement as can be expected in an uncertain subject about the

[15] Aristotle is interested only in the contrast between "at first" and
"now." His statement neither implies nor means to imply anything about
drama that came between these loosely defined limits.

[16] A good statement of Jung's theory of myth can be found in *Essays
on a Science of Mythology*, by C. G. Jung and K. Kerenyi (New York,
1949), 97–109. Freud also, of course, has had great influence on literary
criticism, but not so much in the realm of myth as in that of character
interpretation.

"multiple origin" of myths that are sometimes astonishingly similar not only in spirit but in incident.[17]

If this theory of archetypes is to be accepted, it suggests that such themes, when we meet them in literature, have a very special claim to our interest, for they are a part of our unconscious psychic being, and their power in literature is aided by their evocation of kindred fantasies native and deep-rooted within us. Let us hear Gilbert Murray speak for this view. (It does not matter that he takes his text from the anthropologists, Jane Harrison, Frazer, Ridgeway, rather than the psychologists, for the point of view in this instance is much the same for both groups.) In an essay entitled "Hamlet and Orestes" Murray speaks of "a great unconscious solidarity and continuity, lasting from age to age, among all the children of the poets, both the makers and the callers-forth, both the artists and the audiences." A little later he speaks of

stories and situations . . . deeply implanted in the memory of the race, stamped, as it were, upon our physical organism. We have forgotten their faces and their voices; we say that they are strange to us. Yet there is that within us which leaps at the sight of them, a cry of the blood which tells us that we have known them always.[18]

To many students of literature this way of explaining the literary validity of myth is likely to appear as a deplorable leap in the dark. It is far more comfortable and rewarding to cling to the solid facts of literary tradition; we can see the French

[17] In the various volumes of the collection *Mythology of All Races* (Boston, 1916–1932) there are hundreds of examples of similarities in myths presumably of independent origin. While it is true that there may be more dissemination of myth from one cultural area to another than can ever be proved, it is extremely unlikely that there has ever been enough to invalidate altogether the theory of multiple origin.

[18] *The Classical Tradition in Poetry* (Cambridge, Mass., 1927), 237–239.

classical stage, the English "Seneca men" and their successors, the Romantics, the modern French group of Anouilh, Giraudoux, Gide, Cocteau, and Sartre, and other similar groups clearly deriving inspiration from literary tradition, from the Greeks and one from another, and we may be inclined to rely on the same kind of accounting when we consider the Greek dramatists. Furthermore, mythologists and students of comparative religion are learning that even in preliterate myth the element of deliberate individual literary creation is not inconsiderable.[19] Do we then need this psychological theory to explain the poet's use of myth? Certainly the forces of literary tradition and poetic invention are not to be overlooked; we shall not assume that Sophocles was hamstrung by psychological archetypes any more than by religious duty in selecting a story. But considered as one factor among several, the presumption of a special psychological force in stories of mythology that renders them peculiarly effective in literature is reasonable.

It must be admitted that no very thorough or convincing investigation of the literary consequences of this psychological theory has yet been made. Maud Bodkin's pioneer essay, "Archetypal Patterns in Tragic Poetry," [20] deals with only one "mythologem," the theme of "conflict between generations," which embraces the stories of Oedipus, Hamlet, Orestes and Electra, and Lear. Northrop Frye has more recently spoken for the basic importance of myths of the annual cycle of vegetation in the development of literary genres.[21] In both essays there is a conspicuous shortage of convincing evidence in comparison with the enormous reach of the theory to be sustained.

[19] Cf. Paul Radin, *Primitive Religion* (New York, 1937), where the role of the "religious formulator" in primitive society is stressed.

[20] *British Journal of Psychology*, 21 (1930–1931), 183–202; reprinted as Chapter I of *Archetypal Patterns in Poetry* (London, 1934).

[21] "The Archetypes of Literature," *Kenyon Review*, 13 (1951), 92–110. See also Frye's *Anatomy of Criticism* (Princeton, 1957), especially the section "Theory of Myths."

One caution in such speculations is obviously essential: we cannot hope to find, in so complex and sophisticated a product of thought as a play or a literate story, a single "mythologem" underlying the whole work; [22] it must always rather be a combination of several mythological motifs. In the story of Oedipus, for example, we can identify several familiar themes of myth: the divine child (the exposure and rescue of Oedipus), the cycle of growth and decay (the prosperity and fall of the hero), as well as the "conflict between generations." We get nowhere by trying to understand the story of Oedipus as only an elaboration of the "Oedipus complex." But tentative and assailable though the practice of "myth-interpretation" of literature certainly is, its case is strong enough to deserve consideration: poets do keep turning back upon myth and upon the same types and stories of myth, and when due allowance is made for the force of literary tradition there is still room for belief in an intrinsic literary value in myth. After all, the psychologists have only provided an explanation for what poets have always known by intuition: that, as Aristotle reports, myths—at least certain of them—have a natural force that makes them peculiarly suitable for poetry.

Before going on to consider how this view of myth bears on the plays of Sophocles, we may answer two objections, apart from the disinclination of the critic of literature to accept psychological theory, that may be raised against this belief in the a priori value of myth for Greek tragedy. One objection is that the Greeks themselves did not distinguish myth from history; thus in the *Poetics* it is quite clear that Aristotle regards

[22] Attempts have been made to piece together a primordial "myth of the hero," analogous to Murray's pattern for Greek tragedy and no more convincing. Cf. especially Joseph Campbell, *The Hero with a Thousand Faces* (New York, 1949). Otto Rank's *The Myth of the Birth of the Hero* (Eng. trans., New York, 1952), which deals with only one "mythologem" and seeks to explain its psychological basis, seems to me a far more reasonable and useful approach.

the families of mythology as having existed historically, for he tells us that "in tragedy they keep to actual names, because that which is possible is credible, and, whereas we do not feel quite certain that what has not happened is possible, it is obvious that what has happened is possible." [23] We may answer this objection by observing that the division between myth and history never is clear cut, and that, especially in the kind of mythological story usually classed as saga or legend, the names and some part of the personality of the figures concerned may well be historically real. The distinctive quality of myth, the aspect of it that gives it its peculiar value for literature, is its capacity to express in story form the primary emotional and imaginative workings of the human mind. Insofar as strictly historical events perform this function, they assume the quality of myth; but the mythological value of such events and "families" as Aristotle refers to is likely to have arisen from an accumulated imaginative superstructure upon an often negligible historical foundation, a superstructure composed of traditional mythological themes.[24]

The second objection is this: How can we believe in the intrinsic power of myth when the poet may reconstruct myth almost as he sees fit? The Greek tragic poets freely manipulated their material, Sophocles no less freely than the other dramatists, in spite of what has often been said about his fidelity to the "sacred stories." It would be unwise to disparage the importance of the personal contribution of the poet to his mythological story; in fact, a large part of this study will be occupied with how Sophocles organizes the stories, and why he handles them as he does. Nevertheless the basis for the playwright's work is present in his material, in certain mythological data—the fate

[23] 1451 b 16–18.

[24] On the fusion of historical and mythical elements in Greek myth, see M. P. Nilsson, *The Mycenaean Origin of Greek Mythology* (Berkeley, 1932).

of Oedipus, the theme of revenge in the story of Agamemnon's family, the suicide of Ajax—and these data are of fundamental importance in the drama, not just as events, but as emotional factors which the playwright interprets according to his insight into the nature of man and man's relation to the world. In the long run there can be no separation of the *muthos* of the playwright, his plot in Aristotle's terminology, from the *muthos* of tradition.

Aristotle's insistence, in the *Poetics*, on the primary importance of plot is worth keeping in mind in this connection, for it makes very clear the indissolubility of *muthos* story and *muthos* plot. Again and again Aristotle emphasizes that *muthos* (plot) is first in importance among the qualitative elements of tragedy: it is the soul of tragedy, its *sine qua non*. In Chapter VI he makes clear why he insists on this point and just what dramatic *muthos* means: tragedy imitates action, events in the lives of men rather than men themselves; but these actions are the actions of persons, who act as they do because of their moral and intellectual qualities; there are, then, two causes or sources of actions (πράξεις), namely, moral character (ἦθος) and intellect (διάνοια). *Muthos*, which is the "constitution of the action" (σύστασις πράξεως), actualizes the moral character and the intellect of the agents of the drama; and tragic *muthos* is therefore not only the "synthesis of events" (σύνθεσις πραγμάτων), but the whole complex dramatic action involving persons and events.[25] The very breadth of this definition is a useful check on the tendency of criticism to compartmentalize to an unnecessary degree aspects of drama that are really parts of a single unity.

Going back now to the value of myth as traditional story: If we grant that myths have force of their own, independent

[25] The conclusions about *muthos* drawn in this sentence are not stated by Aristotle, but they follow logically from what he says (1449 b 36–1450 a 4).

of and prior to the contribution of the individual dramatist, what value has this fact for the criticism of a dramatist such as Sophocles who uses mythical plots? We must of course remember that a myth grows with each telling, that it has a literary history as well as a psychological nature, and that, however ancient and powerful the kernel, not only new incidents but new meanings can be added as the story passes from artist to artist. No clearer example is needed than the story of Philoctetes as it grows from the *Little Iliad* through the successive dramatizations of it by Aeschylus, Euripides, and Sophocles, to say nothing of such modern retellings as those of Lord de Tabley in the nineteenth century and André Gide in the twentieth. Perhaps in assessing the value of myth for literature we should say no more than that the power of myth is another real but critically unusable datum like the fact of the ritual nature of the Dionysiac festival for Greek tragedy. But for Sophocles I think we may say something more. At the end of the preceding section it was said that Sophocles as a dramatist "thinks mythically" in a way that Aeschylus and Euripides do not; that while the other two regularly go beyond the implications of the received myth, Aeschylus in a creative way (notably in the *Oresteia* and apparently in the *Prometheia*), Euripides in a critical way (as in his denunciation of divine morals in *Electra, The Trojan Women, Ion, Hippolytus*), Sophocles works within the mythical framework.

This is not to say that out of some peculiar religious zeal Sophocles regarded it as reprehensible to tamper with the traditional stories. He tampered with them as much as the others; among major Sophoclean innovations are the addition of Neoptolemus in *Philoctetes*, Chrysothemis in *Electra*, and Ismene in *Antigone*, all of fundamental importance for the plays in which they occur. But none of them changes the direction or the meaning of the myth; instead, they sharpen the perspective and the emphasis that Sophocles sought within the story.

The introduction of the peasant husband in Euripides' *Electra* is not nearly so telling for the play as a whole as the introduction of Chrysothemis in Sophocles' *Electra*. Yet Euripides' play departs much further from the traditional myth than Sophocles', because Euripides is concerned to criticize the traditional story as a whole, Sophocles to concentrate on one element within it. This Sophoclean way of handling mythological material is very important and very typical and is at the heart of one of the greatest difficulties of Sophoclean interpretation.

Personal anecdotes about ancient literary figures are not usually of any great value for the understanding of their poetry, but the curious story of Sophocles and the snake of Asclepius has some relevance here. As E. R. Dodds says, it "has its bearing on the understanding of Sophocles' poetry." And, unlike most ancient biographical tidbits, it is supported by evidence from a contemporary source. The incident is this: When in the year 420 B.C. the god Asclepius was brought to Athens, he was lodged, pending the completion of his temple, in Sophocles' house; and with him, or more likely in place of him, representing the god, came his sacred snake. It is hard, as U. Wilamowitz observes, to imagine Aeschylus or Euripides entertaining a snake as a house guest. To Wilamowitz, and I think also to Dodds, who cites the incident and Wilamowitz's comment, Sophocles' behavior is reprehensible; Dodds speaks of the whole incident as a "regression." [26] Euripides, in the unlikely event that his fellow citizens had sought to lodge the reptile with him, might have answered that this creeping god, O men of Athens, is of very little value in the cure of diseases. This, at any rate, is what Euripides does with myth in many of his plays. What are we to assume about Sophocles from the incident? Is he so much the typical Athenian that he, unlike the

[26] *The Greeks and the Irrational* (Berkeley, 1951), 193. For evidence concerning the story, see W. S. Ferguson, "The Attic Orgeones," *HTR*, 37 (1944), 88–91.

other men of thought of his day, swallowed every drop of popular superstition? We can search the plays of Sophocles endlessly without finding a clear answer to that question; his outlook is as enigmatic as Shakespeare's toward contemporary popular belief. What we can very definitely say, however, is that the incident tallies with Sophocles' dramatic practice: he accepts, for dramatic purposes, the traditional myths; as a citizen of Athens he accepts without criticism the snake of Asclepius. It does not follow that such behavior marks the limit of Sophocles' perception; rather, it describes his method.

This enigma of attitude and this refusal to take a stand vis-à-vis the mythical material with which he works have been the source of much mischief in the interpretation of Sophocles. (Just so, brains have been racked to determine precisely what was Shakespeare's "attitude" toward the ghost in *Hamlet:* is it a purely theatrical contrivance, is it a moral force or an immoral? Like Sophocles, Shakespeare gives no answer, whereas the ghost of Polydorus, in Euripides' *Hecuba*, is quite clearly no more than a stage device to introduce the play and bind its two main incidents; it does not matter what we think of it because, as a ghost, it has no effective part in Euripides' play.) Perhaps the commonest assumption made by critics is that since in Sophocles' plays the mythical framework is accepted it follows that the message of Sophocles is that mankind must accept these irrational and cruel conditions—the fate of Oedipus, the dilemma of Electra, the baffling oracles of *The Trachinian Women*—must accept them, bow in resignation, and cleave to a life of human humility, ignorance, and inaction. The one great hindrance to supposing that such is the Sophoclean philosophy is the fact that those magnificent creatures, the main characters of the plays, rebel against such acceptance; and without subscribing to the notion that the leading characters are perfect, one may legitimately doubt that Sophocles intends them as examples of how not to live. If, on the other hand, we suppose that in this conflict between the character's action and the fate assigned by myth and accepted without demur by the playwright there is contained a subtle but furious protest against the mythological data, we are interpreting subjectively, with little or no assistance from the text of Sophocles. A third tack is to regard Sophocles' acceptance of the myth as simply a divine apparatus with little effect on the story: Sophocles does not think much about the religious implications of his stories, his concentration is on the human scene.[27] Basically, Sophocles' main concentration is indeed on man; but we shall not arrive at a satisfactory understanding of his plays by closing our eyes to the very substantial part played in them by the forces that surround man.

These are serious problems of interpretation, to which we shall have to return. At this point we need only pursue the one consideration that we have been concerned with in the preceding pages, what Sophocles' distinctive use of myth means for his drama. It might be put in this way: The three lines of interpretation just mentioned all show a certain impatience with Sophoclean procedure, because they are all trying to pounce upon Sophocles' angle in the treatment of myth; but his treatment of myth is not angular. They try to define the attitude of Sophoclean drama toward myth; but Sophoclean drama, one might almost say, has no attitude toward myth—it is myth, and the reason that Sophocles presents the gods and the fate of man as he does is simply that that is the way the story goes—that is the way the myth presents these things. We cannot quite say so; of course Sophocles in a sense stands outside the myth and controls it. But to Sophocles myth is not hypothesis, to be explored, criticized, reshaped, made to yield some specific moral or theological lesson; to Sophocles myth is life, with all its ramifications, its limitations, mysteries, sor-

[27] This is on the whole the view of M. Croiset, *Oedipe-Roi, étude et analyse* (Paris, 1931).

rows, and triumphs. Questions of the rightness or wrongness of the mythological outcome, though certainly not discarded, are enmeshed with so much else that is of vital significance to what Sophocles is saying that they cannot be answered simply and categorically. If we try to answer categorically the question why Oedipus suffers as he does, we are likely to answer that the gods are cruel, or that Oedipus is guilty, or that human life is pitiful. These answers are wrong because they assume that Sophocles presents the myth of Oedipus primarily to offer some such answer, and this is to misunderstand the Sophoclean use of myth. The play of Oedipus means the myth of Oedipus, in all Sophocles' searching and complex understanding of that myth. Sophocles is presenting, to use again Fergusson's words, the "image of human nature and destiny" which the myth conveys and which Sophocles "felt as still alive and significant for his generation."

One further point should be raised in connection with Sophocles' use of myth. In his selection of plots Sophocles has an affinity for the Trojan cycle of legends. In the Introduction to his edition of the fragments A. C. Pearson lists the plays according to their sources and points out that forty-three, more than a third, are drawn from the Trojan cycle, i.e., in ancient terms, from "Homeric" sources. The proportion is substantially higher than it is for Aeschylus or Euripides. In determining what significance this affiliation may have for Sophoclean drama, we must avoid the error made by Pearson, who declares that "these figures"—the forty-three plays on "Homeric" subjects—"confirm the evidence relating to Sophocles' Homeric proclivities." [28] This evidence was marshaled earlier by Pearson and summed up with the opinion that Sophocles'

---

[28] *The Fragments of Sophocles*, I (Cambridge, 1917), xxxi.

most intimate point of contact with the Homeric spirit was his refusal to employ his art for the purpose of fostering religious enthusiasm, or promoting a purer morality, or of freeing the mind from conventional shackles, while he laboured to create afresh the heroic figures of ancient legend, and to present under new conditions the majesty of life which Homer had first portrayed.

The employment of Trojan themes is not at all a confirmation, in itself, of Homeric spirit; whether or not we accept Pearson's summary of the spirit of Sophoclean drama will not depend on most of the forty-three titles from the Trojan cycle, for of these "Homeric" titles only four are Homeric, from the Iliad and the Odyssey, an insignificant proportion of the whole number of Sophocles' plays. Only these four could give the confirmation that Pearson alleges; as sources the other thirty-nine have little bearing on the question, for we have no right to assume that the majestic spirit of the Iliad and the Odyssey was shared by the rest of the early epic poetry. Sophocles' choice of myths does tell us something, however, about his dramatic bent; it reveals that he favored for dramatic treatment the figures and stories of saga, the heroes and their deeds in the quasi-historical, essentially human part of the mythological tradition, for the Trojan story is the latest and most human chapter in the book of Greek mythology.

CHAPTER II

Construction

i. General Patterns of Structure

WHEN we turn to consider the σύνθεσις πραγμάτων in Sophocles, the choice and organization of incidents in the dramas, we must restrict our attention to the seven extant plays. In not one of the many lost plays whose titles and, sometimes, general subject matter we know can we say with any degree of certainty exactly what parts of the story Sophocles used or how he put his play together. We come closer to such knowledge of *Eurypylus* than of any other fragmentary tragedy; but even in it, except for scattered places, we can only guess about the precise material and organization. *The Ichneutae*, as a satyr play, is of no great value for our judgment of the tragedies, and in any case our knowledge of its structure is incomplete.

In the organization of the drama as a whole, there are severe limits to what can be said in description of all seven tragedies taken together. It is tempting but fatal to take *Oedipus Tyrannus* as *the* Sophoclean dramatic type. If we try to squeeze all the other plays into its form, we can only end by misunderstanding most of them. The form of *Oedipus* is simple: a single dominating figure is presented in relation to a series of secondary persons, the priest in the prologue, Teiresias, Creon, Jocasta, the two herdsmen, the chorus; through the interaction of these persons, as they grapple with the two problems of the identity of the murderer and the identity of Oedipus, the action of the play has its existence. *Electra* has very much the same pattern, though in it the main action is enclosed within a framework. Again there is a dominant central figure, Electra, and a series of encounters, with the chorus, Chrysothemis, Clytemnestra, Orestes; and again the action and the meaning of the play consist of and grow with the interplay of the characters in the face of the central event of the drama, revenge for Agamemnon's murder. But *Antigone* and *Philoctetes* are organized very differently from these two plays, and from each other. In *Antigone* there are two dominant figures. Although Antigone may strike us as dominating the play emotionally, so far as structure is concerned she is not at the center of the action in the way that Oedipus and Electra are. There are whole incidents in the drama that do not directly concern her—Creon and the guard, Creon and Haemon, Creon and Teiresias, and the final kommos. In *Philoctetes*, though there is no doubt that Philoctetes is the protagonist, there is obviously an importance in the conflict of three different approaches to the situation of the play, those of Philoctetes, Neoptolemus, and Odysseus. Some parts of this conflict of aims—the prologue, for example—directly concern only Neoptolemus and Odysseus, and so here again the simple pattern of *Oedipus Tyrannus* does not fit.

There are in fact at least four different forms of organization in the seven plays, and these we shall consider in the following two sections of this chapter. Meanwhile we must return to a point raised in the last paragraph. It was said that *Oedipus* and *Electra* are alike in a way that distinguishes them from *Antigone* and *Philoctetes*, but it was implied that all four are alike in one respect; in all four (in fact in all seven plays) the course of the play depends on the interaction of characters (including the chorus), whether or not one character formally dominates the plot. This procedure is not, of course, peculiar to Sophocles, for most dramatic meanings are presented in terms of characters. But in Sophocles dramatic meaning is coexistent with the interaction of characters to a degree that is rare anywhere and unique in Greek tragedy. It is not too much to say that the first requirements for a satisfactory and inclusive comprehension of Sophoclean tragedy are full recognition of this feature of his dramatic method and consistent exploitation of it in the interpretation of the plays.

One important consequence of Sophocles' system of dramatic development through the interplay of characters is that it becomes very difficult to abstract the meaning of his plays, so completely is that meaning bound up with the persons of the drama and with the action. The best evidence of this difficulty is the critics' lack of success in declaring just what a Sophoclean play means. To be told that *Oedipus Tyrannus* teaches us that moderation is best, or that the best of men is fallible, or that it is the fate of man to suffer gives us little satisfaction, and our sense of frustration is heightened by the striking contrast between these sober "lessons" and the strong emotional effect of the play when we read it. Similarly, the celebrated *fabula docet* of *Ajax*, Athena's words to Odysseus in the prologue, "The gods love men of modesty and hate the wicked" (132–133), is irksomely inadequate in comparison with the intuitive response which the great figure of Ajax evokes in us. We feel, and feel rightly, that the meaning of the play is something more complex and more intimately bound up with the whole character of Ajax and the whole action of the play.

Just as it is misleading to view Sophoclean myth as thesis, a means of expressing some specific moral or theological point, so in the relation of character and action to the meaning of the play we find general and abstract solutions unsatisfactory. But we need not therefore conclude, with A. J. A. Waldock, that there is no meaning in the *Oedipus Tyrannus*. There is merely the terror of coincidence, and then, at the end of it all, our impression of man's power to suffer, and his greatness because of this power. The theme is not, then, universal. The theme of *Lear* is universal; but what the *Oedipus Tyrannus* rests on is a frightful groundwork of accident.[1]

Oedipus is, then, just a powerful story, and the excellence of the play depends on the power of the story. This is a circular argument. What gives the story its power is not merely the incidents, which could after all be quite ineffectual in the hands of an inferior artist; not even the most enthusiastic proponent of the innate force of myth would maintain that its literary value operates in spite of the artist. No one would maintain that Dryden's *Oedipus* is as powerful as Sophocles', and yet on Waldock's grounds it ought to be. The power of *Oedipus* depends most of all on the effectiveness with which Sophocles has presented the story, and that effectiveness consists of insights that provide the meaning. Waldock himself states a meaning that has the universality that he denies: "Man's power to suffer, and his greatness because of this power." The way in which this is expressed illustrates exactly the nature of the problem and gives an indication of the kind of meaning that we can discover in Sophocles' plays. It is not an abstractable theme or moral lesson, and the moment we separate the meaning from the person of Oedipus it becomes too vague and general to satisfy us, just as the "moral" of *Ajax* is feeble without the towering figure of Ajax to give life to it.

But to deny the abstractability of Sophoclean meaning is very different from denying universality to it; the problem is ultimately one of dramatic method rather than of special as opposed to universal meaning. Shakespeare is sometimes closer to the Sophoclean way than he is in *Lear*. Let us take *Antony and*

[1] *Dramatist*, 168.

Cleopatra as an example. Much of the interest of the play depends on nontragic elements—the historical panorama, the half-romantic and half-cynical love story, the political framework, the contrast of East and West, the "infinite variety" of Cleopatra; the analogy with Sophocles is therefore very incomplete. But in the person of Antony there is a tragic theme, and it is presented in a manner comparable with the Sophoclean. Antony is tragic, but we can no more abstract a tragic theme from him than we can from Oedipus, because the tragedy involves the entire complex range of Antony's character as it is revealed in the play. The similarity of method is not gainsaid by the fact that Antony and Oedipus are very different.

Sophocles' method can be better described by comparing it with the procedures of Aeschylus and Euripides, who are in the same dramatic tradition and use the same kind of story. In just one extant instance the same mythological material is used by all three, in the story of the revenge for the death of Agamemnon, told in *The Choephoroe* and the two *Electras*.

In Aeschylus' play the central dramatic fact, that which gives the play not only a course of events but its very reason for being, is the accomplishment of the revenge. This is the primary thing; not the behavior of Orestes or Electra, nor the study of the phenomenon of matricide, but the terrible, god-driven, necessary act, as it takes its place in the panoramic study of divine nature and justice that fills the trilogy. The deed is done in Sophocles' play too, but it is certainly not the reason for the play's being. Precisely what the central moment of the play is may be debatable. Tycho Wilamowitz found it in the recognition of Orestes by Electra. This view may be wrong, but it is not capricious or unreasonable, and the fact that this scene can seriously be taken to be the climax is indicative of the nature of the play. Instead of culmination in an all-important act, with all before the act preparatory to it and all after it simply its results, in Sophocles we have a series of portraits of the protagonist running an emotional gamut, with the chorus, Chrysothemis, Clytemnestra, Chrysothemis again, Orestes, and again Clytemnestra (during the matricide scene) providing impetus for Electra's changing moods. This striking difference of emphasis has often been noticed. One critic has even declared that in Sophocles' play "the whole drama takes place within the heroine's soul, its whole interest rests with her feelings." [2] This is an exaggeration; but it is exaggeration in the right direction.

There is interplay of character in *The Choephoroe*. In the long scene, after the recognition, of libation and prayer at the tomb of Agamemnon, the effect of character on character is noteworthy, and there is clear and purposeful differentiation of characters; but the essence of the scene is not what the characters are or what they think, it is a preparation for the deed of revenge. In Sophocles' play the character of Electra, as she disputes, urges, despairs, rejoices, and, finally, when she shrieks "Strike again, if you have the strength!" embraces the meaning of the play. This is not to say that the play is merely character study; if there really is such a thing as pure character drama, it is drama in which the events of the play exist only to display the characters and need have no palpable aim or outcome. Perhaps Chekov's *The Cherry Orchard* and *The Sisters* are character plays, but Sophocles' plays are not. In all of them a course of events is necessarily brought to completion, and our attention is on the characters in relation to these events.

Between the two *Electras* the differences are less apparent but no less fundamental. Both Sophocles and Euripides are interested in the relation between situation and character in a way that Aeschylus is not. Euripides is interested in the kind of person who could do what Electra and Orestes do; his psychological realism and his hostility to the Delphic oracle make the revenge murder, committed upon commonplace people by

[2] Léon Parmentier, *Mélanges Henri Weil* (Paris, 1898), 168.

commonplace people. We feel at least as warmly toward the victims, the nominal criminals, as toward the avengers. Electra is petulant, mean-spirited, shrewish, Orestes an irresolute opportunist; Aegisthus, in the report of his death, which is the one passage where we learn anything about his character, is surprisingly affable and courteous; Clytemnestra can be tricked into a defenseless position because she has the goodness of nature to come to her daughter's aid. The characterization is brilliantly effective, but one cannot say that the play is a tragedy of character in reaction to situation; there are no tragic characters. The tragedy is that false notions of religion should bring such a situation to pass; it is the implications of matricide that give meaning to the play.

In Sophocles the central fact is Electra's response to the entire situation, not alone to the matricide. In both Aeschylus and Euripides it is easier to abstract the meaning of the drama than in Sophocles, because in Sophocles the meaning of the play is so dependent on the nature of its central figure. There are, of course, other things in the play besides Electra's reactions: there is a moral point, though it is somewhat obscured by the emphasis of the play; but all else is oriented to the central fact—Electra.

Another point of direct comparison among the three dramatists is *Philoctetes*. All three wrote plays so named. Euripides' was produced in 431 B.C., Sophocles' in 409. There is no evidence for the date of Aeschylus' play, but of course it came long before 431.[3] Of Euripides' play there remain sixteen fragments, none of more than five lines; of Aeschylus' play there is even less. Our main sources of knowledge about both are two short essays of Dio Chrysostom, one a desultory account

---

[3] F. J. A. Letters, *The Life and Works of Sophocles* (London and New York, 1953), 263, observes that since the play seems to have been two-actor drama, it probably did not come in the last years of Aeschylus' career.

of some aspects of the three plays about Philoctetes, in which, to our misfortune, only Sophocles' play is outlined in anything like completeness, the other a paraphrase of the beginning of Euripides' play. The plots of the lost plays can be partly reconstructed.[4] We know that Aeschylus, departing from the epic tradition, or perhaps selecting from it,[5] has Odysseus sent from Troy, instead of Diomedes, to fetch Philoctetes and the bow and arrows of Heracles after Helenus has revealed that these alone can take the city. Dio tells us that the Odysseus of this play was "sharp and guileful," but intimates that his manner of operation was direct, in keeping with the heroism of old. He assumed no disguise (though he did count on the effects of Philoctetes' suffering to obliterate memory) and somehow prevailed on Philoctetes to go to Troy. How this result was achieved we do not know. From the tenor of Dio's allusive account it is almost certain that the essence of the play was the fated departure of Philoctetes for Troy. Dramatic conflict was obtained by replacing Diomedes, toward whom Philoctetes had no special grudge, with Odysseus, whom he hated.

Dio gives the impression that the form of the play was simple[6] and its meaning direct: fate decreed that Philoctetes must take Troy; Odysseus, by guile, but "old-fashioned" (ἄρχαιος) guile, was the instrument of fate; Philoctetes, no doubt after a struggle of some kind, submitted to fate. It was, then, in all probability, the working out of an ordinance of fate or deity, in which character contributed something but cannot have constituted the essential life.

[4] In the following reconstruction I am much indebted to John S. Kieffer's comparative study of the three plays, "Philoctetes and *Arete*," *CP*, 37 (1942), 38–50.

[5] T. Wilamowitz, *Dramatische Technik*, 269–271, presents evidence suggesting that the epic tradition may have had both Diomedes and Odysseus in the story.

[6] U. Wilamowitz (*ibid.*, 313) says that it was a "dramatized dithyramb."

Dio tells us somewhat more about Euripides' play. Again Odysseus goes from Troy to bring Philoctetes, this time urged to it against his will by Athena and disguised by her (in the manner of the Odyssey, as Dio points out); he goes because he believes that he must to maintain his reputation as a great man. With him goes Diomedes. The reason for the doubling seems to have been that Euripides, while unwilling to give up the fine dramatic possibilities in Odysseus, needed also a figure less hostile to Philoctetes than Odysseus to represent the Greek cause in debate. For—and this is the significant structural feature of Euripides' play—there was also an embassy from the Trojans, led (as we know from the fragments) by Paris. Dio speaks more than once of the "political" nature of the play as well as of its rhetoric. In the debate before Philoctetes one can see how both politics and rhetoric would find ample place! Kieffer suggests that Dio's references to politics mean patriotism and that an important point in the play was Philoctetes' patriotism, his rejection of the Trojan ambassadors, his yielding to the exhortation of the Greeks (with Diomedes as chief speaker?), and, putting aside personal hostilities, his reconciliation with Odysseus. Here is a play not only differently organized but differing basically in meaning from Aeschylus'. Here Philoctetes is confronted with a choice, and his sense of duty to his country conquers the desire for revenge for past injuries, revenge which he could have had at will by favoring the Trojans.

If this description of the general lines of Euripides' play is valid (and it cannot be very far wrong), the play is clearly one in which meaning can be abstracted from character to an even greater degree than in his *Electra*.

Sophocles' play certainly owes much to each of the others: to Aeschylus the conflict between Philoctetes and Odysseus, to Euripides certain aspects of the realism with which the hero's suffering is portrayed. If we had the other plays, more debts would likely appear. The great difference is the introduction of Neoptolemus, whose function it is to mediate between Philoctetes and Odysseus through sharing a part of each of the opposing points of view. He amalgamates them in himself and is the instrument by which a reconciliation of the conflict is ultimately brought about. So far-reaching in its consequences is this innovation that some critics have supposed that the theme of Sophocles' play is the transformation of Neoptolemus, under the influence of Philoctetes, from a naïve and ambitious, though basically high-minded youth to a mature man with an awakened sense of moral values and a profound recognition of the nature of heroism. But the original, Aeschylean conflict is still central, a conflict between on the one hand the authority of the army, personified by Odysseus, and the duty which this authority imposes on Philoctetes, and on the other hand the stubborn, independent, and virtuous will of Philoctetes. It is resolved in two ways: by the mutual effect of Philoctetes and Neoptolemus on each other and by the epiphany of Heracles, the second being a ratification and continuation of the first.

The resolution of the problem is very closely linked to Neoptolemus' transformation. As the young man passes more and more completely under the influence of the stubborn hero, he moves from callow ambition—ready at Odysseus' instigation to compromise his innate sense of virtue for the sake of achieving glory, though not without hesitation and distaste—to complete sympathy with the uncompromising virtue of Philoctetes. Their views on the worthy and the worthless among the Greeks at Troy are identical; the suffering of Philoctetes deeply moves the young man; Philoctetes' trust arouses an answering sense of loyalty that eventually masters all other impulses, even the desire for military glory; and so finally Neoptolemus passes quite into the power of Philoctetes. Odysseus, rejected, can only bluster and retreat. Neoptolemus is prepared to forsake all and make good the promise, false when first made, to take Philoctetes home. But at the same time Philoctetes has in a profoundly important way come into the power of Neoptolemus. To reject Odysseus was easy, but to remain deaf to the pleas of Neoptolemus, who has given proof of his nobility and who finally represents all that Philoctetes most admires, is torment: "What shall I do? How can I reject his arguments when he is intent upon my good" (1350–1351)? Philoctetes in the throes of his dilemma wishes he were dead. But he cannot yield; without a divine mandate he cannot submit, because he has suffered too much. To seal the effect of Neoptolemus' urging requires the appearance of Heracles, who not only embodies the will of Zeus but also that nobility of soul that has been brought to light in the play by the interaction of Philoctetes and Neoptolemus.

Here as in *Electra* the meaning of the play is inextricable from the interplay of characters, and again this method of presentation is the special mark of Sophoclean dramatic form. One cannot properly see the characters of Sophoclean drama except in terms of other characters. Sometimes the relations between characters are less direct than in these two plays; instead of immediate interplay we find a comparison of characters who do not necessarily meet in the course of the play. But we shall see that even in such cases the dependence of characters upon each other for dramatic realization, and the revelation of the dramatic theme through the relations between characters, are no less complete.

The evidence of these two plays gives some initial substantiation to the idea that Sophoclean drama is uniquely dependent on the mutual effect of characters. Further confirmation will be found when we examine the construction of the other plays. It is a consequence of this dramatic method that the meaning of the plays cannot be successfully abstracted from the action. The essential difference between Sophocles and the other two Greek tragic poets is that plot in Sophocles is inextricable from persons whereas in the others—most consistently in Aeschylus

—the emphasis is upon a concept that overrides character. The distinction is not always clear between Euripides and Sophocles, for in Euripides too the connection between theme and character can be very close, as it is in *Medea* and *Heracles*. But more often in Euripides' tragedies there is a separable tragic idea, which may even, as in *Hippolytus* and *The Trojan Women*, be defined in the prologue and given an entity separate from the characters.[7] The Sophoclean method, in all seven plays (*Oedipus at Colonus* is only a partial exception), comes very close to being the sheer, stripped essence of drama as described by Aristotle, "an imitation of an action, performed by men in action."[8]

Dramatic development through character interaction is closely related to the "mythological thinking" which was ascribed to Sophocles in the preceding chapter. There it was maintained that Sophocles' way with myth is not to reshape it, or to turn the story to illustrate a thesis, but to stay within the boundaries and the atmosphere of the traditional myth, to work at it from the inside, so to speak, expanding and illuminating those specific aspects or parts of it that are to his dramatic purpose; and it is upon the characters that Sophocles' work of expansion and illumination is chiefly done. The three great Sophoclean innovations already mentioned illustrate this aspect of Sophocles' art. Ismene, Chrysothemis, and Neoptolemus amplify and realize the central figures with whom they are in interplay. Similarly, the Odysseus of *Ajax*, Creon and Jocasta in *Oedipus Tyrannus*, and numerous other persons of the plays are, one can confidently assume, purely Sophoclean, not always in the sense that Sophocles added them to the story but in that he fashioned them in the particular form that they have in his plays.

[7] On the relation between character and tragedy in Euripides, see Kitto, *Greek Tragedy*, 252–260.
[8] *Poetics* 1449 b 36–37.

ii. The Diptych Plays

It was said above that there are at least four different types of construction in Sophocles' plays, that is, at least four different organizations of the dramatic material. Disregarding relatively slight differences, we may group the plays thus: *Ajax, The Trachinian Women,* and *Antigone; Oedipus Tyrannus* and *Electra; Philoctetes; Oedipus at Colonus.*

The first three plays fall together because they are all clearly divisible into two parts, though not all three are divisible in the same way. To describe this kind of form I use the now traditional word diptych; [9] critics rightly view with suspicion terms that have a mechanical connotation, as though the playwright were consciously choosing one of several standard vessels into which to pour his material, but the word diptych is brief and convenient, and I know of no better designation for these plays as a group. In *Ajax* there is a division between the part culminating in Ajax's death and the part having to do with his burial. To determine the exact dividing point in the action is impossible: the lament over the hero's body by Tecmessa and the chorus, joined later by Teucer, belongs to both parts and serves as a transition. In *The Trachinian Women* there is a sharper break. The nurse's report of Deianeira's death ends with a generalization very much like the choral tags usual at the end of a drama: "Foolish, therefore, is he who reckons for two days, or more; there is no to-morrow until one has successfully passed through the present day" (943–946). Yet in this play too there is some degree of linking; the nurse refers to Hyllus' grief for both parents, and the stasimon that follows her speech unites the two catastrophes in its lament:

[9] The word has become a part of the vocabulary of modern Sophoclean criticism; cf. Webster, *Introduction,* 102–103; Kitto, *Greek Tragedy,* 116 (rejecting the use of the word); Waldock, *Dramatist,* 50–61.

πότερα πρότερον ἐπιστένω;

The division is nevertheless very marked, chiefly because the contrast in personality between Deianeira and Heracles is so violent. In *Antigone* there is no palpable division in the action. After Creon's debate with Haemon and before his scene with Teiresias, both of which belong primarily to Creon's part in the play, there occur Antigone's final episode (the kommos of 806–888 and 929–943 and her final iambic scene, 883–928) and the "Danae" ode, which belongs to Antigone's part.[10] But the double nature of the play is none the less clear: there are two persons whose fates contribute to the tragic meaning; though interdependent they are yet distinct, and the dramatic form reflects this distinction.

This double form, whether the duplication is of theme as in *Ajax* or of persons as in the other two plays, is significantly different from the form of *Electra* and *Oedipus Tyrannus*, where a single figure and a single theme are dominant throughout. It might be said that there is a thematic change in *Oedipus* from the search for the murderer of Laius to the search for Oedipus' identity, but these are two stages in a single development, without any division in structure corresponding to what is found in the three plays now under discussion.

What is the significance of this diptych form? If we are to understand Sophocles' methods of achieving dramatic meaning, we cannot disregard the point. Diptych structure has often been denied existence by critics and been regarded as an accident or an involuntary fault of structure. Among recent critics Waldock has given particularly close attention to the matter, devoting several pages to what he calls "the problem of unity." [11] Noticing that three plays of Sophocles and four

[10] The relevance of the ode is discussed below, pp. 210–211.
[11] *Dramatist*, 50–61.

of Euripides are diptychs, he suggests that these plays exhibit a basic difficulty of form experienced by the Greek playwrights and that Greek tragedy, with its strict concentration on a single action without subplots (as opposed to Elizabethan form), has difficulty finding matter enough to fill out the necessary length of the play: "It is a little harder for him [the Greek dramatist] to *brake* his play, to keep it from moving ahead too fast." Thus in *Hippolytus* Phaedra cannot be kept in the play to the end; her story simply runs out, to the detriment of the play. And in *Ajax* the second part is simply filler; the playwright, having exhausted the "initial charge" of the drama, must reload with a new charge before the play has run its due course. Sometimes, however, stories are found "of a peculiar build, that seem as if made for the use of Greek dramatists: the example of examples is the story of Oedipus."

This is an issue of fundamental importance. If this view is right, we had better stop talking about Sophoclean form in terms of conscious dramatic art, for Sophoclean form, and Euripidean, is accident, not art. It is easy, however, to show that Waldock's criticism is inapplicable to either Sophocles or Euripides. In *Hippolytus* and *Hecuba* (two of Waldock's examples) there can be no question but that the division is deliberate; it is necessary for the meaning of the play in each case, and the prologue of each play shows that Euripides so regarded it. In *Hippolytus* the design is especially clear, for in the prologue Euripides tells us just what he is going to do and why; and his intentions not only justify but necessitate both Phaedra's and Hippolytus' fate.[12] We may say that he would have done better to concentrate on Phaedra, but we have no right to consider it an accident that he did not. The suggestion that the form of *Oedipus* is a happy accident rather than a credit to Sophocles is at best ex-

---

[12] On the unity of *Hecuba*, see my paper, "Hecuba and Nomos," *TAPA*, 78 (1947), 62–68.

tremely improbable. We cannot properly say that the story of Oedipus was of a build made for the use of Greek dramatists for the simple reason that we know nothing whatsoever of the build of the story before Sophocles—we are not now talking about mythological material, but about the shape of Sophocles' play; what gives it its peculiar build is what Sophocles has done with the story. The Sophoclean form *is* the peculiar and excellent build that we perceive.

Finally, a word about the relàtion between diptych form and the shortage of material. We have already seen that Euripides clearly wanted to bring in the two parts of two of his diptychs, simply because what he had to say necessarily involved in the one case the fate of both Phaedra and Hippolytus and in the other the sacrifice of Polyxena and Hecuba's revenge for the murder of Polydorus. We can offer in addition a sort of mathematical refutation of Waldock's charge. In *The Trojan Women* Euripides uses a whole series of incidents (the play is a "polyptych" if we wish): the taking of Cassandra, the murder of Astyanax, the incident of Helen, the sacrifice of Polyxena, and the assignment of Hecuba to Odysseus. On the basis of Waldock's argument, we should be able to assume that he did so in order to have plenty of material. Is it not strange that in spite of this mass of material, the play is among Euripides' shortest? The confusion is increased when we turn to Sophocles' *Electra* and find the playwright deliberately compressing and excluding great lengths of perfectly usable dramatic material, and yet writing a longer play than some of his diptychs.

The notion of "initial charge" and its exhaustion will not work; indeed it is based on the irrational assumption that Sophocles had to begin his plays at some specified point; that he had to start *Ajax* and *Antigone* just where he did, even though by moving back a little in the myth he could in each case have availed himself of an abundance of material to dramatize. Kitto had already pointed out that "there is no difficulty in making a play about Ajax," [13] nor, one can add, about Antigone, or Creon, or Deianeira, or Heracles. Waldock's explanation will not account for diptych form. The Greek dramatists had control over their material, as we know from the freedom they assumed in adapting stories to their purpose, and we have no right to suppose that Sophocles did not write diptychs for a purpose. The diptych is a deliberate form, not a failure of form. Whether the diptych plays are failures is of course another question. We may prefer the more compact form of *Oedipus Tyrannus*, but we must not suppose that the three diptych plays are unsuccessful attempts to achieve the form of *Oedipus*.

Diptych form is very closely connected with the quality of Sophoclean structure that we have already noticed, the habit of presenting ideas by the interplay of characters. Sophocles always thought in terms of contrast in the construction of his plays, and this is as true in *Oedipus Tyrannus* as in *Ajax*. We come to know Oedipus through his relations with Creon, Jocasta, Teiresias. But in *Oedipus* through a series of such relations a portrait of the main figure in the face of the situation of the play is created, and it is this that conveys the dramatist's meaning, whereas in *Ajax* and the other diptychs the meaning of the drama is conveyed in terms of a central contrast: between Ajax and Odysseus, Deianeira and Heracles, Antigone and Creon. In each case a single contrast is the basic fact of the play. The nature of these contrasts will be described presently.

A further distinction must be made. In only one of these three plays of double form, *Antigone*, do the two principals involved in the contrast actually meet; hence only in this play is there any direct interaction between the characters. In the other two the interdependence is of a more remote though no less important kind; it is in the final effect of the play on the mind of the audience that the interaction of Ajax and Odysseus

[13] *Greek Tragedy*, 119.

(who do not really *meet*, in the prologue) and of Deianeira and Heracles comes into being. In the action of the play the relationship is one of comparison or contrast, not direct conflict. But the technique is essentially the same as in the other plays: we cannot properly understand the tragedy of Ajax without observing the contrast between him and Odysseus, and so also with Deianeira and Heracles.

All three of these contrasts have been noticed by many critics. But strangely enough, so far as I know not one critic has made full use of this simple fact of form in the interpretation of all three plays. Detailed examination of the character relationships must wait until the next chapter, where fuller confirmation of the following comments on the three plays will be found. Our present concern is with the main outlines of the plays.

First let us consider *Ajax*. Ajax is a powerful figure of "soldierly greatness" and "spiritual daring" [14] but possessed of little reflective wisdom. His military virtue is everything to him; this gone, he is at an end, and his only solution is a magnificent refusal to compromise with anything: with the plea of Tecmessa for common sense and a spirit of grace, with the chorus's urging of moderation and submission. Ajax dies bitter, unforgiving, unrepentant, but splendid in his devotion to an ideal (however limited) and in the unwavering firmness of his spirit. He is a study in greatness, but his greatness is limited by his narrowness of outlook. The first part of the play emphasizes these two aspects of the hero. In the prologue with Athena and in his scenes with the chorus and Tecmessa we see his vigor of spirit, his pride, and his devotion to a soldierly concept of nobility. We see also the bitterness of his spirit, especially in

[14] *Ibid.*, 118. Kitto takes proper account of the diptych form of *Ajax*, and my account of the play owes much to his excellent pages on it. But I cannot agree that there is no rehabilitation of Ajax in the second part of the play.

the great "deception" speech (646–692) and in the final monologue before his death. His nobility is apparent, but it is narrow,
as we see when it is expressly contrasted with a humbler and
more gracious kind of nobility in his scene with Tecmessa.
His suicide is the natural, inevitable culmination of the first
part of the play.

Critics often slight the part of the play following Ajax's
death, mainly because they do not give due weight to the role
of Odysseus.[15] The real issue is not the debate between Teucer
and the leaders but the point of view expressed by Odysseus,
which takes us back, by pointing a profound contrast, to that
of Ajax and explains more fully the meaning of his lofty but
restricted view of life. Teucer is a shadow of his brother, adding no new ideas and necessarily less impressive; it would be
poor dramatic management for him to rival Ajax. The sons of
Atreus are as narrow as Ajax, and they are, unlike Ajax, mean-
spirited. What is needed is someone of breadth, honesty, and
impartiality, who can recognize and express Ajax's greatness.
This need is supplied by Odysseus. He is no hero, and therefore does not blur our impression of the magnificence of Ajax.
Toward Agamemnon he is conciliatory, yet firm in opposing
his bullying and ironically tolerant of his shortsightedness. With
Teucer he is understanding; when Teucer cannot accept his
offer to help in the burial—it would be untrue to Ajax, who
hated Odysseus—Odysseus understands at once and has only
praise for Teucer's loyalty: "It was my wish; but if you will
not have me join the task I say farewell, and praise your deed"
(1400–1401). This appearance of Odysseus was prepared for
in the prologue and is the necessary final word on the tragedy
of Ajax. What Odysseus does at the end is a realization of what
he says in the prologue: "I pity him, though he is my enemy
. . . for I see that all of us who live are only phantoms, insub-

[15] In Reinhardt's *Sophokles,* for example, there is no mention of the
part of Odysseus at the end.

stantial shadow" (121–126). The same compassion and humanity motivate both initial statement and final action.

Alone, the first part of the play would be insufficient. No doubt we divine in it Ajax's heroic nature, but the harshness and violence of his behavior leave matters incomplete and turbulent. At the end, through the wisdom and tolerance of Odysseus, who "hated him, when hatred was fair" (1347) but who can accord to his greatness a full, almost reverent recognition, the bitterness and distraction are resolved. The limits of Ajax's soldierly greatness remain, but the lasting worth of his uncompromising nobility shows up more clearly and with a certain tranquillity. It is Ajax, not Odysseus, who achieves real sublimity; there is no doubt about who is the central, and the great, figure of the play. But the dramatic manifestation of his greatness is brought about by the contrast between him and Odysseus.

Ajax tells the story, not of a great warrior's death, but of his character in action, and both parts of the play contribute to the portrayal. It is a single dramatic structure in two parts, not a play followed by an epilogue to bring the whole up to standard length.

If we fail to recognize the diptych nature of *The Trachinian Women*, we must choose between equally unsatisfactory alternatives: it is a play about Deianeira, followed by a disconnected and wildly distracting epilogue on the suffering of Heracles,[16] or it is a play about Heracles in which an introductory incident constitutes an inordinate amount of the action.[17] That there is a marked contrast between Deianeira and Heracles is unmistakable, a contrast between gentleness, selfless devotion, ir-

[16] So the play is interpreted by Ivan M. Linforth, "The Pyre on Mount Oeta in Sophocles' *Trachiniae*," *Univ. of Calif. Publ. in Class. Phil.*, 14 (1952), 255–267. Linforth calls the Heraclean part an "afterpiece."

[17] This is the interpretation of Kitto, *Greek Tragedy*, and Bowra, *Sophoclean Tragedy*.

resoluteness, and helplessness on the one side and harshness, un-yielding self-centeredness, power, and certainty of purpose on the other. Yet just as in *Ajax*, only more so, this contrast has been regularly disregarded in the interpretation of the play.

Recognition of the contrast and interpretation of the play on the assumption that the diptych form is the result of design, not of accident or Sophocles' ineptitude, do not solve all the problems of *The Trachinian Women*. The exact meaning of Heracles' nature in this play is difficult to assess. Is his end a rejection by his father Zeus, as Hyllus thinks, or does Sophocles intend us to know, from hints and trends, that Heracles in his final agony is on the road to deification? This problem will occupy us later. But recognition of the diptych form does permit us to get the two parts of the play in sensible relation to each other. As in *Ajax*, so here at the death of Deianeira we are left with an in-complete understanding of the tragedy. We understand that Deianeira is a figure of pathos, fallen into disaster through the failure of her own well-intended act; and we see that she has a touch of the sublime quality of heroism, not unlike Ajax, worlds apart though they are in all other respects.[18] But the implications of her pathetic fate are made clear only in Heracles' scene. We are left, at her death, with the insistent question: Why did Deianeira suffer so cruelly?

The final part of the play gives us the answer. It was because in trying to interfere with the actions of Heracles she was grappling with forces too great for her. Only for Heracles can the baffling and misleading oracles and the truthful lie of Nessus give meaning and pattern. For Deianeira to become involved in this unmanageable sweep of events means destruction; she is not "child of Zeus," as we are insistently reminded throughout the play that Heracles is. The final part of the play does more than present the second half of a very penetrating contrast be-tween Deianeira and Heracles; it fulfills, through the contrast,

[18] See below, pp. 114–115.

the tragedy of Deianeira. We are shown with cruel clarity the nature of the tangle of forces with which she is implicated, and her helplessness takes on a new meaning, symbolizing the inadequacy of purely human endeavor to control the course of things.[19] Her nobility also is enhanced. By the contrast not only of Heracles' crude selfishness but also of his superhuman purposefulness—he knows full well what the final words of the play mean, that "none of these things is without Zeus"—her purely human firmness of purpose and moral integrity acquire greater poignancy and heightened beauty.

What of *Antigone?* It is of a somewhat different structural type, for in it a direct encounter between the principals is the central scene of the play. There can be no shadow of doubt that Sophocles wanted to create two opposing forces of about equal weight in the drama. The achievement of this design required that the two forces be given careful development both before and after their moment of clash. Hence Antigone's prologue scene with Ismene and Creon's structurally corresponding encounter with the chorus and the guard; hence also the continuation of these two lines of development: Antigone with Ismene again and the chorus, Creon with Haemon and Teiresias. To regard Antigone as an overgrown minor figure, in basic conception like some of Euripides' martyrs (Polyxena in *Hecuba,* Macaria in *Heraclidae*), is unsatisfactory. This detailed and many-faceted study is different in kind; indeed in the emotional sense Antigone dominates the play.

The double form serves much the same purpose here as in the other two plays. Antigone's fate only attains completely explicit meaning in relation to Creon's fate; she needs Creon as Ajax needs Odysseus, Deianeira Heracles. When Antigone leaves the scene, her part in the play is by no means finished; there are unanswered questions: Why does Sophocles subject

[19] But the helplessness of Deianeira and of other Sophoclean central figures is not unalleviated, as the next chapter will try to show.

her to so terrible a fate? Why is the chorus, though sympathetic, stern and partially condemnatory of her act? Antigone herself is shaken by the attitude of the chorus, though she eventually goes to her death courageously in the conviction that she has done what was right. There is, then, an air of incompleteness, a need for answers. Creon's fate supplies the needed commentary. When finally he is brought by Teiresias to see that his conduct has been unwise and wrong, he loses all firmness, all conviction; oblivious of his own former idea of "law," he now gives in entirely to Antigone's. And when, inevitably, his capitulation proves to be too late, and everything tumbles around him—"everything is aslant in my hands" (1344–1345) —Creon is completely, pitifully shattered. The kommos which ends the play is filled with his repentance and self-recriminations. Where Antigone was shaken by the chorus's severity but recovered because she still had a conviction to sustain her, Creon has nothing left and collapses.

There is thus a contrast between two kinds of "failure" in the eyes of the chorus, that is, in the eyes of Thebes. In this play the chorus have an unusually important role; that is why, unlike the choruses of *Ajax* and *The Trachinian Women*, the Theban elders are impartial and judicious. We are not free to infer that the chorus here represent Sophocles' view but only that they represent the Theban view, the view of law-abiding citizens who are involved in what is going on and have an interest both in the laws of Thebes and in the laws of human decency. Antigone has broken what is, right or wrong, a law of Thebes. The chorus disliked Creon's edict, and they admire the fidelity and piety of Antigone's act of burial. But (rather like the Dioscuri at the end of Euripides' *Electra*) though they think the deed should have been done, they do not like the fact that it was done contrary to law. Hence their judicial attitude toward Antigone. With Creon their attitude is different.

As soon as the illegality of his law is clear to them through the words of Teiresias, they are able to combine their sympathy and loyalty on Antigone's side, and they turn on Creon with unabated scorn. Their final condemnatory words on Creon (1347–1353) are to be taken closely with their "judgment" on Antigone (872–875).

The measure of Antigone's insight and of her firmness is only made fully apparent by the contrast of Creon's abysmal failure; only through the comparison of their attitudes toward their fate and of the choral attitude toward each is the meaning of the play made clear. It may be objected that the question of Antigone's rightness is not answered; the half-condemnation of the chorus still stands. This is true. Sophocles did not mean to give any precise answer as to the rightness of Antigone's act in the political and practical sense in which the chorus were judging right and wrong. What the play does make clear is that Antigone was great in her devotion to what she considered to be right and to be her duty. The contrast with Creon is not aimed at solving a problem of conduct but is meant to reveal the nature of Antigone's high-minded conduct and to point up the difference between nobility and the lack of it; and the course of nobility always partakes of ultimate rightness.

Diptych form is, then, in vital relation to the dramatist's aims in these three plays. In each play the center of the action is a contrast between two persons, which gives both meaning and shape to the play. Can we find in the incidence of diptych form any evidence for the development of Sophocles' dramatic art? Of the three plays, two are generally regarded as the earliest extant plays. *Antigone* is known from ancient evidence to have been produced before 440, quite probably in 442;[20] *Ajax*, on

[20] Sophocles was probably victorious in the year he produced *Antigone*; cf. Snell, *TGF* 1, p. 7.

linguistic and stylistic grounds, is thought by most critics to be earlier. *The Trachinian Women* is without definite moorings, but recent opinion has tended to place it early rather than late, before *Oedipus Tyrannus* rather than after. Some, finding Euripidean qualities but nevertheless regarding it as relatively early among the extant plays, have compromised by placing it third, after *Antigone* and before *Oedipus*, in the period 438–431. The older view regarded it as very late, and among modern scholars Perrotta and Kitto continue this tradition. Reinhardt, finding archaic qualities, speaks boldly for a very early date, before *Antigone*. In spite of its "Euripidean" tone I am inclined to agree with him.[21]

We cannot take it as any proof of chronological proximity that *The Trachinian Women* has formal similarities to *Ajax* and *Antigone*. We have no idea how many plays Sophocles may have written in this form and cannot therefore assume that he wrote no diptychs after *Oedipus*. It is, therefore, mostly conjecture when I suggest that having once turned to the more unified type of *Oedipus* Sophocles continued to use this form, even when the dramatic material which he used could well have been adapted to the diptych form. This is not the case, clearly, in *Oedipus* or *Electra*. But it is eminently true of *Philoctetes*. Here again there are two opposing points of view embodied in two dramatically strong and adaptable figures, Philoctetes and Odysseus. The fact that Sophocles forms this play more after the pattern of *Oedipus* than of the diptychs is just possibly an indication of a development in his dramaturgical thinking.

The diptych form is, then, certainly a factor of prime importance for the understanding of the three plays where it occurs; and it may mark a recognizable stage in the course of Sophoclean dramatic art. But above all, it is a definite and deliberate dramatic shape, not a makeshift to save a faltering plot by shoring it up with another theme.

[21] See the Appendix for a discussion of this dating.

iii. Oedipus Tyrannus *and the Later Plays*

The form of *Oedipus Tyrannus* has all too often been regarded as *the* Sophoclean form. Rather, it is the most perfect and most successful; and it is the simplest. In a series of scenes, with Oedipus dominant in all, the characters, acting on each other as they grapple with the situation before them, gradually develop the life and power of the play; this life consists essentially of the nature of Oedipus as it emerges in the course of the revelations brought about by the plot. This simple structure, with its concentration on the single figure of Oedipus, we may call a *linear* dramatic style in contrast to the parallel or (in *Antigone*) intersecting form of the diptych plays. Along with greater simplicity of form there are greater range and more subtlety in the depiction of the chief character. Oedipus' changes of mood and changes of purpose during the play—first searching for Laius' murderer, then warding off a fancied plot against himself, then, after Jocasta's fateful mention of the "place where three roads meet," in fear of his own guilt and in search of his own origins, and at the end responding to the complete self-recognition that he has reached—this variety is very different from the single-minded devotion of Ajax, Antigone, and Deianeira. The same combination of simpler dramatic form and more complex presentation of the main figure is found in *Electra*. It is a natural development. Simplicity of plot means greater concentration on one person, which in turn results in more intricate presentation of that person.[22] But the matter should really be stated the other way

---

[22] In *El.* there is some return from the variety of mood and interest that characterizes the depiction of Oedipus to the single-mindedness of Ajax and Antigone. For Electra throughout is dominated by the one thought of revenge. But the analysis of Electra's character is so intense and detailed that in this respect too the play is closer to *OT* than to the earlier plays.

around: wishing to submit one figure to more searching study, Sophocles adopted a type of structure better suited to his purpose. It would have been quite possible for Sophocles to dramatize the story of Oedipus as a diptych had he chosen to; we can see the lines that such a form could have followed from the dramatic material of *Oedipus*. It would only take a different Creon—a more substantial figure, more directly and tellingly in conflict with Oedipus, and one raised further in importance above the other secondary figures—to change the whole emphasis of the play. In the next chapter we shall see how Sophocles deliberately fashions Creon as he is in order to serve the dramatic form he chose to use in this play.

We need not linger over *Oedipus* at this point while we are discussing general form. The effectiveness of this simply formed play depends on its remarkable and sustained tension, a dynamic aliveness that is brought about by the interaction of the characters, by the dramatic force of the magnificent choral odes, and by a unique vivacity and subtlety of language throughout. In the following chapters we shall examine these aspects of the play.

One is conscious, on comparing *Electra* with the corresponding plays of Aeschylus and Euripides, of how greatly Sophocles has compressed the story and of how much he has excluded from it in order to make his play the drama of Electra, not of Orestes or of the revenge. As in *Oedipus Tyrannus* the protagonist dominates a series of scenes, even the scene of Clytemnestra's death, where logically we might expect Orestes to be the more prominent. The part of the play from the recognition to the end is an excellent example of the subtlety of Sophocles' structural art. Orestes is to carry out the act of revenge. It is he, therefore, who must in a practical way take the lead, and in this sense he does so: in the kommos following the recognition (1232–1287) he is the one who urges dispatch and sees the danger of time lost in unguarded rejoicing; Electra is carried off by a lyrical ecstasy at the recovery of her brother. The difference is marked—as it usually is in a kommos—metrically: Orestes speaks in iambics, Electra in lyrics (including many dochmiacs, the lyrics of extreme emotion), and the more passionate outbursts of Electra quite naturally (if a little illogically) claim our main interest. So also in what follows: even at the moment of Clytemnestra's death, when Orestes is the one acting, Electra keeps the center of the stage, and Sophocles contrives what is, in effect, a dialogue between mother and daughter. In the last scene Electra's tigerish playing with the unsuspecting Aegisthus and her final expression of pent-up hatred of the usurper overshadow the quiet and businesslike action of Orestes.

In another respect too the form of this play seems to be kept in the likeness of *Oedipus* by a tour de force rather than because it best accommodates the incidents. *Electra* is in part what we shall see more fully developed in *Philoctetes*, a play of intrigue. The element of intrigue is, of course, the plot of Orestes and the paedagogus, above all the false report by the paedagogus of Orestes' death. Now this plot logically involves Orestes, the paedagogus, and Clytemnestra, not Electra at all; it is aimed to deceive Clytemnestra and implement the revenge. Yet when the report has been made, the main dramatic upshot is its effect on Electra. We are shown Clytemnestra's reaction, but this is over with quickly. Far more important is the emotional effect on Electra: the second scene with Chrysothemis springs from it, and, when the plea for aid in that scene fails, Electra's resolve to fight on alone; the effectiveness of the recognition scene—where Electra is of course dominant—depends on her belief that Orestes is dead.

Electra is in form closely akin to *Oedipus* but has elements that are really foreign to that structure. *Philoctetes*, though preserving important features of the "linear" style, is sufficiently different from it that it must be regarded as a third type of Sophoclean dramatic construction, a triangular form. This

play uses three interrelated characters to embody the action
as no other Sophoclean, indeed no other Greek, tragedy does.
The triangularity is the result of the introduction of Neoptolemus into a naturally dual pattern, the story of how Odysseus
brought Philoctetes to Troy. In this story Neoptolemus ought
properly to be a minor figure, the helper of Odysseus. Instead,
he towers over Odysseus in dramatic importance, though
Odysseus is felt as a presence all through the play, even in the
character of Neoptolemus. Although Philoctetes is clearly the
protagonist, his relations with the others are from the point
of view of structure quite unlike those of Oedipus with the
other persons of *OT*. In one sense we can still speak of linear
form in that Neoptolemus, Odysseus, the pretended merchant,
and the chorus bring out aspects of Philoctetes' nature as they
impinge on him. But the way in which the relationships are
handled is new. In Philoctetes we do not look only, or even
decidedly more, at the results of these scenes on the protagonist.
The effect of Philoctetes on Neoptolemus and of Odysseus on
Neoptolemus is almost as important, though ultimately to be
sure the changes wrought in Neoptolemus—the course of his
emotional development—come back upon Philoctetes in their
effect. Because the latent nobility of Neoptolemus overcomes
the ambition and the disregard for moral scruples to which
Odysseus has schooled him, a decisive emotional change takes
place in Philoctetes. The principle of development is the same
as before, but it is worked out through a different system of
construction.

The element of intrigue is very strong in *Philoctetes*. The
whole plan of the action springs from the problem of how to
catch Philoctetes. It cannot be done by force or persuasion;
therefore a trick must be used. Hence the elaborate lie, or series
of lies, told Philoctetes by Neoptolemus, and hence the incident
of the merchant. But we cannot write off the play as simply
the working out of an ingenious trick. It could have been so

written and still have made fine drama. Some critics would so interpret the play and are rather impatient with those who "read into it" further meaning.[23] The trouble with this view is that it does not answer to the spirit of the play. The growth of Neoptolemus before our eyes into a εὐγενὴς ἀνήρ, and the answering change in Philoctetes from a solitary outcast, distrustful and bitter, into a man who sees before him a hero's destiny and can accept it—these are more than high-spirited adventure or ingenuity. They make the play a moving study of character confronted by a decisive and challenging situation and responding to the challenge with the insight and firmness of a great man; and this is tragedy in the Sophoclean sense. The action of *Philoctetes* explodes beyond its apparent "initial charge" (to use Waldock's phrase); out of what seemed to be a special problem of deception springs a universal problem of nobility.

As an example of how the merely external events of the play are transcended by its spirit, let us look for a moment at the function of the merchant incident. Certain useful structural purposes underlie it: the incident keeps Odysseus before our minds and thus prepares for his eventual reappearance; and the dangers threatened by the merchant's report that Odysseus is coming in search of Philoctetes pave the way for the handing over of the bow to Neoptolemus, since Philoctetes is impressed by the need of immediate action. But a far more important reason for the incident is its effect on Neoptolemus. Before the appearance of the merchant the stratagem was moving ahead smoothly, and Neoptolemus had given no signs of uneasy conscience. But immediately after the incident he shows reluctance to go on with the deception; the wind, he says, is adverse (639–640), though just a little earlier it was favorable (466–467). It is as if, having seen the situation more objectively now that the scheme has become more elaborate and he has been on the sidelines (during the "merchant's" long speech) rather than

[23] Cf. especially Waldock, *Dramatist*, Ch. x.

in the center of the action, Neoptolemus begins to waver; above all he is reacting, we may suppose, to the messenger's incidental reminder that Philoctetes must come willingly to Troy before the city can be taken (611–613). It is not that Neoptolemus now thinks that the trick will not work but that he is now beginning to see what later on he sees more clearly and expresses, namely, that the trick he is abetting is in direct contrast to the heroism that Philoctetes breathes and that can alone answer to the true meaning of the oracle. The shift of mood is slight, but it is the beginning of Neoptolemus' transfer of loyalty, and even by the end of this episode he is speaking, in all sincerity, words that sort very oddly with the activity he is supposed to be engaged in. In response to the friendliness and trust that Philoctetes has shown him, he says, in heartfelt reply: "The man who learns to return good acts for good is a friend more valuable than any wealth" (672–673). Even the very heart of the stratagem has become part of this further, more universal theme.

Oedipus at Colonus is in still another distinct form. It is closer to *Tyrannus* than to *Philoctetes* in that the central figure again dominates every scene and the action develops entirely in and through him. But it is unlike *Tyrannus*, in fact unlike any other Sophoclean play that we have, in an important respect: *Oedipus at Colonus* is essentially the illustration of a theme given in advance, rather than the development of a theme by a course of incidents. In *Philoctetes*, for example, we do not know that through the agency of Neoptolemus Philoctetes is going to experience a profound change of mood, even if we do know that the result of the play must be that Philoctetes goes to Troy. In *Oedipus Tyrannus*, though we may know the story beforehand, we do not know what it is going to mean (except externally) for the character of Oedipus. But in *Colonus* we discover in the prologue what the potentialities of the old Oedipus are: that he has a special power to bless those who accept him and to curse those who reject him, once he has reached the grove of the Eumenides. The whole play is essentially the expansion of this double theme of blessing and curse; it is a very impressive and panoramic fulfillment, with the stirring action when Creon abducts Oedipus' daughters, the somber power of the scene wherein Oedipus curses his sons, and the thrilling moment when the old blind man, led by a divine inward light, strides unerringly to the place assigned for his rendezvous with deity, leading the way for the others. In fact *Colonus* is more crowded with incidents and depends more for its effect on physical action and stage devices than any other Sophoclean play.

In its difference from the other plays, *Colonus* is like some plays of Euripides—*Hecuba, Hippolytus,* and *The Trojan Women* are examples—where the theme is clearly stated in the prologue and the ensuing action illustrates that theme. To call *Colonus* Euripidean may seem paradoxical, and of course it is not in most ways Euripidean: the personality of Oedipus, the nature of the choral odes, and the kind of theme that is dramatized are not Euripidean. But in this one significant aspect of form it is unique in Sophocles, and several times paralleled in Euripides.[24]

A word of further description of this double theme is in order. First, the two parts of the theme are united in Oedipus and are in fact simply two aspects of his daemonic power.[25]

[24] U. Wilamowitz, in T. Wilamowitz, *Dramatische Technik*, derives the form of the play from Euripides' *Philoctetes*. (He ascribes to Tycho the idea of this derivation.) The chief similarity of form consists in the presence of two opposing sides bidding for the favor of the tragic hero. The structural similarity is marked enough to be worth noticing, but the fact that twenty-seven years elapsed between the two productions, during which period a large number of plays were produced of whose form we know nothing, makes the assumption of direct influence questionable.

[25] Ivan M. Linforth, "Religion and Drama in *Oedipus at Colonus*," *Univ. of Calif. Publ. in Class. Phil.*, 14 (1951), 75–195, in a searching examination of the play, denies that there is evidence for heroic or daemonic power in Oedipus. (Cf. especially pp. 114–129.) Linforth's skepti-

The double power is described in the prologue. After the Colonean stranger, from whom he has learned that he has now reached the sacred place of the Eumenides, has left, Oedipus addresses a prayer of peculiarly hushed solemnity to the goddesses, beginning ὦ πότνιαι δεινῶπες. These opening words, by their hint of the paradoxical double power of the Eumenides-Erinyes, "Cherishing goddesses of grim aspect," already suggest the double nature of Oedipus' daemonic destiny, and throughout the play he is in strange and impressive rapport with the goddesses in whose grove he has found rest.[26] In the prayer he goes on to say how he was told by Apollo that he would some day find rest at their holy place and would "bestow blessings on those who have received me, destruction on those who sent me here, who drove me forth" (92–93). The course of the play illustrates the realization of this double power. With Theseus, who receives him graciously, symbolizing Athens, and with his daughters, who have been his defenders in his helplessness, Oedipus has a relationship of calm and gracious friendship; they are "those who have received" him, and in the play they receive the blessing of his grace. For Creon, who represents the spirit that has driven him out of Thebes, and for Polyneices, his disloyal son, he has nothing but hatred and curses. Every incident of the action is a contribution to the display of this strange double power of Oedipus.[27]

---

cism seems to me excessive, but his study is an excellent reminder that there are other things in the play beside religion, and his analysis of the play is most valuable.

[26] The Eumenides are kept in prominence, for example, in the incident of sacrifice (461–509) and in Oedipus' curse on his sons (1391). For an interesting discussion of the part of the Eumenides in *OC* and of other religious matters connected with the play, see R. P. Winnington-Ingram, "A Religious Function of Greek Tragedy," *JHS*, 74 (1954), 16–24.

[27] This is essentially the interpretation of the play offered by Bowra, *Sophoclean Tragedy*.

Such are the four methods of construction that Sophocles uses in the seven plays that we have. Had we seventy, we might find forty forms, so little is Sophocles restricted to a single pattern. But we can make one general distinction of value for the understanding of the plays: there are three plays of double form, where two analytically distinguishable parts of the play present two different aspects of the theme; in four plays a single dominant figure holds the action together and gives it continuity.

iv. Restriction

In comparison with most later drama Greek tragedy as a whole is notable for the extent to which it excises or compresses all aspects of the story that are not strictly necessary to the theme of the play.[28] In *Antigone*, for example, the heroine and Haemon are betrothed; we know that they love each other, from a few indications: the one suggestion of Antigone's emotional attachment in lines 568 and following,[29] Haemon's championing of Antigone (where, however, the theme of love scarcely comes into the open and is mostly conveyed by implication, especially by the choral ode following Haemon's scene with Creon), and, the most overt indication, Haemon's suicide after finding Antigone dead, and his loving embrace of her dead body (1223–1225 and 1236–1237). It is significant that by far the most direct and emphatic token of this love occurs when it has an immediate bearing on the main theme,

[28] There are good notes on this feature of Greek tragedy in Jebb's introductions, especially his introduction to *OT*.

[29] Line 572 is Ismene's in all MSS. Many editors, beginning with Aldus and including Pearson, give it to Antigone. There are excellent arguments either way. As Letters, *Life and Works*, 166–167, observes, Antigone does not need the line; we know from Ismene's words just above (570) that the love of Antigone and Haemon is mutual and strong. For our present discussion it does not matter much which sister speaks the line. A. Bonnard, *La Tragédie et l'homme* (Neuchâtel, 1951), 85–86, argues excellently for the ascription to Ismene.

in the messenger's speech; here it is altogether to Sophocles' purpose to underline in this way the fact that Creon's stubbornness has brought sorrow and ruin to everything that is dear to him; the same purpose is later served by the suicide of Eurydice.

It is illuminating to compare this severe restriction with a later treatment of the story, Anouilh's *Antigone* (1942). Anouilh means to follow the plot and the spirit of Sophocles' play closely, but he cannot refrain from expanding the theme of love considerably, in Antigone's conversations with Ismene and by the insertion of a love scene, even though this theme has just the same bearing on the main theme as in Sophocles. Some will object that my example is not fair, on the grounds that romantic love has no place in classical Greek literature. The objection is not valid in this instance because the fact of romantic love is unquestionably present here, though it is not of course the dramatist's prime concern. In any case, the principle of dramatic construction that concerns us now can be substantiated with other examples. In view of *Alcestis* and *The Trachinian Women*, it can hardly be alleged that the Greeks found no place in literature for marital devotion; and in *Oedipus Tyrannus* we find a close parallel to our example from *Antigone*. We know that Jocasta's love for Oedipus is a very strong feeling; we know it not because any statement is made by anyone in the play to that effect or because any scene is devoted to revealing the fact, but because of Jocasta's maternal protectiveness of Oedipus. Here again the subordinate matter has a place only when it is a part of the main theme.[30] The friendship of Pylades and Orestes and the consequent part of Pylades in *The Choephoroe* are another example of the same attitude: in Pylades' one short, vital speech, the fact of his friendship with Orestes is

[30] The love theme is much expanded in such later Oedipus plays as those of Dryden and Voltaire (who complicates the theme by bringing in Philoctetes as an old suitor of Jocasta's).

supremely important, and yet the playwright has not found it necessary to amplify this fact.

Everyone at all familiar with Greek tragedy is aware of this compression of subordinate matters and accepts it as a part of Greek tragic form. There are, however, some instances of this technique where it is not so immediately clear that what is happening is simply a result of the conventions of the genre, and some of these cases are responsible for serious confusion about Sophocles' dramatic intentions.

First let us notice a minor example of this technique which is clear, though not always recognized for what it is. It is in *Antigone*. When Teiresias is warning Creon of the inevitable consequences of his folly, he tells him that he will lose his son (1064–1067) and that there will be "wailing of men and women" in his house (1078–1079); then he adds:

> And all the cities are stirred with hatred, whose
> mangled corpses have had funeral rites from dogs
> and wild beasts, or some winged creature which carries
> the stench of impiety to the city hearth. [1080–1083]

In these lines we receive the new information that Creon has refused burial not only to Polyneices but to all the enemy dead. There is in terms of the myth nothing surprising in this. Euripides makes a play out of it, *The Suppliants*, and in the handbook of mythology ascribed to Apollodorus it is given as one of the incidents of the story of the Seven Against Thebes. It is altogether likely that the incident was a standard part of the legend from early times. Where Sophocles has diverged from tradition is in omitting mention of it in the earlier part of his play. For this exclusion he had an obvious reason: to mention the general interdiction of burial would have dissipated our sense of the enormity of Creon's treatment of Polyneices in particular and would have distracted our attention a little from this one important fact, the fate of Polyneices. But now, when it is very much to the point to have everything crashing upon Creon's head, it is useful for Sophocles to bring in this other fact.[31]

By bringing in the incident later on, Sophocles permits us a glimpse of this interesting technique of suppression in a very minor case. Clearly he does not mean us to assume, when he suppresses the incident in the early part of the play, that the other invaders were buried; he does not mean us to make any assumption at all about their fate.

There is a more troublesome instance of the same procedure in *Electra*. Endless debate has gone on concerning Sophocles' attitude toward the act of matricide. Most critics have assumed that since in this play no Furies appear, and Orestes seems relatively untroubled at the end, Sophocles is presenting the story simply as a grim but god-sanctioned and righteous act of revenge. We have already discussed ways in which the form and emphasis of this play are quite unlike those in Aeschylus and Euripides. Sophocles is dramatizing, not the revenge, nor the act of matricide, but the story of Electra as she is affected by her years of resistance to Aegisthus and Clytemnestra, by the return of Orestes, and by his consummation of the revenge. All other elements of the traditional story are, in accordance with the habitual dramatic method of Sophocles, excluded as irrelevant. To have included in the play the consequences—if any—of Orestes' murder of Clytemnestra would have been to make the play something other than what it was intended for, something other than the play of Electra. We do not know what Sophocles thought about Orestes' deed in relation to Orestes

---

[31] The casual mention of the death of Megareus (1303) is to the same point. In this instance the interesting thing is not just the matter of suppression but the fact that Sophocles could apparently expect his audience (or his reader) to grasp even this brief allusion to a part of the myth that lies outside his plot.

himself. We can neither assume that Orestes is considered guiltless by Sophocles nor that he is doomed to Furies or remorse. What we should expect is an indication of what all these things mean for Electra. Consideration of this difficult problem will find place in our discussion of the characters, in Chapter III.

In *The Trachinian Women* scholars generally assume that we have a bitter or hostile portrait of Heracles, in which he is not deified in the traditional manner, the mortal part of him burnt away in the funeral pyre on Mount Oeta; that, instead, he dies in agony, a "mortal" death. The assumption is not warranted. It is fathered by the conviction that the play is about the death of Heracles. Above, we have seen that the diptych form shows that the action is centered elsewhere; the play is about Deianeira and Heracles in relation to each other, and aspects of the two which do not concern each other have no place. Heracles is unquestionably regarded throughout as son of Zeus and a being of significant destiny; his whole nature and fate belong to a realm of being far beyond the powers of Deianeira to cope with. But the final fate of Heracles is no part of Sophocles' play. We cannot assume either apotheosis or inglorious death but must take Heracles as we find him in the play, not as we suspect, without guidance from Sophocles,[32] he may turn out just beyond its end. Sophocles' repeated use of deliberate restriction should warn us against making such assumptions, especially when we can clearly see his reason for this rigid restriction, namely, to maintain the dramatic balance that is an essential part of this diptych action. By these restrictions Sophocles leaves unanswered questions that we should like very much to have answers for. But we must not supply the

---

[32] In lines 1208–1210, when Heracles says that Hyllus will, by burning him, become his "healer," there seems to be a passing allusion to the apotheosis—not emphatic enough, I think, to be dramatically important, but certainly clear enough to forbid our supposing that Sophocles means us to believe that his Heracles died forsaken by Zeus.

answers; the very impossibility of finding a generally satisfactory answer warns us against the attempt.

Closely akin to the matter of restriction, indeed another facet of this technique, is the question as to what facts in the story, apart from those that are openly part of the action of the play, belong to the theme and are therefore to be taken into account in our reception of the play. The answer is, theoretically, obvious: what the playwright tells us, he wants us to consider, and what he does not tell us (no matter how standard it is in the legend), he wants us to disregard. In practice, however, it is not always easy, to judge by the different assumptions critics have made, to know what is dramatically relevant and what is not. In *Oedipus Tyrannus* how shall we decide what parts of Oedipus' earlier career belong to the play? Was his marriage to Jocasta an instance of fatal hastiness and self-confidence that Sophocles means us to take into our consideration of his character in the play? Careful discrimination is necessary. We have no right to construct a picture of Oedipus as a boy and trace his psychological development from that age. But we certainly do have a right to use the incident of his dissatisfaction with his seeming parents' assurance that he is their child, his consequent trip to Delphi, and, following on this, his self-imposed exile from Corinth. We have a right to say that here are confirmations of the traits that we see elsewhere in the play: the consuming desire of Oedipus to know the whole truth and his strong tendency to rely on his own judgment. We have a right, also, to observe not only the fact that he killed Laius, but the manner in which he did so; in the description of the incident (806–813) we see abundant evidence of his quickness of temper and his impetuousness, confirming the evidence of events within the play.[33] We ought to take cognizance of this

[33] A number of critics have denied the propriety of using this passage as evidence for Oedipus' temper, because, they say, the incident was purely a matter of self-defense on Oedipus' part. (Cf. Whitman,

evidence for the simple reason that Sophocles presents us with this evidence; it is not Sophocles' habit to present dramatically meaningless facts.

But we must, on the other hand, avoid behaving like detectives and trying to build up a case against (or for) Oedipus out of matters that the playwright does not bring to our attention. Therefore we must not criticize Oedipus for not having found out more about his predecessor on the Theban throne, or for having been so indiscreet as to marry, and at that a woman old enough to be his mother. However well they may accord with Oedipus' impetuousness and want of caution, these facts are not evidence for these qualities simply because—for the obvious purpose, if no other, of obscuring the latent incongruities of the story—Sophocles does not make them a part of his play. *Oedipus Tyrannus* must not be interpreted as though it were a fragmentary biography of a real person; Oedipus, so

---

Sophocles, 268; Letters, *Life and Works*, 218; and others.) But if Sophocles meant us to think this, why does he so deliberately stress the violence of Oedipus' retribution on Laius and his party? Sophocles does not include such details of realism unless he means them to have dramatic relevance; when he has Oedipus tell us, "He [Laius] paid *no equal penalty.* . . . I killed them all" (810–813; the passage has the same feeling of swift violence as Deianeira's report of Heracles' dispatch of Nessus, *Trach.* 566–568), he is creating a strange and unintelligible picture of an act of pure self-defense. If this is not evidence of anger and impetuous behavior, I cannot imagine what would be. It is instructive to contrast Oedipus' report of the incident in his defense of his past in *OC* 960–1002, where the poet clearly means to indicate that it was an act of self-defense; this, of course, suggests nothing for *OT*. The words in *OT* are not evidence of criminal intent or behavior on Oedipus' part; but this is not the point at issue.

In the magnificent performance of *OT* in Yeats's translation in the Shakespearean Festival at Stratford, Ontario, in the summer of 1955, this speech of Oedipus' was one of the great moments of the play. Perhaps the director, Tyrone Guthrie, overstressed the passage; but nobody, I think, could see that performance and doubt that Oedipus' report of the event at the crossroads is profoundly important for the depiction of his character.

far as this play is concerned, is what Sophocles says or otherwise reveals about him in the course of the play.

In other words, it is essential to distinguish what is properly a part of the drama from what is ἔξω τοῦ δράματος, and the only possible division is between what the playwright gives us and what he conceals. There can be no chronological division: events before, as in *Oedipus Tyrannus,* and even events after, as in *Philoctetes* (the fulfillment of Philoctetes' destiny, which we are told will come about) and in *Oedipus at Colonus* (Oedipus' future gift of protection to Athens), may be within the drama; events contemporary with the action may be outside.

An instructive example of the latter case occurs in *Antigone.* On reading the play or seeing it performed, one is not struck by the fact that there are two burials of Polyneices; we are aware of it, but we do not normally attach any importance to the fact. Sophocles does not mean us to be impressed by it, and nowhere in the play stresses the duplication. He needed it for the action of the play, but that is all. In the clinical atmosphere of the study, however, such an interesting symptom does not go unanalyzed. (Nor do I suggest that it should; only that analysis should not lead to improper use of the evidence.) The reason for having Polyneices' body buried twice is sufficiently clear and has been adequately explained by critics: Sophocles wanted two effects from the act of burial, Antigone's defiance of Creon and Antigone's capture. To combine them in a single scene would mean attenuating the force of the first of the two desired effects, if not of both. On the first depends Creon's initial interview with the guard, an incident of great value for our understanding of Creon; from the second comes the great scene between Antigone and Creon and indeed all the rest of the play. Therefore Sophocles has the burial repeated. The explanation is simple and the device obvious and highly successful. The fact that analysis discloses the mechanism detracts nothing.

From false emphasis on this simple dramaturgical device have sprung two wrong interpretations: that the second burial is

intended by Sophocles as the *hamartia* of Antigone (representing undue willfulness and stubbornness) [34] and that it was Ismene
who first buried Polyneices.[35] The first of these is an error of
judgment. It is wrong to put interpretative stress on an aspect
of the action that the playwright is minimizing; to do so is to
confuse dramatic interpretation with detective work. The second misinterpretation is the wildest nonsense. It misreads the
character of Ismene and destroys the isolated heroism of
Antigone; above all it necessitates a crass misuse of a line of the
play. Ismene, in her small moment of heroism, blurts out δέδρακα
τοὔργον. This is half a line; and on this half-line the whole interpretation depends. One has only to read the rest of the line,
εἴπερ ἥδ' ὁμορροθεῖ (536) to see at once that Ismene spoke in
hyperbole; her "participation" is in spirit only.[36] It is almost un-
believable that two reputable critics, independently and almost
simultaneously, proposed this fantastic interpretation, acceptable
neither as literary criticism nor as criminal investigation.

[34] Minnie Keyes Flickinger, "The Ἁμαρτία of Sophocles' Antigone,"
Iowa Studies in Classical Philology, Vol. 2 (1935). It seems worth while
to mention here a suggestion made by S. M. Adams in *CR*, 45 (1931),
110–111, and repeated in his "The *Antigone* of Sophocles," *Phoenix*, 9
(1955), 47–62, that the first burial was brought about by divinity, by
means of a dust storm. There is not, in my opinion, enough evidence in
the play to substantiate this idea, but it has the merit of being far more
in accord with the sense of the play than the other notions discussed
here. Cf. now also Kitto, *Form and Meaning*, 153–154. Kitto discusses
the double burial at length, maintaining its relevance to the theme, which
is emphasized throughout *Form and Meaning*, of parallel human and
divine action. On pp. 152–178 Kitto considers a number of structural
features of the play, including the double burial.
[35] W. H. D. Rouse, "The Two Burials in *Antigone*," *CR*, 25 (1911),
40–42; J. E. Harry, "Studies in Sophocles," *Univ. of Cincinnati Studies*,
ser. 2, 7 (1911), 20–25.
[36] Robert F. Goheen, *The Imagery of Sophocles' Antigone* (Princeton,
1951), 45, 139–140, translates "I did the deed, even though she rows by
my side." (Goheen, however, does not proceed to misinterpret the spirit
of Ismene's words.) But εἴπερ does not mean "even though" in Attic
Greek. It means "if, indeed," and is often virtually equivalent to "since,"
though it cannot have the latter meaning here.

Here then is a physical fact that is not a dramatic fact. Physically there were two burials; dramatically there was only "burial" divided in two in order to achieve two separate purposes.

Let us notice one more example of this Sophoclean technique of restriction, this time with reference to an event before the action of the play. In *Ajax* the protagonist several times complains that he was unfairly deprived of the armor of Achilles: he says that he was "dishonored" (98); calls it "my armor" (100); suggests that the Atridae were guilty of favoritism toward Odysseus (441–449). Agamemnon, on the contrary, indicates that the issue was decided by a vote, in which Ajax was worsted (1243–1244). Which are we to believe? A good many critics, understandably sympathizing with Ajax, have spoken as if it were a clear and incontrovertible fact that the award was an injustice to Ajax.[37] For this assumption there is absolutely no warrant in the play. Sophocles leaves the issue vague, and here again we can readily see that he had excellent reason for so doing: the justice or injustice of the award is not part of this play; what is a part of it is the conviction of Ajax that he has been wrongly treated and of the leaders that Ajax did not deserve the prize. The vagueness is intentional and dramatically valuable, and it is wrong for us to try to go beyond Sophocles and settle the question of justice.

v. Oracles and Dramaturgy

We are here interested in oracles primarily from the point of view of their place in the organization of Sophocles' plays.

---

[37] Cf. Whitman, *Sophocles*, 76; Linforth, "Three Scenes in Sophocles' *Ajax*," *Univ. of Calif. Publ. in Class. Phil.*, 15 (1954), 1–28 (cf. p. 25, "the arms of Achilles, which should have come to him [Ajax]"); Opstelten, *Pessimism*, 51, referring to *Aj.* 1135–1136. But line 1136 is not an admission by Menelaus that Ajax was cheated; it means, as Jebb takes it, "At the hands of the judges, not at mine, he had that fall."

When so considered they deserve a place close to the matters discussed in the preceding section; they are, in fact, a special branch of the technique that we noticed there. We cannot, however, entirely overlook the possible religious element in Sophocles' use of oracles and the effect that this element may have upon his plays.

Oracles, perhaps not all of them but at least all that we find in Sophocles, may be divided into three categories. They may be ways of presenting truths about the conditions of life or about human character in a way that has a religious coloring or context. For example, the oracular treatment of Cleobis and Biton and of Trophonius bears the implicit lesson that death at a moment of supreme happiness is the highest good. Oracles may also consist of advice: the answer to the Athenians that they are to trust to their wooden walls. Or, commonest of all, oracles may simply declare what will happen: Croesus, if he attacks the Persian power, will destroy a mighty empire. Such oracles are frequently ambiguous, sometimes constitute a test of character (will the man who has consulted the oracle have the sagacity to understand the answer?), but seldom, if ever, enforce events or acts of character. This last point is particularly important in connection with Sophocles. In his plays events do not take place because the oracles say that they will; on the contrary, the oracles say that events will take place because they are going to. There is no fatalism involved in the oracular utterance itself; the oracles need not say why the events will take place, and they may come about because of human character. The fulfillment of most Sophoclean oracles does, in fact, require the force of human character, though it may also involve divine will. To what extent Sophocles' use of oracles is a reflection of a personal religious outlook is impossible to say and does not matter here. What we can know beyond doubt is that in his way of handling oracles in his plays he shows a good deal of freedom of invention and a consistent tendency to dovetail oracular material with the natural outcome of character. A brief survey of the chief oracles and related phenomena in the plays will clarify these assertions.

In *Ajax* there is no oracle; but Calchas' prophetic statement that the hero is subject to the divine wrath for that one day is of the same nature. Calchas' announcement does not in the least make Ajax's suicide inevitable; he could have stayed in his tent and been safe. The suicide requires two things, the anger of the gods which caused Ajax's madness and the character of Ajax.

The oracular element in *The Trachinian Women* is interesting above all for the way in which it is handled by the playwright; we shall come back to this presently. There is really only one oracle that matters, that concerning Heracles' "rest" after a certain period of time and after the fulfillment of the final task on which he is engaged when the play begins. What is the meaning of this deceptive oracle, in which the promised rest turns out to be the peace of death? Rather than a mere prank of divine cruelty upon Heracles it seems to be an oracular statement about the character of Heracles: the restless, ever-toiling hero can have no rest so long as his mortal life goes on. The other oracle in the play, that Heracles' death will be at the hands of one no longer living, scarcely calls for consideration; it has no religious significance certainly, and its place in the play is only that of a signal to Heracles, whereby he can know that the end of his life is at hand.

In *Antigone* Teiresias' prophecy and warning to Creon are no doubt religious and reveal the displeasure of deity with Creon's conduct. There is no question here of capricious oracular power or fate: Creon's conduct gives rise to the divine displeasure, and Teiresias' statement reports this displeasure.

In *Oedipus. Tyrannus* there are two oracles: the response to Creon, reported in the prologue, and the oracle given to Oedipus in his youth. Of the first we need say little. It asserts the technical guilt of Oedipus by declaring that the murderer of Laius must be driven from Thebes. But of this there is no question and therefore the oracle has no peculiar religious power or meaning; it merely gives information. The other oracle, proclaiming that it is Oedipus' fate to marry his mother and kill his father, is the best known of all Sophoclean oracles and the one which most accounts for the common attitude that things happen in Sophocles because oracles declare that they must. Here we cannot separate the content of the oracle from its manner of presentation, for in this oracle the essential feature of Sophocles' presentation is his modification of the traditional content. According to the archaic, pre-Sophoclean, and better-known version of the oracle, a dire fate is imposed on Oedipus because of Laius' insistence on begetting a son, against the will of the gods; in fact the chain of causes sometimes goes back to an earlier offense of Laius.[38] Sophocles wanted no part of this motif of inherited guilt and therefore dropped from his version of the oracle the traditional cause—a very significant omission. (Even when in *Oedipus* the corresponding oracle to Laius is mentioned—that the son he sires is destined to slay him—there is no cause given.) The traditional cause of Oedipus' suffering is thus erased from Sophocles' play, and we must not try to spirit it back in.

To what cause Sophocles wants us to ascribe the fate of Oedipus is a problem that has elicited many and various answers and is often regarded as the key to the play. But what if Sophocles never intended there to be an answer? What if the fate of Oedipus is simply a mythological datum, to be accepted and built into the study of Oedipus without comment or solution? We can enjoy the play most fully, and best avoid misunderstanding it, if we take the simple approach that these questions

[38] H. W. Parke and D. E. Wormell, *The Delphic Oracle*[2] (Oxford, 1956), 298–300. Strictly speaking, there are three oracles in the play, for the response given to Laius and that given to Oedipus are separate oracles, though the content is essentially the same.

suggest. I doubt, however, if one can read all seven of Sophocles' plays without yielding to the temptation to supply some answer to the question of Oedipus' fate. But the answer will probably be based on an impression gained from all the plays; it will therefore belong to a more subjective and more abstract realm of criticism than we are now concerned with. In the next chapter we shall find confirmation of the common view that whatever the answer may be, it must not be separated from the person of Oedipus; his fate is not independent of his character. For the moment it is relevant to emphasize that it is not the oracle that brings about the events but the events that permit the oracle. Furthermore, this famous oracle is no more sacrosanct and immutable than others that Sophocles uses: when Jocasta reports the oracle (711–714), she "knows" only the part that applies to Laius. What this means, in terms of Sophocles' use of the oracle, is that at that point in the play Sophocles wants to reveal only this half of the oracle, for it is enough to set the wheels of discovery in motion.

In *Electra* the first thing to observe is that the oracle does not concern Electra. She needs no oracular backing and is impelled by no oracular demand; her actions and her feelings spring from her own character. Therefore in this play about Electra the oracle can have only an indirect bearing; it can only tell us whether Orestes is justified in his revenge, supported by Apollo's will. In assessing Sophocles' attitude toward oracles this in *Electra* is a particularly valuable guide: whether Sophocles believes in the truth and the religious force of oracles or not, we see in this play very clearly that he is at least capable of thinking in quite different terms, even in a story where oracular influence was traditionally present. He could, had he been concerned to support the validity of oracles, have contrived to make his tragic heroine base her inflexible resolve for revenge on the need for obedience to the oracle; instead, he has her base it on her own will and her own moral judgment.

In *Philoctetes* there is no oracle but one prophecy in several installments; here, as in *The Trachinian Women*, the most interesting thing is Sophocles' way of presenting the matter, of which more presently. There is no religious value in this prophecy of Helenus, which states merely that Troy cannot fall without Philoctetes' presence in the Greek army. This is surely a commentary on Philoctetes' greatness, just as his possession of the weapons of Heracles is. (In Sophocles, Philoctetes acquired the weapons directly from Heracles, though the usual tradition was that they came to him via his father Poias.)

The very theme of *Oedipus at Colonus* is, as we have already seen, embodied in an oracle that is stated in the prologue (87–95); and this same oracle is several times repeated, or paraphrased in part, elsewhere in the play. This oracle depends on the character of Oedipus and on the recognition by deity of the power and value of that character. It is because Oedipus is what he is that he is granted the strange and great power of bestowing blessings and ruin. Here again matter and presentation are inextricable, as Letters has acutely pointed out: it is significant for Sophocles' use of oracles that he does not hesitate to attach a completely new and different paragraph to the old oracle portending disaster to Oedipus.[39] Are we to assume that Sophocles meant us to know about this ultimate rewarding of Oedipus when he used the oracle in *Tyrannus?* Of course not. In that play it suited his dramatic purpose to have only the gloomy prophecy; in this play he wants a further, restitutive clause, and so he adds it without hesitation.

There is no reason for believing that Sophocles was tyrannized over by oracles, and no reason to suppose that the presence of numerous oracles in his plays indicates a tendency to rely primarily on the power of fate or deity, as expressed through

[39] Letters, *Life and Works*, 294–295. Letters is the first critic, so far as I know, to have made the simple but important observation that this oracle in *OC* is represented as being part of the famous oracle of *OT*.

oracles, for his view of human life. In the great majority of cases the content of the oracle tells as much about character as it does about divine will or fate. Whether or not Sophocles had a personal belief in the religious value of oracles is, of course, another matter; it is altogether probable that he did, like most men of his day, but the evidence of the plays is quite inconclusive. What matters for us as students of Sophoclean drama is the fact that oracles in the plays of Sophocles are invariably shaped to fit the dramatic context, and not vice versa. We are therefore justified in assuming that when Sophocles presents oracular information in a unique and unconventional way he is doing so for his own reasons as a dramatist, and we shall see that in two plays, *The Trachinian Women* and *Philoctetes*, he uses oracles in a way that is closely similar to his method of restriction.

In *The Trachinian Women* the oracle telling of what is to happen to Heracles comes out piecemeal and rather confusedly. In the prologue Deianeira's reference to the oracle seems to indicate that it has to do specifically with Heracles' expedition against the city of Eurytus (74–81); when next she refers to it she says only that Heracles has told her that at the end of fifteen months from the time of his last departure he will either die or live in peace thereafter (166–169); and when finally Heracles speaks of it he says merely that it was prophesied that "at this time now living and present" he would have release from toils (1169–1171). These are minor differences, but the inexactness is not without significance. More striking, and more important for Sophocles' use of oracles, is the fact that in the choral ode following Hyllus' report of his father's agony, the Trachinian women speak with detailed knowledge of the oracle, mentioning something that neither Deianeira nor Heracles ever refers to, that the oracle was given twelve years before its fulfillment. How did they know about the oracle? Earlier, Deianeira speaks to them as if they were strangers to the whole situation.

Jebb thought that "the inconsistency of detail was simply overlooked by the poet." [40] Possibly so; but it may be more accurate
to say that the poet counted on his audience to overlook the inconsistency, while he went ahead and used whatever parts of the
oracle suited his purpose at various points in the play.[41] This is
Jebb's view of the use of the oracle as a whole in the play,[42] and
I think that it is certainly right. Toward the beginning Sophocles
uses it, in the mouth of Deianeira, to increase the sense of foreboding that fills her mind and is an essential part of the setting;
at the end it helps Heracles tie matters together and realize
that his death is at hand; in between it is used in a choral ode
to grace and substantiate the chorus's reflections on what has
happened.

Is this not precisely the same kind of dramatic method as in
the matter of burial in *Antigone?* Just as in that play "burial" is
distributed according to the necessities of the dramatic action,
so here "oracle" is similarly parceled out when and as the development of the play demands.

Our final example of this aspect of Sophoclean method is
the prophecy of Helenus in *Philoctetes*.[43] Here again there is
one original statement several times reported in the play, and
each time a little differently, according to the exigencies of the
moment. Here again there are elements of illogicality in the
knowledge shown by different persons, but as in *The Trachinian*

[40] Edition of *Trach.*, p. 123.

[41] He even alters it, when he chooses, to suit his dramatic purpose: in
lines 166–169 Deianeira makes the "peace" specifically an alternative to
death, because at this point the ambiguity of the oracle's possible meaning is useful to heighten the doubt and suspense that are maintained
throughout the first part of the play; in lines 1169–1171 the same oracle
is reported as offering only "surcease from toils," and Heracles goes on
to equate this surcease with death. It is idle to ask which version is correct. Each one is dramatically correct in its place.

[42] Edition of *Trach.*, pp. xli–xlii.

[43] For a valuable discussion of this point, see Kitto, *Form and Meaning*, Ch. iv, *passim*.

Women these illogicalities have dramatic point. The prophecy, given in its fullest form in the speech of the pseudo-merchant, declares that the Greeks will not take Troy until they bring Philoctetes, by persuasion, from Lemnos to Troy (610–613); from other versions we get the information that the weapons of Heracles are also essential (113). In addition to the prophecy, there is also certain related information concerning the disease of Philoctetes and its destined cure; whether this information is known by oracle, prophecy, or some other means is never specified.

From this body of extraordinary knowledge, Sophocles draws whatever parts he needs at any given moment, often without regard for strict probability; here again, as in *The Trachinian Women*, it is probably safer to ascribe the illogicality to Sophocles' design than to oversight. (The discrepancy between Neoptolemus' statement that the Asclepiadae will cure Philoctetes [1333–1334] and Heracles' that he will send Asclepius to do so [1437–1438] is perhaps an oversight, though even here it is not unreasonable to find a dramatic point: Neoptolemus' version of the cure is more naturalistic and less miraculous, since the Asclepiadae are the traditional physicians of the Greek host; Heracles' promise to send the god of healing himself is in keeping with the exalted tone of the entire epiphany and emphasizes the divine interest in Philoctetes' destiny.) In the prologue Odysseus speaks only of the need for the weapons in Philoctetes' possession—they and Neoptolemus are destined to take Troy (113)—not a word about Philoctetes. The reason is clear: Odysseus is trying to steel the young Neoptolemus to carry through the deception, and he quite naturally stresses the glory that will come to him. We need not assume that Odysseus does not know the rest of the prophecy; we are best off making no assumptions about such matters. In the parodos Neoptolemus, in answer to the chorus's expression of sympathy for Philoctetes' suffering, declares that the suffering was imposed by heaven and will end only when the hero "bends the shafts of the gods" against Troy (191–200). In view of Neoptolemus' apparent ignorance about Philoctetes in the prologue, this sudden revelation of knowledge not gained from Odysseus is a little surprising, though not impossible. But why is Neoptolemus ignorant in the prologue, knowledgeable in the parodos? Because in the prologue Sophocles wanted to stress the influence of Odysseus over him; the youth is to be the learner, the receiver of knowledge, not the knower. In the parodos, on the other hand, Sophocles wants us to see him steeled against the sympathy he would naturally feel for Philoctetes; the knowledge displayed here by Neoptolemus helps to explain, in terms of his character, how he is able to continue to deceive Philoctetes for so long. Also, of course, Sophocles is in this way able to give his audience pertinent information without interfering with the progress of the action.

Later on the bogus merchant adds the vitally important fact that Philoctetes must come to Troy and must come willingly (610–613). It has already been suggested that the main dramatic purpose of this speech is its effect on Neoptolemus; so far as the action of the play is concerned, this is the first moment at which Neoptolemus knows this part of the prophecy, and his behavior from this point onward indicates that his emotional reaction to the new information is strong. Finally, when Neoptolemus at the end has returned the bow to Philoctetes and appeals to him as a friend to come to Troy, he needs every persuasive argument possible, and so Sophocles grants him full and authoritative knowledge of the prophecy and of the conditions of the healing of the wound (1329–1335); and again we are most unlikely, when we watch the play, to ask how it is that Neoptolemus, who began in such boyish ignorance, can now speak with such oracular firmness and fullness.[44]

[44] It may seem a questionable liberty of criticism to assume that the inconsistencies under discussion were both undetectable by the audience

Throughout, Sophocles uses the prophetic and supernatural knowledge exactly as it fits his dramatic design, excluding whatever does not suit the immediate purpose, adding and changing at will, in a manner that does not always answer to the demands of strict logic but makes excellent dramatic sense, provided we do not demand logic and strict realism in inconspicuous dramaturgical details. If we do make such demands, then Sophocles will not measure up. But neither will most of the supreme poetic dramatists. By such standards Ben Jonson and Alfieri excel Shakespeare and Sophocles.

vi. *Dramatic Rhythm and Scene Building*

Hitherto we have been examining matters pertaining to Sophocles' methods in the over-all structure and organization of the plays. Now we turn to more specific questions within the dramatic framework: how the series of scenes in a dramatic action is held together in a pattern and given continuity and tension; and how the individual scenes achieve their effect.

Each of these two aspects of the dramatist's art has a special means for its achievement. For guiding the rhythm of the play the chorus is Sophocles' greatest and most flexible instrument; for scene building the interplay of characters as they develop relations of conflict or harmony is of highest importance. The character relationships and the qualities of the major characters as they emerge from these relationships have also an important bearing on the continuity and tension of the whole. In addition to these two aspects of the drama, other elements of Sophocles' art make important contributions: the repetition of themes and other effects of diction, the famous Sophoclean irony, the underlying religious and moral outlook. All these as-

---

and deliberately inserted by the dramatist for dramatic purposes. No doubt some sharp-eyed and analytical spectators may have been aware of Sophocles' inconsistencies. And perhaps there are some inconsistencies that were pure accidents, though I doubt if these are numerous.

pects must be considered, in more or less detail, in following chapters. In this section, our attention will be restricted to a number of miscellaneous considerations.

In each of Sophocles' plays there is some one *event* which we would immediately single out if asked what is the main thing that happens in the play: the death of Ajax, the injuring of Heracles by the poisoned tunic, the burial of Polyneices, Oedipus' discovery of his identity, the revenge on Clytemnestra and Aegisthus, the winning of Philoctetes, the mysterious disappearance of the aged Oedipus. These events serve as points of cohesion and in an external way provide the necessary drive to keep the play moving. It is significant for Sophocles' dramatic method that in only one play is the event identical with or even at the center of the dramatic theme. In *Oedipus at Colonus* the entire play leads up to the consummation of Oedipus' daemonic status; it is announced in the prologue as about to come—only in *OC* is the theme explicitly stated in the prologue—and the intervening incidents of the play are preparations for it or illustrations of its meaning. The course of the drama is not unfairly described by Waldock as a matter of "filling out"; [45] this does not mean that the intermediate parts are otiose or lack vital connection with the theme. What it means is that they do not, in the usual Sophoclean way, create the theme; they expand and illuminate it.

In the other plays the procedure is different. In *Ajax* the central event, the death of Ajax, arises from the humiliation of the warrior and the need that he feels to save his honor; his death in turn gives rise to the question whether he is to have decent burial. Surrounding the event, then, are two *situations*, both of which are parts of the theme, the conduct of Ajax. In *The Trachinian Women* the disaster to Heracles arises from Deianeira's misguided effort to recover Heracles' love; it gives rise to the revelation of Heracles' fate, and in the description of this situa-

[45] *Dramatist*, 219.

tion Heracles' nature is revealed. Again the two situations convey the theme, the contrast of the natures of the two principal figures. In *OT* the central event springs from a search for the cause of the plague and is the cause of Oedipus' new assessment of himself. The search and Oedipus' reaction to the revelation constitute the theme, the heroic conduct of Oedipus as he is confronted first by the problem and then by the knowledge of himself. In *Electra* the theme is the revelation of Electra's soul as she reacts to a series of situations which derive from the revenge (the event), both in anticipation of it and in its consummation. In *Philoctetes* the taking of Philoctetes occasions the stratagem which in turn brings about the development of Neoptolemus' true character; and this in turn is the cause of Philoctetes' change of attitude, which alone gives meaning to the accomplishment of the event. The theme is the reorientation of Philoctetes under the influence of Neoptolemus.[46] Except in *OC*, the theme of each play, that which raises it beyond its existence as a mere series of happenings and gives it a universal meaning, is more closely allied with situation, or, more precisely, with character in situation, than with any single, central event. The closeness of relation between event and situation varies; the relation is loosest in *Electra*, as we should expect; it is closest (apart from *OC*) in *OT*, where event and situation are almost identical.

It is sometimes said (the remark derives from Goethe, I believe) that in Sophoclean tragedy the tone of the play is always established in the prologue. We have seen that this is true in *OC* in a sense in which it does not apply to the other plays. It would be more accurate to say that one important element of the drama is always set in motion in the prologue. There are two different relationships between the prologue

[46] In these one-phrase definitions of themes I do not pretend to describe the meaning of the plays but only to indicate the main threads of significant dramatic development.

and the rest of the play: in three plays, the first episode continues the action begun in the prologue; in the other four, prologue and first episode inaugurate parallel actions which are eventually integrated by later developments in the play. For example, in *OT* the prologue introduces the initial situation, the plague, and the related command from Delphi that Laius' murderer be cast out. The first episode continues to develop the same theme, as Oedipus sets to work to discover the murderer by his proclamation to the people and by summoning Teiresias. *Antigone* begins quite differently. The prologue is Antigone's; in it she presents her passionate reaction to the decree of Creon and her resolve to bury Polyneices. In the first episode it is as if a new play were starting; there is not a word about Antigone, while Creon's character and intentions are revealed to us. Then in the second episode the two parallel developments are united in a conflict between the two opposing forces that we have been shown.

The division between parallel and continuous development is not identical with the division between diptych plays and plays of single development. *Ajax* is like *Antigone*, but *The Trachinian Women* is not. In *Ajax* the prologue reveals the madness and error of Ajax before the eyes of Odysseus, and thus the incident is among other things a preparation for Odysseus' all-important return at the end of the play. The first episode introduces a different aspect of the situation, the madness and misfortune of Ajax as they appear from the point of view of Ajax and those devoted to him, Tecmessa and the chorus. In this play the parallel developments are not wholly integrated until the final scene, when Odysseus returns. In *The Trachinian Women* the fears and premonitions of Deianeira, her devotion to Heracles, and her hopes for his return fill both prologue and first episode. In this play the fact that the entire first half looks forward, quite literally, to the appearance of Heracles makes it unnecessary for any specific preparation to be made for his appearance by a parallel development of situations.

OC is, as is inevitable from the nature of the play, another example of continuous plot development, the first episode expanding the situation begun in the prologue. The prologue of *Electra* introduces Orestes and the paedagogus (and the silent Pylades) and sets their plot in motion. At the very end of the prologue Electra is heard, and the parodos begins with her threnody. The parallel developments are finally united in the recognition scene. It is worth observing that this play, though in its concentration on a single person so like *OT*, is in this aspect of form unlike it, a further indication of the dislocation of its theme in relation to the central event of the story from which it comes. *Philoctetes* is an incomplete example of parallel development. The prologue presents Odysseus and Neoptolemus, the first episode begins another aspect of the theme, the relationship of Neoptolemus and Philoctetes. This is a true parallel development. But since the meeting of Neoptolemus and Philoctetes is actually the result of the stratagem concocted in the prologue, the first episode is also continuing the action of the prologue.

In the manner in which transition is made from one incident to another there are marked differences among the plays. Here we may distinguish between *Ajax* and *The Trachinian Women*, and the other plays; for in these two plays there is a pronounced degree of jerkiness in transition that is not to be found elsewhere in Sophocles. In *Ajax* the protagonist goes through two remarkable changes of mood in the course of three episodes. At the end of the first episode Ajax seems to have decided beyond doubt to take his own life. Then after a stasimon comes the famous speech of deception (646–692). Whether or not this speech marks a real change of heart is debated; we shall return to the question in the next chapter. But that there is a change of mood that significantly affects the rhythm of the play is obvious.[47] Another ode follows, and the report of the messenger sent by Teucer; then comes Ajax's final soliloquy, when he is on the point of suicide. The striking thing is that the alterations of mood take place not during the episodes but between them, off stage as it were.

Similarly in *The Trachinian Women* Deianeira undergoes a change of attitude between successive episodes. At the end of the long first episode, in her speech to Lichas (436–469), she insists that she will not be troubled by the knowledge of Heracles' love for Iole: "Not to know, that is what would wound me; what terror is there in knowing? Has not Heracles wed many other women before?" Yet at her next appearance she declares that she cannot bear the prospect of sharing Heracles with another woman (545–546). In the course of the speech Deianeira tells us why she has had this change of heart. But this is still very different from the style, for example, of *Philoctetes*, where the change in Neoptolemus under the influence of Philoctetes takes place before our eyes. There is, in *Ajax* and *The Trachinian Women*, a sealing off of moods by episodes that is unlike the smooth and gradual manner of the later plays.

Such instances of relative awkwardness formed an important basis for Tycho Wilamowitz's interpretation of Sophoclean art as an intense and exclusive concentration on the effectiveness of individual scenes; characterization in a modern, psychologically realistic form is unknown; it does not matter that Ajax and Deianeira change their minds suddenly and without warning because in reality there is no Ajax or Deianeira. Wilamowitz's theory has prima-facie plausibility with regard to these two plays, but its weaknesses as a general critique of Sophoclean dramatic style become apparent when he maintains, against the

[47] Even the change of mood has been doubted recently by Erik Vandvik, "Ajax the Insane," in *Serta Eitremiana* (Oslo, 1952), 169–175. Vandvik argues, not convincingly, that Ajax is mad throughout the play and that his sudden changes therefore mean nothing.

clearest evidence, that Neoptolemus' change of heart is equally unmotivated and unprepared for. As critics of Wilamowitz's theory have shown, the theory does not in fact properly apply even to *Ajax* and *The Trachinian Women*. (Some consideration of the reasons for these sudden changes will occupy us presently.)

A third somewhat disconcerting change of mood is that of Antigone, in her lyrical lament in the kommos and in her final iambic speech (891–928), the speech that offended Goethe so, and Jebb, and many critics since. Our discussion of that speech will be deferred until we examine the character of Antigone; but we may for the present notice that it is in its general effect not unlike the changes of Ajax and Deianeira.

What do these abrupt changes mean for Sophocles' dramaturgy? There are two complementary answers. First, it is typical of Sophocles' method of dramatizing to have elements of contrast everywhere. The scenes of his plays are generally built out of the contrasting ideas, aims, and moods of the persons; and in the course of the drama there are contrasts of situation from episode to episode. We shall find that in Sophocles' characterization, in his handling of the chorus, in his diction, this element of contrast is at the very core of his dramatic method. Whether or not the Hegelian theory that conflict is the essence of tragedy can adequately be adapted to all tragedy, there is no doubt that it is one valid form of tragic drama; and it is a conspicuous part of Sophoclean form. Sophocles deliberately uses sudden shifts of intention or attitude as a means of securing variations and contrast in the pattern of his dramatic form. These *volte-faces*, however much they may startle or annoy the critic, are products of conscious technique.

The second answer has to do with the evolution of form in the course of Sophocles' career. It is surely not by accident that it is in the earliest play that this jerkiness in the technique of structural contrast is most evident. Of course *Ajax* is no *Jugend-*

werk but the work of an experienced and mature playwright, and in general conception it shows no ineptness. But we know virtually nothing about the earlier plays except some titles; what we do know about Sophocles' dramatic career is that it was for some time a course of constant experimentation, the dramatist working in two preliminary styles before he found in the third the form that suited him best. There is nothing fantastic in supposing that *Ajax* may have been one of the earliest plays cast in the form that Sophocles describes as ἠθικώτατον καὶ βέλτιστον.[48] *The Trachinian Women* has this same abruptness of style, and this feature of it is one of the reasons why I regard it, with some misgivings, as an early play. *Antigone* is a natural third in this company. In *OT* Sophocles has found other, more natural and explicit ways of conveying changes of mood, very brilliantly, for example, in the case of Jocasta in the third episode, from triumphant self-confidence (952–953) to horrifying knowledge and complete despair (1071–1072). Yet he has not sacrificed the element of effective contrast, as for example in the contrast in mood between Oedipus and Jocasta in this same scene. Is it not reasonable to assume that the change from jerkiness to smoothness of transition and from an enigmatic and unexplained presentation of moods to one that is explicit and clear constitutes evidence of a real development in technique? This does not mean that the earlier manner was accidental, nor that it is inferior—only that the course of Sophocles' mature development was, in the matter of dramatic form, from a stylized, motionless series of scenes to a smooth, compact, and more unified structure. The change from diptych to single form is of the same sort.

[48] In his study of this problem, "Sophocles on His Own Development," *AJP*, 61 (1940), 385–401, Bowra suggests that *Ajax* may be the last example of the second Sophoclean style, τὸ πικρὸν καὶ κατάτεχνον τῆς αὐτοῦ κατασκευῆς, on the basis that the language of *Ajax* is not ἠθική. But it is important to remember (as Bowra himself points out) that the sentence does not refer only to diction.

In the construction of scenes there are a number of habitual methods peculiar to or typical of Sophocles. In the following brief review of these our examples will be scattered and not at all complete, since our purpose is to illustrate a number of individual related points, not to treat these aspects of Sophocles' dramatic art exhaustively.[49]

A number of episodes are divided in two, in such a way that each part serves a different purpose. As in the structure of the plays as a whole, here again we find differences from play to play in the way in which transitions are made. The third episode of *Ajax* is sharply divided, the first part containing the report of the messenger sent by Teucer from the council place of the army and the consequent beginning of Tecmessa's search for Ajax, the second the suicide speech of Ajax. There is a change of scene and of characters as well; there is no effort to dovetail the two parts of the episode. There are a good many scenes in the other plays with the same division, but never again is there this abruptness. In *The Trachinian Women*, for example, the long first episode falls into four parts: the messenger's arrival and report; then—separated by a short lyric passage (205–224)—the arrival of Lichas with the captives and his report on Heracles; then, when Lichas has gone into the palace, the messenger steps forward again to contradict Lichas' report; and finally Lichas comes out again, is challenged by Deianeira and the messenger, and admits that his first report was untrue. In these transitions there is not the same stiffness as in *Ajax*. Each part develops from the preceding; and the messenger, though he stands wordless throughout Lichas' first report, is by no means otiose, for he is an interested, indeed in-

---

[49] A number of points treated very cursorily here are discussed at greater length by Webster, in Chapters V and VI of *Introduction* and in two articles: "Plot Construction in Sophocles," *CR*, 46 (1932), 146–150, and "Preparation and Motivation in Greek Tragedy," *CR*, 47 (1933), 117–123.

dignant, listener, and when he speaks to Deianeira and then doughtily accosts Lichas, the spirited way in which he speaks reveals the indignation that has been building up as he watches and listens.[50]

There are a number of other such divided episodes. An excellent example, where transition is smooth and where the second part grows out of the first inevitably, is the second episode of *OT*. There are two distinct incidents, first Oedipus' quarrel with Creon, then Jocasta's attempt to comfort Oedipus, which is the beginning of the revelation. Transition is made during the kommos (649–696), when Jocasta enters as peacemaker. The second episode of *Electra* is another instance. The first part of it is a dispute between Electra and Clytemnestra; the second contains the paedagogus' false report of Orestes' death and the reaction to it of Electra and Clytemnestra. The two matters are distinct, yet the second is brought very close to the first in that the contrasting reactions of the two women to the report arise naturally from the spirit of the preceding incident and are, in fact, a further illustration of their personalities as they have been revealed in the dispute. Furthermore, a strong link is provided by Clytemnestra's prayer, which both forms the culmination of the first part and provides a highly dramatic prelude to the paedagogus' report. Finally, in *Philoctetes* the first episode is divided, with the merchant's report bringing about the transition. We have already discussed the profound change in Neoptolemus between the two parts of the scene. So natural is the development in this case that we are hardly conscious of the division.

The foregoing examples from *OT* and *Electra* bring us to

---

[50] We cannot know from the text whether or not the indignation that is apparent in his words was, in ancient production, expressed also before he speaks. It may have been, by gestures. In any case, the audience knows afterward what he felt, and in the final impression of the scene his indignation makes his silent presence effective.

another technique in scene building, the introduction of messengers' reports and other similar long speeches. The messenger's report was a convention of Greek tragic form and needed no preparation. When the *exangelos* comes out to describe Jocasta's death and Oedipus' self-blinding, no one familiar with Greek tragedy experiences any sense of impropriety at his unannounced appearance; in fact we are waiting for him, as we are for the messenger in *Antigone* who reports the misadventures of Creon when he has set off to right the wrongs he created, and for the messenger in *OC* when Oedipus has left the scene. We do not know who these men will be, but we know that they will come. But when a similar speech occurs in a situation that is not conventional, Sophocles takes care to have the speech adequately prepared for. In *The Trachinian Women* the nurse's description of Deianeira's death is virtually a conventional messenger's speech (the situation demands a messenger's speech), and for it there is no careful preparation, though we have at least seen and heard the nurse in the prologue. There is also a long speech by Hyllus, which is not at all in the convention; what we are waiting for is not a report, but Heracles. Consequently the speech is prepared for in the prologue, when Hyllus is sent out by Deianeira in search of Heracles. So also with the false reports in *Electra* and *Philoctetes*, by the paedagogus and the supposed merchant respectively. Both are tricks and therefore different from conventional messenger's speeches. Hence both are carefully motivated: in each case the later appearance and to some extent the tenor of the speech are planned in the prologue.[51]

In *OT* there may appear to be no preparation for the Corinthian, who, although he delivers no long speech, plays a messengerlike role in that he brings news that has a decisive bearing on the drama. Is this an instance, in the very heart of

[51] On preparation in general, see Webster, *Introduction*, 104–107, and the two articles mentioned above in Note 49.

the play that is above all regarded as a masterpiece of dramatic structure, of structural ineptness? No, provided the part of the play that immediately precedes the arrival of the Corinthian has made its intended mark. As he appears, Jocasta has just finished a prayer to Apollo. As if in answer to that prayer (but in ironical answer to it, as we later know), the Corinthian comes. This is preparation of a telling kind.[52] In *Ajax* the messenger sent by Teucer is not prepared for, and his arrival does not strike one as necessary and expected, as does that of the *Antigone* messenger for example. This is certainly the dramatically crudest entrance in Sophocles. In *The Trachinian Women* the messenger is equally unannounced, but the final effect is smoother, both because the arrival is much earlier in the play and because, like the Corinthian in *OT*, the messenger remains in the action and develops out of his stock-messenger beginning into an interesting and useful minor character.

More peculiarly Sophoclean is the use of such "messenger" speeches, whether conventional or not, to achieve varied effects on the persons to whom they are addressed. Sometimes there is a strong contrast in the way in which two listeners receive the news. The finest example of this contrastive effect is at the end of the paedagogus' speech in *Electra*. Clytemnestra, after some initial sign of maternal feelings (which we have no right to think spurious), is relieved and triumphant; to Electra the news of Orestes' death brings utter gloom and despair. In *Philoctetes* Neoptolemus and Philoctetes react very differently to the merchant's "warning" that Odysseus is sailing from Troy to take Philoctetes. Philoctetes reacts as he was intended to by the plotters, with alarm and renewed eagerness to

---

[52] Very probably the Corinthian appears in the orchestra even as Jocasta prays. Thus from his first appearance he has dramatic force. The messenger speech of *Electra* has this kind of preparation too. For further discussion of the preparation provided for the *OT* messenger by what precedes his appearance, see below, pp. 212–213.

leave Lemnos; Neoptolemus at this point suffers his first misgivings about the deceit he is practicing on Philoctetes; as we
have noticed, he now hesitates, though before he was all eagerness. Similarly in *Antigone* Creon and the chorus react differently to the guard's report, and, in the third episode of *OT*,
Oedipus and Jocasta are affected in opposite ways by the information brought by the man from Corinth. In this last case
there is no long speech, but the structural principle is the same
and is here put to extremely effective use. The difference in reaction of the two hearers contributes largely to the atmosphere
of the following stasimon and the next episode, in which Oedipus
finally learns the truth about his origins.

A closely related technique is the silent withdrawal of a
character on hearing a report. The best example of the silent
withdrawal is in *The Trachinian Women*, when Deianeira, on
hearing Hyllus' speech describing the suffering of Heracles and
condemning her for what she has done, leaves the stage without
a word, though the chorus urge her to stay and justify herself. Sophocles twice again uses this exquisite theatrical trick,
though never again, I think, so perfectly. Eurydice withdraws
silently after hearing of Haemon's death (*Antigone* 1244–1245),
and in *OT*, at the end of the episode mentioned just above,
Jocasta leaves with no explanation, only a shriek of despair for
herself and Oedipus. In each case suicide follows withdrawal.

We know from various bits of ancient evidence that Sophocles
had a lively interest in the externals of dramatic presentation;
that it was he who introduced scene painting and that he made
certain innovations concerning costumes and properties.[53] In
reading the plays we do not always notice the effect of such
external attributes, though in performance they are of the
greatest importance to any drama, in spite of Aristotle's rather
lofty attitude toward them in the *Poetics*. In the latter part

[53] Cf. Aristotle, *Poetics* 1449 a 13 and the anonymous *Vita Sophoclis*,
4–6.

of *Ajax*, for example, the scenes between Teucer and the two
sons of Atreus in turn are, on reading, rather disappointing—a
little too long for their dramatic life, the characterization comparatively wooden, the dispute at times trifling. Critics remind
us of the Athenian zest for debate and of the attractions, for
an Athenian, of the anti-Spartan intimations of the scenes; the
reminders are in place, but they do not make the scenes first-
rate. A more important reminder is given by Bowra: that the
body of Ajax is on stage throughout, lending a deeper intensity
to Teucer's fight to maintain his brother's part.[54] The presence
of the body is not the only important part of the staging of
this incident. Before the second of the two scenes Teucer carefully instructs the child Eurysaces to sit by the body as a suppliant, clinging to it and holding suppliant locks taken from his
own, his mother's, and Teucer's heads. The pathos of the following scene (for it does have some) depends not a little on
the tableau: the body, beside it the child as suppliant, nearby
Tecmessa mourning, Teucer standing before all to brave the
hostile commander.

In *The Trachinian Women* the highest kind of dramatic value
is obtained from the group of captive women sent on by
Heracles, above all by the figure of Iole. Though she does not
speak, Iole plays an important part, and her silence is capitalized
on by the dramatist. Her youthful beauty is a contrast to the
fading charms of Deianeira; [55] she is a symbol of the destruction
wrought by love; and she is a constant reminder of Heracles'
faithlessness. There is another instance of an effective silent
presence, in *Antigone*. All through the last scene of Antigone
—her kommos, her last iambic speech, and the choral ode after

[54] *Sophoclean Tragedy*, 50.
[55] We are kept conscious of the contrast by Deianeira's frequent
references to Iole (e.g., 307–313, 381, 547–551). On the importance of
Iole, see Adolf Beck, "Der Empfang Ioles. Zur Technik und Menschen-
gestaltung im ersten Teil der Trachinierinnen," *Hermes*, 81 (1953), 10–
21.

she has been led away—the silent, menacing figure of Creon stands by, keeping the contrast between him and Antigone visibly before us.[56]

The opening scene of *OT* is greatly aided by the tableau. Before and on the palace steps the Theban people are seated, bearing suppliant boughs and calling on Oedipus to help them. The appearance of Oedipus from the palace to tower over the throng, the father of his people, contributes a good deal to our initial impression of the august might and dignity of Oedipus. In *Electra* the most thrilling moment of the final scene depends on a physical detail. The shrouded corpse of Clytemnestra lies on stage; Aegisthus, thinking that it is the body of Orestes, lifts the shroud, sees the face of Clytemnestra, and knows in a flash of horrified comprehension that he faces death. This is an extraordinarily brilliant moment of theater;[57] and its brilliance is a strong reminder of Sophocles' interest in more than just the text of his plays.

Philoctetes and *OC* have more in the way of scenic effects than any other of the seven plays. Critics usually point to Euripidean influences, and so far as concerns the manner of these effects, they may be correct in doing so. That theatrical effects to a similar purpose were within the dramaturgical scope of Sophocles without prompting from Euripides is clear from the examples given from earlier plays. In *Philoctetes* the rocky landscape, the cave, the pus-filled rags, the lameness—all these things are very probably Euripidean realism; but they are also Sophoclean adaptation of scenic effect to dramatic purpose. The loneliness of Philoctetes, the rigors of his ten-year exile,

[56] There is no reason to suppose that Creon leaves the orchestra during this part of the play, as Kitto points out (*Form and Meaning*, 146–147, 165). Jebb, in the analysis in his Introduction to *Antigone*, p. xiii, has Creon enter in Episode Four without having had him exit after his scene with Haemon.

[57] Kitto, *Greek Tragedy*, 175: "Perhaps the most shattering *coup de théâtre* ever invented."

his helplessness—all help to account for, and to underline, his stubborn refusal for so long to accept his fate. They serve also to arouse our sympathy for the hero and, perhaps more important, to arouse the sympathy of Neoptolemus.

In *OC* the setting in the grove of the Eumenides symbolizes Oedipus' strange intimacy with deity and his own coming daemonic stature. The ragged helplessness of the aged blind man with his staff, leaning on his daughter's arm, is an important means used by the playwright to enhance the theme of the play, the illustration of Oedipus' nature and its contrast of external weakness and inward power. After the gradual rise in dignity and power of Oedipus throughout the play, his withdrawal from the scene, as he leads the way off with confident strides, depends not a little for its impressiveness on the mere matter of physical action and spectacle.

The immediately preceding pages, devoted to miscellaneous and on the whole secondary aspects of dramatic construction, have been in the nature of a digression from the main considerations of the chapter, though I hope that the digression has brought some substantiation to the principal points. Before going on, as we shall in the next three chapters, to an examination of elements of Sophoclean drama that can be distinguished from the actual structure of the plays—though they are not by any means separate from it—it may be helpful to recall in a sentence or two what has been arrived at concerning forms and procedures in the structure of Sophocles' plays. We began by noticing that Sophoclean drama is distinguished by its dependence, for the expression of its themes, on the interaction of characters, regardless of the specific shape of a given play. But we observed also that there are various forms, differing distinctly from one another, among the tragedies, and that these forms can be roughly categorized as the "diptych" and the "linear" types. These forms are intimately related to the varying dramatic purposes of the playwright. We noticed, further, that a distinctive feature of Sophoclean form is its intense concentration on a small area of material, to the exclusion, sometimes, even of material which we may regard as necessary for the sake of clarity. It was maintained, also, that by numerous means, of which the interaction of character is the most prominent, Sophocles achieves in his plays a continuous sense of antithesis, brought about sometimes by the contrast of more or less separate elements and sometimes by direct clash; and we saw that these antitheses pervade the relationships both of characters and of the parts of the drama.

CHAPTER III

Character Portrayal

i. Character and Dramatic Structure

IN a preliminary definition of Sophoclean drama in Chapter I it was suggested that the special mark of Sophocles' procedure is the delineation not of character in and for itself, but of noble character faced with, and in its special way responding to, a situation that serves as a complete and ultimate revelation of its nature. In discussing the form of his plays, we noticed that in Sophocles to a degree greater than in Aeschylus or Euripides the development of a tragic action depends on the interplay of characters. It is time now to examine in some detail Sophocles' methods of building dramatic action by this play of character on character.[1]

---

[1] The concept of character in drama tends to be elusive. The necessary beginning point for its study is a firm recognition of the fact that characters (πρόσωπα, *personae*) are not actual persons but elements of the playwright's work; they are altogether created and fully controlled by him and by the requirements of his artistic purposes. The characters are simply the agents in the drama, the *dramatis personae*. Therefore all drama must have characters, *personae*. But "character" means also personality, especially that part or aspect of personality that corresponds to the Greek term *ethos*—what is sometimes called "moral character." To speak of character portrayal is to consider the kind and degree of personality, especially "ethical personality," *ethos*, invested by a playwright in the agents of the drama, and his reasons for depicting the agents as he does.

It is possible to schematize Sophocles' plays in lists of contrasts, as Webster has done in his suggestive chapter "Character-Drawing," [2] and we realize that the implications of these lists for Sophoclean technique are not slight when we see that they touch on nearly every part of every play apart from messengers' speeches and choral songs. Webster's extravagant-seeming declaration that "Sophocles constructs his whole play of character contrasts" is almost justified, though it is necessary to add that "contrast," though conspicuous in Sophoclean character relations, is not in itself an adequate description of them. But to go on to say, as Webster does, that the same character relationships are repeated from play to play, forming a Sophoclean "stock in trade," is on the whole misleading. The contrasts, for example, between Creon and Haemon, Heracles and Hyllus, and Oedipus and Creon (*OT*) are all designated by Webster as "prejudice *vs.* reason." But it is only in a very partial way that these three relationships are similar, and what similarity they have is mostly external; all three are other things besides prejudice *vs.* reason, and in their other qualities they are not alike. Any such unqualified listing of groups of character relationships is bound to be an oversimplification.

It is not possible to give an adequate account of the more important character relationships without some individual analysis of them, because both the major characters and their relationships are without exception complex. Even among secondary figures there are few that give the impression of being "mere foils," even though the secondary figures are indeed regularly foils. It is not so much that Sophocles was not content to leave even an unimportant figure without some real and individual personality—though this may be true—as that the intricacy of all major Sophoclean characters calls for some corresponding elaboration in the figures by whom they are revealed. Figures such as the guard in *Antigone*, the Corinthian

[2] *Introduction*, Ch. iv.

in *OT*, and the Colonean stranger in *OC* have distinctive personality; and we shall see that the peculiarities of their personalities are useful for the portrayal of the major characters with whom they are in interplay.

If the argument that in Sophocles dramatic meaning is especially dependent on character interaction is valid, our understanding of Sophoclean drama will rest to a very large extent on our comprehension of the characters and above all of the character relationships of the plays. I hope, therefore, that the reader will accept as necessary the following rather long and at times minute examination of the character relationships. As I have already suggested, abstract grouping of the relationships according to types will not serve our purpose; we need to see the characters in context and shall therefore study them *in situ*, proceeding from play to play, though it will not in all cases be necessary or even advantageous to keep to the strict order of events in the plays.

ii. Ajax

The main contrast of the play, as we saw in Chapter II, is between the somewhat monolithic warrior heroism of Ajax and the humane sagacity of Odysseus, with the two appearances of Odysseus serving as a frame for the action. Within, there is first a presentation of Ajax with his supporters, Tecmessa and the chorus of Salaminians, and then of Teucer, representing his brother, in the face of the hostile Atridae. Both intervening sections contribute to the comparison of Ajax and Odysseus.

In the prologue Athena, Odysseus, and Ajax speak. We need not spend time on Athena in discussing characterization, for she is not in the usual Sophoclean sense a character. So far as her relationship to the two men is concerned, she is an instrument to bring to light their characteristics. A good deal has been made of her "cruelty" to Ajax,[3] but in fact she is not cruel but

[3] Cf. Reinhardt, *Sophokles*, 22, and many other critics.

impersonal and dispassionate and as ready to let Odysseus err as to let Ajax.[4] The difference, so far as matters of personality are concerned, is in the attitude of the two men to her. In herself she represents the anger of deity against Ajax, and this is not a matter of character.

We need not labor the point of this initial contrast between the wild arrogance and cruelty of Ajax and the piety of Odysseus. The two men are in this scene virtually personifications of *hybris* and *sophrosyne*. Odysseus is in awe of Athena and commits himself to her hands; Ajax greets her with bluff familiarity (91–93), offers her favor rather than reverence, and contradicts her to insist on his own will. Odysseus refuses to mock a stricken foe, even when lured by Athena's leading question, "Is it not sweet to mock one's enemies" (79)? Instead, he is moved to sympathy: "I pity him in his wretchedness, though he is my foe" (121–122). Ajax is pitiless, in his imagined triumph, toward the enemy he believes to be at his mercy: "This, and no less penalty, shall he pay" (113).

There could hardly be a more shocking contrast of spirit or one more uncompromisingly harsh to Ajax. But it should not prejudice our view of the play, or of Ajax, and make us suppose that the whole drama is a revelation of heinous, unthinking guilt over against the model of safe-mindedness; we must remember that this behavior of Ajax's is a part of his humiliation, and thus part of the initial situation from which the play takes its rise. The Ajax of the prologue is mad; we can only estimate him properly by seeing what elements of Ajax mad are still present in Ajax sane. And there is a significant difference; in the rest of the play there is not the same blind passion. Yet the portrait of the prologue is by no means foreign, for Ajax never does show reverence, humility, or a repentant spirit. In later references to Athena he speaks of her "torture" and "injury" of him, and there is no thought that his humilia-

[4] Cf. lines 75, 79.

tion was for any fault of his own. His later references to Odysseus show just as little change of spirit; he assumes that Odysseus will gloat over his misfortunes (382) and never shows any comprehension of Odysseus' nature.

But why so wild an initial portrait of Ajax and so stark a contrast? For one thing, the play thus opens with a scene that is extraordinarily vigorous and gripping, and this is always a dramatic advantage. Moreover, by the very extremity of his conduct, Ajax is presented as a tremendous figure, a spirit of heroic proportions, however wrong he may be. It is as though Sophocles were putting to his audience the question of the meaning and value of human personality on this colossal scale.[5] Just as some of Dante's tortured souls, like the proud heretic Farinata, win us by their magnificence, so Ajax, in contrast with safe-minded Odysseus, is at once culpable and splendid. The contrast is not, therefore, only between arrogance and moderation; it is also between heroic force and normal human conduct.

The contrast between Ajax and Odysseus is resumed at the end of the play, with Teucer representing his brother. Meanwhile a series of subordinate relations amplify and in some ways modify the impression of Ajax created in the prologue. In the first part of the play the most important of these is Ajax's scene with Tecmessa. Before it, in the kommos (348–429), the chorus have warned Ajax not to boast (386), and reminded him that "at god's disposal all men laugh or grieve" (383). In a slight way they continue the part of Odysseus.

Tecmessa is a much more substantial person than the sailors. Indeed she is a most underrated character. By Ajax she is treated harshly and peremptorily. Even when later he is certainly affected by what she has said, his confession that he has been moved is unwilling and contemptuous: "My words grow wom-

[5] Essentially the same technique marks the prologues of *OT* and *Antigone;* in these plays as in *Ajax* the initial presentation of the protagonist is strikingly impressive.

anly under this woman's influence" (651–652). And earlier, in a much-quoted *mot*, he sums up his attitude with "Woman, silence is woman's adornment" (293). This statement (which is, by the way, reported to us by Tecmessa) has had a prodigious influence on the attitude of critics toward Tecmessa, and even on notions about the treatment of women in Athens. We are told that Ajax's attitude is normal for an Athenian and that Sophocles is simply depicting what was a common attitude. As a corollary, critics usually treat Tecmessa with the same offhandedness as Ajax does, writing off her great speech to Ajax as merely an appeal for pity.

The position of women in Athens has nothing to do with the case.[6] If it could be shown that Ajax's attitude toward Tecmessa is typical of how the relations between husband and wife are depicted in Sophocles' plays, then we might suppose he was mirroring a current attitude. But the totally different attitude of Oedipus toward Jocasta shows that we cannot generalize:[7] the relationship of Ajax and Tecmessa springs from the immediate situation of the play. There is evidence in the play that Ajax's treatment of Tecmessa in this crisis is not even normal for him. To begin with, the chorus maintain an attitude of respect toward her throughout. They have words of praise for her advice to Ajax (526); they turn at once to her for leadership when news of Ajax's danger comes (784); it is Tecmessa who takes charge of the dead Ajax when he is found and who

[6] The notion that Athenian women were hopelessly downtrodden has been sharply questioned by Kitto, *The Greeks* (Harmondsworth, 1951), 219–236. For the old attitude, see (among others) J. Donaldson, *Woman, Her Position and Influence in Ancient Greece and Rome* (London, 1907), 49–76.

[7] Cf. *OT* 577–580. In *Ajax*, incidentally, if we are to imagine the audience nodding in accustomed agreement when Ajax declares that silence is woman's adornment, what are we to suppose they thought when in the next scene Tecmessa delivers, without apparent hesitation, a *rhesis* of forty lines?

covers up his body. (It would not be proper to ascribe all this to dramatic exigencies, for no capable playwright will solve problems of dramatic economy at the expense of the meaning of his play. There are other ways out of such difficulties; in this case the chorus could reasonably have done all that Tecmessa does.) These companions of Ajax have no lordly attitude toward Tecmessa, and Ajax himself has not always treated her with such disdain. When she learns that Ajax has after all gone to commit suicide, Tecmessa laments that she is "cast forth from the favor of earlier days" (808), words that strongly suggest that she was accustomed to his affection and respect. We ought to be ready to give Tecmessa a considerate hearing, even though at this point Ajax does not.

In the scene between them, Tecmessa's appeal is not only an entreaty; she presents a concept of values and of duty significantly opposed to that of Ajax. Ajax speaks first (430–480), announcing his decision to commit suicide. He says that he has hopelessly disgraced his father and himself, that he is hated by all, that he has no way of redeeming himself by continuing his life, and that it is therefore base to go on living. He sums up his case with the declaration that the truly noble man must live nobly or die nobly:

$$\text{'Αλλ' ἢ καλῶς ζῆν ἢ καλῶς τεθνηκέναι}$$
$$\text{τὸν εὐγενῆ χρή. πάντ' ἀκήκοας λόγον. [479–480]}$$

Tecmessa replies (485–524) with a set of opposing ideas. By her own example she shows that even the nobly born must yield to fate; true reverence for his parents demands that Ajax live, not die and forsake them; what he proposes to do will disgrace him in that he is deserting his wife and child; to his complaint about his misfortunes she opposes the misfortunes that he will inflict by his death on her and their son; finally, to his idea of the εὐγενής she opposes her own—the man who remembers benefits bestowed upon him, the man of χάρις:

Χάρις χάριν γάρ ἐστιν ἡ τίκτουσ' ἀεί. [522]

The contrast of ideas is emphasized by the repetition of the word εὐγενής in the last line of each speech. Only once does Tecmessa make a direct appeal for pity (510); her speech taken as a whole is a logical one, and through it we see the narrowness of Ajax's resolve, as well as his inflexible and courageous firmness; in his resolve to die he is disregarding much that is honorable and a part of his duty as a man.

The two speeches provide an excellent and a neglected example of Sophoclean technique in the portrayal of character. There are many such thorough comparisons of ideas—between Antigone and Ismene, Antigone and Creon, Oedipus and Creon, Oedipus and Jocasta, Electra and her mother and her sister, Philoctetes and Neoptolemus, to mention only the most obvious—throughout the plays, and we are not really reading the whole of Sophocles' plays unless we recognize the complexity of his presentation of characters and their relations. The present scene is no mere rejection of a woman's plea for pity, and if we are content to take it as such we are seeing less than Sophocles means us to see. It is an outlining of two different ways of thought. Tecmessa's way is mild and unheroic, impossible for a warrior to accept; but we have no right therefore to close our eyes to its logic and its moral force.

It would be unthinkable for Ajax to take any overt account of Tecmessa's ideas. He is in no mood to hear any advice, least of all advice that counsels gentleness and compromise. In his next long speech (545–582) his attitude and resolve are substantially unchanged, though in his solicitude for Eurysaces, which gives rise to the speech, and for his parents (569–573) the influence of Tecmessa's words is perhaps operative; thus in spite of his intervening harshness we are to some extent prepared for his changed attitude when next he comes out of his tent, because we have seen that he is capable of a gentler mood.

In the famous speech of lines 646–692 Ajax indirectly recognizes the cogency of Tecmessa's arguments when he speaks of the change and submission of all things and when he permits himself to speak in a reflective and even gentle vein. Further consideration of this speech will be left until later in this chapter.[8]

After the incident of the messenger, the suicide speech, the finding of Ajax's body, and the lament over it, none of which directly concerns us at the moment, come Teucer's scenes with the Atridae. Both scenes contain a good deal of bickering and less-than-fascinating detail, but they are necessary to the action, both because they restore dignity to Ajax by a rehearsal of his greatness in contrast with the meanness of his adversaries and because they necessitate Odysseus' reappearance, with its essential contribution to the action.

Teucer, with his pugnacious independence of spirit, his readiness to match both Menelaus and Agamemnon in vituperation, and his wry comments on the testiness of old Telamon, has his own personality, but in essence he is the proxy of his dead brother. The keynote of his stand is summed up by Teucer himself at line 1125: "With justice on his side, a man can be proud in thought." Menelaus' most specious argument is that fear and obedience are necessary in an army or a city (1071–1086), but he is clearly more interested in violent retaliation than in justice (1087–1088), and the chorus at once objects to his sophistic attempt to justify his own *hybris* (1091–1092). Finally Menelaus is jockeyed by Teucer into admitting that his feelings against Ajax are of personal hostility (1134). Menelaus is not so much a symbol of "authority," as Webster calls him,[9] as a symbol of the same kind of vindictiveness that Ajax was guilty of, without the grandeur of spirit that characterized Ajax.

The scene with Agamemnon is in the same mold, though dramatically a little stronger because Agamemnon is more sub-

[8] Cf. below, pp. 160–162.   [9] *Introduction*, 88.

stantial: even though his attitude is much like Menelaus', he does represent decisive authority in himself, not a mere shadow of it. The scene gives Teucer an excellent chance to recall to everyone's mind some of the great deeds of Ajax during the war (1272–1287), thus enhancing the hero's prestige. From our present point of view, the most important aspect of the scenes is the fact that they are Sophocles' way of bringing into relation Ajax and his enemies, balancing the earlier part of the play in which we saw Ajax with his supporters. It is typical Sophoclean style to achieve further elaboration of the character of his protagonist by character interaction. The scenes both add to our knowledge of Ajax's qualities as a warrior and permit us to distinguish between his nobility of character and the meanness of the Atridae.

Odysseus' reappearance brings the argument to an end. It brings also a sharp criticism of the Atridae, and the emphasis on justice recalls and confirms Teucer's defense of his brother. Odysseus tells Agamemnon not to let violence overcome judgment (1334; a clear reflection on the violent behavior of Menelaus, already criticized by the chorus); not to hate beyond just measure (1335); not to violate the laws of the gods by refusing burial (1343–1344). His calm, farsighted prudence is antithetical to the petty and selfish vindictiveness of the Atridae, just as his piety and moderation were antithetical to Ajax's wild excesses in the prologue. One short passage exemplifies the contrast clearly. In answer to Agamemnon's question, "Do you really bid me let them bury the man" (1364)? Odysseus answers,

I do; for I too shall some day come to this.

Agamemnon's answer is most revealing:

All alike! Each man works for himself.

Incapable of understanding the higher selfishness of Odysseus, who sees in the fate of Ajax the potential fate of all men (he has expressed the same insight in different words in the prologue, 125–126) and therefore advises tolerance, Agamemnon can only grasp the concept of narrow personal advantage. And Odysseus leaves him to his stupidity (1367).

There is criticism of Ajax too in this second appearance of Odysseus. Ajax was as incapable of a wide and tolerant view as his enemies are now shown to be. At the end Teucer fittingly carries on this narrowness of view when, in spite of his surprised gratitude to Odysseus, he will not let him take a hand in the burial of Ajax, "lest this be odious to the dead man" (1395). He is faithful to his brother's spirit, and the gap between Odysseus' way of life and Ajax's remains unbridged. There is another passage that sharply points up the difference between Odysseus and Ajax. At line 1359, Odysseus, still in debate with Agamemnon, declares, "Many a man now friend will be a foe sometimes." His conclusion from this reflection is that a change from friendship to enmity should not blind one to a man's worth (1361–1363). Ajax expressed a similar thought in lines 678–683 in the course of his reflections on the mutability of all things. But his conclusion was significantly different—that all friendship is, therefore, a hollow and treacherous thing (682–683). Ajax lacks Odysseus' ability to look beyond personal relationships with a broad and humane perspective on life; he scorns this attitude and sees in it only shifting unreliability. The point of structure here is worth noticing too: Odysseus, in effect, directly answers words of Ajax that in their context seemed monologic. This kind of contrast at a distance we shall see in *The Trachinian Women* also.

Though there is no rigid or obvious schematization, *Ajax* is largely unfolded by means of character interplay. In contrast with Odysseus and Tecmessa and through Teucer's wranglings with the Atridae, Ajax's heroism comes to life in its grandeur and in its limitations. He signally lacks the gentleness of spirit, the χάρις, that Tecmessa stands for; and he falls far short of Odysseus in breadth of vision, humaneness, and moderation of spirit. Yet by his very rejection of these qualities, or his blindness to them, he stands forth the more clearly in his devotion to his concept of honor, in his firmness, and in his magnificence of spirit. To the sons of Atreus, as limited in outlook as he and without his greatness of soul, he is immeasurably superior. It is too much to say that the whole play is a "paean" of Ajax; [10] Sophocles' presentation of the violent warrior hero is more complex than that. He is a great man, he dominates the play, and he wins our sympathy; but he is an incomplete man, and it is from his incompleteness that his tragedy arises.

iii. The Trachinian Women

As in *Ajax*, one central contrast dominates the action and the structure of *The Trachinian Women*. The contrast is between Deianeira and Heracles; but the development of the contrast depends in part on the subordinate contrasts in each of the two parts of the play; Deianeira with the nurse, Hyllus, the chorus, the messenger, Lichas, and Iole; Heracles with Hyllus, who represents Deianeira, as Teucer represents Ajax. In this play there is no frame as in *Ajax*. None is needed, for the entire first part of the play keeps Heracles constantly before our minds; and the contrast between him and Deianeira is carried far along before he makes his appearance. There is between Deianeira and Heracles a double contrast: first, there is a contrast between Deianeira's devotion to Heracles, her gentle graciousness of spirit, and her unselfishness, and Heracles' obliviousness to the interests and the feelings of anyone but himself, and his harsh violence; and, secondly, Deianeira's impracticality and uncertainty of self contrast with Heracles' more than human effectiveness, the inevitability of his career.[11]

Deianeira's opening speech reveals her anxiety about Heracles

[10] Whitman, *Sophocles*, 79.

[11] This central contrast of the play is discussed in my paper "The Dramatic Unity of Sophocles' *Trachiniae*," *TAPA*, 72 (1941), 203-211.

and her sense of foreboding, and it shows too her innate timidity. Her first terrible suitor the river god, the battle in which Heracles won her, and her marriage with the ever-wandering hero—all these have caused her a life of brooding and trouble: "Ever I breed fear upon fear" (28). Surrounded by vague terrors she waits, not knowing what to do. The nurse's answering speech breathes an entirely different spirit. The nurse is a slight figure in the play, but we see at once that she has a distinctive personality, and we see exactly why Sophocles has endowed her as he has: she is chatty, eager to help, thoroughly practical, just the reverse of the gentle Deianeira. Why not send Hyllus to look for his father? she promptly suggests (55–59). Deianeira's warm gratitude for this rather obvious counsel testifies both to her impracticality and to the generosity of her nature. Hyllus too, on his appearance, points to his mother's helplessness in the domain of action: he already knows, to her great surprise, something about his father's whereabouts (69–71). In this conversation another, and more creditable, characteristic of Deianeira's appears—the simplicity with which she assumes her complete dependence on Heracles (83–85) is a charming indication of her devotion to him; life without Heracles is beyond her comprehension.

Of the prologue as a whole we may say that, whatever may be its Euripidean characteristics, it is a typical Sophoclean scene in that the character relationships in it are designed to emphasize specific traits of the main figure. We shall see that these traits are further displayed later in the drama and serve an important part in conveying its meaning.

Deianeira's next speech (141–177)—it is nominally addressed to the chorus, but its dramatic relevance lies with Heracles—continues especially the theme of her devotion to Heracles: she fears that she may be "deprived of the best of mortal men" (177). The messenger now enters, with happy news. But Deianeira, though she finally tells the chorus of maidens to greet the word of Heracles' approach with a song, is slow to accept the report as really good news and asks, "How is it that Heracles himself is not here, if he prospers" (192)? She never does overcome her brooding sense of uncertainty.[12] When Lichas arrives, almost at once she turns in compassion to the unhappy captive girls he has brought. When the chorus call on her to rejoice, her answering speech (293–313) is not so much an expression of happiness as a magnanimous and sympathetic lament for the hard fate of the wretched girls before her. At once she singles out Iole, conspicuous for her beauty and her spirit (313), tries to find out her name from the evasive Lichas, and finally bids her go into the house, "that she may be as content as possible, and not be grieved by me along with her other sorrows" (329–330). The contrast between the sympathetic Deianeira and the silent girl who is the cause of her present undoing is a firmly drawn and unmistakable element of the play; and yet it is managed with such delicate reserve that we are not likely to be fully conscious of it until in the next episode Deianeira emphasizes the contrast.[13] At this point the messenger exposes Lichas' false report and reveals the truth about Heracles' latest undertaking, and the identity and significance of Iole. Here the chorus provide a contrast for Deianeira. She, as we should expect, receives the heavy news with bewilderment, but without reproach for either Heracles or Iole. The chorus, on the other hand, express instant and lively resentment of Heracles' behavior:

> May evil-doers perish, or such of them as practice
> secret evils! [383–384]

[12] Cf. line 228, χαρτὸν εἴ τι καὶ φέρεις. Wilamowitz, *Dramatische Technik*, 134–135, denies that the phrase suggests hesitation and cites parallels. But none of his parallels contains the vital word καί, which is just what marks the suggestion of doubt.

[13] Cf. Beck's article in *Hermes*, 81 (1953), 10–21.

On the reappearance of Lichas there is a spirited scene when the old messenger, championing Deianeira, takes it upon himself to force the truth from the unwilling herald. The characterization of both is delightfully sharp and vivacious, in welcome contrast to the dullness of Teucer's scenes with the sons of Atreus. It is noteworthy that even in so slight an encounter as this the personalities are clearly and purposefully drawn, not just for the sake of their own effect, but for their bearing on each other. They are, in a dramaturgical sense, made for one another. The messenger is a plain and forthright peasant; Lichas is very conscious of his dignity as a herald and his difference from the messenger. Breaking in upon Deianeira's gentle and ineffectual interrogation of Lichas, the messenger shouts, "Look here, man! Who do you think you're talking to" (402)? and proceeds to force the truth from him. Lichas wriggles and evades, affects hauteur and declares his questioner mad, but he cannot escape. Deianeira is now convinced that the messenger's charge is true and insists, in her moving speech in lines 436–469, on knowing the whole truth.

One characteristic that has been prominent in Deianeira in relation to all other persons is her simplicity. There is no subtlety in her; in contrast with the deceptiveness of Lichas, the false position of Iole, the initial want of frankness of even the messenger, her utter guilelessness is marked. When in this speech she assures Lichas that she will not be moved by the knowledge that Heracles is in love with Iole, we should be most circumspect about assuming that she is telling a falsehood, in spite of her contrary reaction in the next episode. The speech has been regarded as inconsistent with Deianeira's character elsewhere in the play. But it is perfectly natural: uncertainty in a matter of such profound importance for one's happiness is always unendurable (545–551).[14] Heracles has had his women

---

[14] Cf. Jebb's comment quoted below, p. 162.

before (460), but now there is a special reason for fear: Iole is young, just approaching womanhood; Deianeira's beauty is fading (547–549). There is inconsistency no doubt between the present speech and the first of the next episode. But it is just the kind of inconsistency that is perfectly natural to this gentle, irresolute creature. We shall find Heracles very different.

Deianeira, realizing that she cannot endure to share Heracles with Iole, resolves to try to regain his love, and so she smears a robe with the gore from the wound that Nessus died of long ago at Heracles' hands. It was foolish of Deianeira to trust the centaur; and when it is too late to do any good, she recognizes her folly (705–708).[15] Here is inconsistency again, and again it is in keeping with the character of Deianeira throughout the play. Even when she sends the robe, she suspects that she may be wrong and tries to encourage herself by the supposition that it will be a concealed wrong (596–597).[16] The inconsistency of her thinking is deliberately emphasized by the repetition of this notion of concealment; later, she declares that she would never advise a deed to be done in uncertainty (669–670). Sophocles obviously means us to see that Deianeira is inconsistent.

In just one thing she is consistent, firm, and courageous—in

[15] On this point and for a valuable discussion of the differences between Euripidean and Sophoclean dramatic intrigue, see Friedrich Solmsen, "Das Intriguenmotiv in den Tragödien des Sophokles und Euripides," *Philologus*, 87 (1932), 1–17.

[16] Whitman, *Sophocles*, 266, proposes to understand αἰσχρὰ πράσσειν (596) as meaning "suffer evil" rather than "do evil." Even without other evidence this would be somewhat improbable, for it gives the sentence an unnatural sense ("For in darkness, even if you suffer evil, you will never fall into disgrace"), and there is other evidence, all indicating that the phrase means "do evil": the discussion a few lines above of κακαὶ τόλμαι (582), which Deianeira wishes to avoid but which she clearly feels her use of the philter to resemble; and the virtual repetition of the phrase at line 667, where there is no possibility of the meaning "suffer evil." Lines 669–670 are to the same effect.

her devotion to Heracles. Just as it was this that guided her conduct in the earlier part of the play and that led her, the irresolute, to take a chance with the anointed robe, so when the chance seems likely to fail terribly, it is this alone that gives her firmness and direction: if Heracles dies from the venom of Nessus, she too will die. There is no hesitation and no uncertainty. Her concept of nobility is as solid and unshakable as that of Ajax when she declares,

> This I have resolved: if Heracles dies, by that same
> force I too shall die; for to live with reputation gone is
> not to be endured by one who values nobility of life
> (μὴ κακὴ πεφυκέναι). [719–722]

Deianeira is true to her resolve. When Hyllus returns to tell of Heracles' suffering and to call down the vengeance of heaven upon his mother (808–809), Deianeira leaves without a word of self-defense, in spite of the chorus's efforts to induce her to speak on her own behalf. Deianeira has no interest in defending herself, for self means nothing to her; Heracles, and the perfectness of her devotion to him, mean all, and having failed in this devotion, even though unwittingly, she is finished with everything. In the nurse's description of her suicide we have a final substantiation of her loving, selfless, and devoted nature: after passing through the house, weeping at the sight of the servants and the household objects—tokens of her married life —she throws herself upon the bridal bed, apostrophizing in her final words the symbols of her wifehood: "O bed and bridal chamber, farewell now forever" (920–921).

Unselfish devotion, graciousness to all, impracticality, timorousness, but single-mindedness and strength in her love for Heracles—such are the characteristics of Deianeira. There is nobility of a genuine Sophoclean kind in this, feminine though it is.[17] But the person of Deianeira makes only incomplete dra-

---

[17] There has always been extreme uncertainty among critics as to just

matic sense until the answering picture of Heracles is added. During the first part of the play we have been given a fairly definite, though sketchy, impression of Heracles. His life has been one of toil and wandering (31–35); his strength is great (19–21); he is the son of Zeus (19, 140, 288, and elsewhere). But there is a quality of brutality and capricious violence in his deeds as they are reported in the first part: his drunkenness (268), his murder of Iphitus (269–273) and of the innocent Lichas (779–782), his obvious indifference to his own son's welfare in demanding help for himself (797–798). This impres-

what Deianeira is and means. Bowra is impressed above all by what he regards as her unwomanly refusal to submit to her husband's will and accept the concubine; Whitman strangely pairs her with Oedipus as a model of "sheer intelligence." The view of her that I offer has the merit of being based very much on the evidence of the text, which is more than can be said for either Bowra's shrew or Whitman's blue-stocking. I suspect that one basic reason for difficulty about Deianeira is the fact that she is a surprising, and not altogether satisfactory, tragic hero. Allardyce Nicoll, in a passage where he clearly does not have *The Trachinian Women* in mind, declares (*The Theory of Drama* [New York, n.d.], 158): "The feminine in high tragedy must either be made hard, approaching the masculine in quality, or else be relegated to a position of minor importance in the development of the plot." It is a fact that most great tragic heroines do indeed have about them a quality of hardness; Nicoll instances Antigone, Clytemnestra, Bérénice, Phèdre, Hedda Gabler, and Rebecca West. It is a conspicuous fact that Sophocles made this mistake, if it is a mistake, only once that we know of. Per-haps the dissatisfaction that has often been voiced about *The Trachinian Women* (notably and influentially by A. W. Schlegel in the *Lectures on Dramatic Art*) arises above all from the fact that Deianeira is in the tradition of Tecmessa rather than of Clytemnestra, Antigone, and Elec-tra and yet is burdened with the dramatic responsibilities of the latter group. If we recognize the paramount importance of the contrast with Heracles, we both relieve Deianeira of some of her burden of centrality and see why she is as she is rather than like other Sophoclean tragic heroines.

There are, of course, "tragic heroines" who are in essence victims; at their head comes Euripides' Alcestis. The above comments do not apply to them because their role is totally unlike that of a Sophoclean tragic hero or heroine; they belong to a different kind of tragedy.

sion is enormously strengthened when the suffering Heracles appears. His hatred of Deianeira for what she has done is unbridled; his self-praise and self-pity are boundless. He is an impressive figure indeed, but what a grotesque one! If there were no dramatic context to help us determine its meaning, we could make little sense of the portrayal. But it is a perfect contrast to the picture of Deianeira. His self-centered boasts and cries make Deianeira's delicate self-effacement the finer. Reinhardt has observed their contrasting apostrophes: she, as we have seen, of the symbols of marriage, he of his back, and breast, and arms (1090)! [18]

The continuation of the final scene fully confirms the contrast. We might, conceivably, suppose that the initial portrayal of Heracles is intended merely as a dramatic tour de force, something huge and terrible and overwhelming, to fill the stage and stagger us, with no further meaning than its own tremendous spectacle. But the following scene with Hyllus, who does his best to justify Deianeira all along, points the contrast so that we cannot disregard it. For Hyllus' words in defense of Deianeira Heracles has no ears at all. Her good intentions leave him unimpressed (1136–1137). All he heeds is the mention of Nessus: his death through the centaur fulfills a prophecy of old (1159–1161), and it is only this fact, the fact that immediately concerns him, that means anything to Heracles. In his disposal of Iole the same ruthless selfishness is clear. Overriding his son's horrified rejection of the idea of marriage to one who has been the instrument of both his parents' death, Heracles goes his way, oblivious of all personal feelings except his own. The utter want of grace, of thought for anyone else, above all the complete indifference to Deianeira once he finds he has no cause to hate her, are the complete reverse of all that we saw in Deianeira.

But there is another element of contrast too. Deianeira was impractical and irresolute, unable to cope with the flow of

[18] *Sophokles*, 68.

events about her. Heracles is quite the opposite. In his dispatch of Nessus, as it is reported by Deianeira (565–568), we catch a glimpse of the marvelous effectiveness and the unhesitating directness of this tremendous figure. His behavior upon learn-, ing that it is Nessus who has brought about his death is similar in its sureness and energy. At once his course is clear; he makes his demands of Hyllus and will not be denied, in spite of his son's wavering. There is something more than human in this aspect of Heracles' personality, and it is not by accident that references to his father, Zeus, are common in the play. Heracles is in fact a part of the mighty sweep of events by which Deianeira is overwhelmed. When Hyllus, reluctantly consenting to marry Iole, says, "I could never appear base in obeying you, father" (1250–1251), he is not only recognizing the rectitude of filial obedience, but acknowledging that Heracles is somehow akin to the will of the gods; what Heracles demands has a quality of inevitability and of ultimate rightness, however strange and terrible from the human point of view.

We cannot allow this second element in Heracles' nature, and in the contrast between him and Deianeira, to lead us too far. The play does not include the apotheosis of Heracles. It clearly states his sonship to Zeus and implies that his status is more than human. Beyond this the playwright does not go, because the main emphasis of the central contrast of the play is not on the more than human reach of Heracles' nature but on the human qualities of Deianeira. To the other kinds of contrast which we have noticed, this part of Heracles' nature makes an important addition: in this respect he becomes a part of Deianeira's fate, an element in the bewildering and destructive forces which entangle Deianeira.

iv. Antigone

That a contrast between Antigone and Creon lies at the heart of the drama can be taken for granted. Our task in this section will be to examine two matters: the complexity of this contrast, and the subsidiary character relationships and their effect on the action. We shall review first the secondary contrasts and end with the main clash between Antigone and Creon.

Antigone and Ismene are together in two scenes, in the prologue and at the end of the second episode. The contrast between them is not that of devotion to a cause *vs.* timidity; it is more complex than that and more revealing of the character of Antigone. Of course Antigone is devoted and has a cause; and Ismene, by contrast, is timid. But to what, exactly, is Antigone's devotion, and what does it indicate about her? The contrast with Ismene helps us to answer these questions. In the prologue Antigone's first concern is not for religious duty, which looms so large in her scene with Creon. Her first reaction is a personal one; the matter is one of family loyalty, where, she feels, Creon has no right to intrude. Antigone is intense, as we see from the opening line on; her greeting to Ismene has more of intimacy and passion than of loving gentleness.[19] To Creon's clumsy interference with her duty to her family, she responds with instinctive hostility. She is furious that Creon should seek to legislate to her in a matter so personal to her: "Such conditions they say the worthy Creon has proclaimed for you and me—yes, even for me" (32–33)! The burial of Polyneices becomes for her the very touchstone of nobility, and she declares that Ismene by her attitude toward it will show "Whether you are of noble nature (εἴτ᾿ εὐγενὴς πέφυκας) or base though your parents were good" (38). Like Ajax and Deianeira, Antigone has an unhesitating devotion to her concept of what is becoming to the εὐγενής.

In all this there is no thought of the ἄγραπτα νόμιμα; up to this point Antigone has not reflected and has not formulated her instinctive idealism. She is not to be thought of as primarily a

[19] Goethe's famous description of her as "most sisterly of souls" is right, provided we do not equate sisterliness with gentleness.

philosopher or an embodiment of the reasoned way of life. By the contrasting reaction of Ismene we understand more clearly what Antigone is. Ismene's conduct is equally instinctive. Suddenly confronted with a bold and illegal scheme, she shrinks at once, for her instinct is to obey, just as surely as Antigone's is to exercise her own will: she is a woman, and cannot fight against men (61–62); she must obey (47, 59, 79); Antigone's plan lacks common sense (68); those below will forgive her for not acting (65–66); she cannot act βίᾳ πολιτῶν (79). So far as moral attitude is concerned, there is no fundamental difference; Ismene is as aware as Antigone of the wrongness of Creon's edict. The difference is in personality: Ismene is without the imperiousness, willfulness, and single-mindedness of her sister; she is prudent and sees other aspects of the situation. Antigone has eyes for only the one issue that is to her all-important.

There is another contrast between them. When Ismene shows reluctance to act, Antigone becomes instantly hostile. She declares bitterly that she would not now accept her sister's help if it were offered (69–70); when Ismene advises silence and says that she too will be silent about the plan to bury Polyneices, Antigone angrily bids her tell it to all (84–87). Antigone promises Ismene the hatred of their dead brother and of herself (93–94); Ismene in the last words of the prologue assures Antigone of her love, mad though she may be. It is Ismene, then, who has something like the gentleness and affection and patience that we have seen in Tecmessa and Deianeira; relatively, Antigone is hard, abrupt, intolerant, and in this she is like Ajax. It is the natural concomitant and price of her firmness and single-mindedness.

The second incident continues the contrast. To Ismene's unexpected and courageous attempt to assume joint responsibility for the burial and to share the punishment, Antigone's response is a passionate rejection. Both reactions are, superficially, strange; but both are in place. We soon learn Ismene's

reason: so warmly does she love her sister that she cannot face
life without her (548), and this is what inspires her with courage. Antigone's conduct is a continuation of what we saw in the
prologue. The harshness with which she here spurns Ismene
is no different from her impetuous scorn there. Antigone knows
that Ismene is even yet not in real sympathy with her spirit. For
Ismene is acting out of affection; Antigone's drive comes instead from her concept, at first intuitive, now formulated, of
noble conduct.

Does Antigone suffer by the contrast? As a specimen of
normal, gentle womanhood, perhaps she does. But it is a part
of her towering strength to cast aside such normality; just as
Ajax, in contrast with Odysseus and Tecmessa, is lacking in
χάρις, so the firmness and devotion of Antigone cut her off
from much that is gracious and attractive. It is at least in part
because she is without the intolerance of an Ajax or an Antigone
that Deianeira is not altogether right as a tragic hero. Critics
who want an Antigone against whom no breath of criticism
can be uttered tend to undervalue the interplay between the
protagonist and her sister; Jebb, for example, saw in their second
meeting only an effort by Antigone to save Ismene from death,
disregarding the whole atmosphere and nearly all the implications of the incident. But we shall not understand Sophocles'
protagonists by closing our eyes to those aspects of their portrayal that do not satisfy our preconceived specifications.

Leaving Antigone's encounters with the chorus (which are
very important) for attention later, we turn now to Creon.
His first appearance brings his "speech from the throne" and
then his contretemps with the guard. In the solemn opening
speech there is nothing palpably wrong, and perhaps if we were
to hear it without the rest of the episode we should find nothing
to criticize. We later realize that even in this first speech there
is a revelation of Creon's nature that is not altogether attractive. He is a little too pompous, too given to maxims, too eager

to justify himself; and hence the speech lacks the profound dignity of (for example) Antigone's statement about the Unwritten Laws. The first obvious disclosure of Creon's nature comes with the guard's report of the burial of Polyneices' body. The encounter between Creon and the guard gains dramatic force from the ripple of humor which it contributes.

This scene is sometimes used as evidence against the much-repeated observation that there are no scenes of comedy in Greek tragedy. But it is a confirmation rather than the reverse: there are a good many scenes in Greek tragedy in which an element of humor is joined to a perfectly serious purpose, and this is one of them.[20] Is this not really the case in most tragedy? A difference is sometimes made between Greek and Elizabethan tragedy on the grounds that the latter has scenes· of comedy, the former has not. In *Hamlet* some of the scenes with Polonius —his farewell scene with Laertes (I, iii), and the baiting of Polonius by Hamlet in II, ii—have a comic element, but they are not comedy for its own sake, and we know this very well by the end of the play, when Polonius and his family have suffered madness, moral disintegration, suicide, and ignominious death.[21] The difference between Shakespeare and Sophocles is not between the presence and absence of a certain effect but, as in so many aspects of the drama of these two periods, between amplitude and conciseness.[22] The comic elements in *Hamlet* stand by themselves, to be related to the tragedy later; our

[20] Other instances in Sophocles: the manner of the Corinthian in *OT*, Episodes Three and Four; the clash between Lichas and the messenger in *Trach.*; the sudden reappearance of Odysseus at *Philoc.* 974.

[21] Harley Granville-Barker, *Prefaces to Shakespeare*, 3rd ser. (London, 1937), 49, has this comment on *Hamlet*, I, iii: "They [Polonius and his children] lavish good advice on each other; but the dark machine is already moving, in which they are, all three, to be caught and broken."

[22] Kitto, *Form and Meaning*, 225: "The essential difference between the Greek and the Elizabethan drama may be expressed in the formula Concentration, not Extension." The whole chapter, "Greek and Elizabethan Tragedy," 199–230, is worth consulting on this point.

present bit of comedy in *Antigone* coincides with the serious dramatic development. Both are to the same purpose and bear the same relation to the spirit of the drama.

The guard is a solemn fool, thoroughly frightened for his own safety but incapable of presenting anything but a ludicrous appearance.[23] Creon's impatience with him, his futile anger at his report, his immediate suspicion of bribery, and his long tirade on the evils of money, reveal with merciless clarity his want of dignity and self-confidence. We know now that Creon, in spite of the grandiose nature of his first speech, is a man of little stature. But it is wrong to suppose that the principle on which he bases his stubborn refusal of burial is brutal or deliberately mean. Creon has his concept of right, and until far on in the play he does not even suspect that there is any discrepancy between his notion of right and the will of the gods. His infuriated amazement at the chorus's suggestion that the gods may have had a hand in the burial (280–287) is neither assumed nor unnatural. To Creon, the state is under the care of the gods and an insult to the state is an insult to the gods. He seriously believes that his exemplary "punishment" of Polyneices' corpse is for the good of the state. His essential wrongness lies in his limited concept of what is good for the state and his fatal stubbornness in clinging to this concept against all opposition and all reason.

The encounter with the guard reveals above all Creon's shortcomings of character. In the incidents with Haemon and Teiresias the contest is on somewhat more abstract grounds, though the personal commentary also continues. Haemon represents the voice of Thebes, as well as the cause of Antigone. After Haemon's opening words of filial respect (635–638) Creon

---

[23] His *rhesis*, lines 407–440, reporting the circumstances of the mysterious burial, has nothing ludicrous about it. Except for the closing lines, which are to some degree in character, the speech has the usual impersonality of the conventional messenger's report.

launches on an elaborate vindication of his course of action and a denunciation of insubordination. But the finale of the speech is nothing more dignified than the fear "lest we be called the inferiors of women" (680). When Haemon alleges that his father is acting against the will of the *polis* (733), Creon, angry and illogical, takes refuge in explicit tyranny: "Is not the *polis* regarded as the property of its ruler" (738)? As Haemon is led to say, Creon wishes only "to speak and not to listen to the answers" (757). Creon's anger suggests his lack of real self-confidence; and this is confirmed when at the end of the scene he shows his first sign of retreat: acting on a hint by the chorus, he will spare Ismene (770–771). This is the first slight withdrawal from his own will; he withdraws gracelessly, and without any acknowledgment of having been touched consciously by Haemon's logic.

The Creon-Teiresias scene proceeds along similar lines. In each scene Creon's opponent begins with well-meant advice and ends with anger and warnings; Creon begins with specious logic that is only disguised stubbornness and ends, the pretense removed, in anger and abuse. Teiresias represents the will of the gods, and he does so with an impressive authority that cannot really be resisted. Creon's attempt to do so is pure stubbornness; he can only proceed, with little sign of inner conviction, to impugn Teiresias' skill as a prophet. Resistance is useless, and even Creon has to see this, though he does not do so until the prophet has left in fury and Creon has further revealed his own folly.

In the scene between Antigone and Creon, Antigone is presented in a more wholly admirable light than in her scenes with Ismene. Sophocles' purpose in so proceeding is clear; nothing must mar the moral triumph of Antigone over her antagonist. But is the picture of her in this scene, calm, orderly of thought, "born to join in loving, not in hating," quite consistent with what we have seen elsewhere? Essentially it is so, provided we clearly understand what Antigone's words in this scene mean. Of the beauty of her statement of devotion to the unwritten laws of the gods, when she is challenged by Creon, there can be no question. This is the noble outcome of what was, in the prologue, still inchoate and instinctive feeling. There is no inconsistency, but development and fulfillment. Creon does not really answer her at all. With a burst of maxims (473–478) he scourges her for insubordination; her conduct and her justification of it are in his eyes nothing but *hybris* (480–483). He is simply too limited even to comprehend her motives. In the stichomythia that follows, the ideas of the two antagonists about reverence, good and evil, friend and foe, are shown to be in different realms of thought. Antigone maintains that it is no impiety to respect a brother (511); Creon considers respect for Polyneices to be impiety toward Eteocles (514). Their notions about piety are simply not in the same world. To Antigone it means respect for a kinsman and religious duty (511); to Creon it has only a political meaning: both man and burial are to him impious, because they are opposed to his concept of law (513, 515). Eteocles is καλός, Polyneices κακός, on the basis of their political behavior. When Antigone queries, "Who knows if these things are honored below" (521)? she is, in effect, challenging the ultimate importance of these political distinctions. Creon then asserts that a foe is always a foe, even in death:

οὔτοι ποθ' οὑχθρός, οὐδ' ὅταν θάνῃ, φίλος. [522]

and Antigone makes her celebrated reply:

οὔτοι συνέχθειν, ἀλλὰ συμφιλεῖν ἔφυν. [523]

These two lines are a summary of the difference in ideas between Antigone and Creon, and they are emphatically marked and linked by the anaphora of οὔτοι and by the striking similarity of their phraseology. To Antigone, Creon's political, worldly wisdom means nothing; she moves in a different atmosphere, and her concern is with family loyalty, not with political loyalty. And this is what her beautiful words basically mean; not that she is a gentle, loving peacemaker (we know from the prologue that she is fiery and passionate and ready to hate when she thinks hatred is due), but that she scorns as superficial Creon's world of political obsession.

There is also in the scene a distinct contrast of character. Creon, as we have noticed, has maxims forever on his lips; Antigone's speech is markedly simple, direct, and genuine. Creon has his everlasting fear of damage to his prestige, especially at the hands of "women"; Antigone is tranquil in her single-minded conviction.

The chorus of *Antigone* is unusually important for the thought of the play. As elders of Thebes the chorus have a lively personal interest in what is going on; they are concerned both with religious rectitude and with the welfare and stability of the state. They are throughout aware of the moral excellence of Antigone's piety, and from the beginning they have qualms about Creon's edict (210–215). But they will abide by the law of the land, and they believe that it is right to do so. Hence their criticism of Antigone's act in spite of their sympathy for her; her piety they admire, her disobedience they censure as headstrong and ill-judged (872–875); their censure is expressed by their declaration that she has offended against *Dike* (853–855). But for Creon, once they have been assured, through Teiresias' indisputable words, that his law is wrong in the eyes of the gods (and hence is no true law of Thebes, as Creon himself has finally to recognize), they have nothing but reproach and condemnation. Final choral tags do not ordinarily have more than a very general relevance to the theme; but in this play the chorus's final words (1347–1353) are a direct criticism of Creon for his impiety, his folly, and his pride. This passage and their judgment of Antigone (872–875) form a pair of comments of great significance for the theme of the play: with Antigone they are divided between sympathy and reproach; with Creon their attitude is of unmixed condemnation.

Finally, a word about the manner in which each of the two principals reacts to the disaster that befalls both; for here again there is marked contrast. Antigone, after some evidence of human frailty in her kommos and in her last iambic speech (891–943),[24] leaves to face death with pride and self-confidence (937–943). Creon is completely broken; in his kommos at the end there is nothing but despair, self-abasement, and recognition of his error and folly.

v. Oedipus Tyrannus

In this play there is no basic pair of characters as in the diptych plays, but the importance of character interaction for the revelation of the theme is no slighter. Another kind of contrast contributes greatly to the action of the play, a contrast between the revealed and the unrevealed or, as Reinhardt puts it, between seeming and reality.[25] In the customary Sophoclean manner this contrast is joined with one of will and personality: while Oedipus strives constantly to cut through the mystery and know the truth, a whole series of persons tries to hide the truth from him—Teiresias, Jocasta, the Theban herdsman, and, in the time before the action, Oedipus' Corinthian foster parents. The theme is centered in the person of Oedipus, and the function of the subordinate persons is to reveal his nature. We must consider in detail three of these persons, Creon, Jocasta, and Teiresias. The relationship of each of them to Oedipus is a work of dramatic genius.

The first major interplay of character is in Oedipus' scene with Teiresias; but in the prologue there is some contrast between the magnificent and self-confident king and the respectful but eminently god-fearing priest who speaks for the Theban

---

[24] The passage is further considered below, pp. 163–165.
[25] *Sophokles,* 108 and *passim* in his chapter on *OT.*

people. The priest very explicitly differentiates his respect for Oedipus from his piety to the gods (31); and in referring to Oedipus' victory over the Sphinx he does not fail to mention the aid of heaven (38). Oedipus, by the end of the prologue, has become most vehement in his promises of what *he* will do: he will be the avenger of the land and of Apollo too (136); he for his own sake will rid Thebes of the pestilence (138, note the touch of egotism suggested by the expression αὐτὸς αὐτοῦ); he, in fact, will do all (145).[26] His final words soften the effect of complete self-reliance somewhat (σὺν τῷ θεῷ, 146), but there is an air of dominant confidence that differs markedly from the piety of the priest, whose last words recall once more this spirit when he calls upon Apollo, sender of the oracle, to be the deliverer (147–150). We must not cry *hybris;* up to this point, at least, Oedipus is not guilty of any impropriety of spirit. But neither must we disregard the clear meaning of this initial slight contrast of spirit; it is a significant hint of the powerful and impetuous self-reliance that marks Oedipus' nature as it is revealed later in the play.

We have seen the structural principle of Oedipus' scene with Teiresias in operation twice before, in the Creon-Haemon and the Creon-Teiresias scenes of *Antigone*, but the present scene is much bolder in execution than either of the others and, because of the infinitely greater stature of Oedipus than Creon, far more engrossing. Here, following the pattern of the earlier scenes, the prophet begins well intentioned, the king respectful and calm. Indeed the extreme reverence of Oedipus toward Teiresias (he addresses him as σωτήρ and ἄναξ and declares ἐν σοί ἐσμεν) is very unlike his imperious manner in the prologue and his anger later in the scene. It is quite clear that Sophocles

---

[26] ὡς πᾶν ἐμοῦ δράσοντος. The usual sinister meaning of πάντα δρᾶν is not to be forgotten here. This is among the first of the many striking verbal ironies of the play.

is aiming at a striking contrast between the mood at the beginning of the scene and that at its end. (In this too the pattern follows the *Antigone* scenes—in this case the Creon-Haemon scene especially—but again the *OT* scene has a great deal more verve.) Oedipus, obstructed by Teiresias' refusal to talk, soon flies into a terrible rage (334–335) and presently accuses him of complicity in the crime (348–349). This in turn stings Teiresias into declaring that Oedipus is himself the murderer that he seeks. By now Oedipus is in a towering rage, and Teiresias can shout aloud the whole truth without any chance of Oedipus' discovering it: the two men are moving in different channels of thought, though each is impelled in the direction he takes by the influence of the other. Oedipus hears Teiresias and reacts, and yet he does not really hear. Or does he? Is there, behind the indignation and rage that fill this scene and the next, with Creon, a lurking fear that what Teiresias has said is right? If so, it is a less explicit fear than that which Sophocles makes us realize that Creon feels in *Antigone*, where we know from his behavior at the end of his scenes with Haemon and Teiresias that his angry self-defense has no firm inner conviction. With Oedipus, the fear, if such there is, is deep within and unconscious.

The revelation of Oedipus' anger and his too ready suspicion of Teiresias have implications for the character of Oedipus that are not to be disregarded. Toward the end of the scene there is a subtle and most revealing display of Oedipus' egotism. A reference by Teiresias (436) to the parents of Oedipus catches the king's conscious ear, though the foregoing declarations of his guilt have found him apparently deaf. Oedipus is for the moment all attention (437), and we think that now he must learn his parentage. But the prophet answers enigmatically (438), and Oedipus reproaches him for doing so (439). Teiresias asks if solving enigmas is not Oedipus' special skill (440); and this reminder of his triumph over the Sphinx so engrosses the king's attention that he forgets all about his original question and the moment of possible revelation passes unfulfilled.

The contrast between the outward magnificence and inward blindness of Oedipus and the outward blindness and inward sight of the prophet is one of the given attributes of the scene, and Sophocles does not waste this natural opportunity. (Comparison with *Antigone* is instructive: there, though the same opportunity existed, Sophocles did not use it. This is one measure of the difference between the Creon of *Antigone* and the Oedipus of *OT*. Creon is not great enough for the irony to be dramatically telling; Oedipus is.) Oedipus taunts Teiresias with his blindness, saying that he has "eyes for profit only, blindness in his craft" (388–389); Teiresias' answer is a magnificent consummation of this play on sight and blindness:

σὺ καὶ δέδορκας κοὐ βλέπεις ἵν' εἶ κακοῦ. [413]

With Creon, Oedipus has two scenes, and the second is no less important than the first for its revelation of Oedipus, though its effect is easier to overlook. The first follows the Teiresias-scene and is like it in form, though Creon has not the fire and authority of the old prophet and hence the dramatic pitch of the scene is much lower. Creon, as everybody knows, is the moderate man. His role is to stress, by his unfailing modesty and calm, the extravagance of speech and the self-reliance displayed by Oedipus. This aspect of their relationship needs little mention. Oedipus is angry from the start; Creon pleads only for a fair hearing (543–544). In contrast to Oedipus with his wild suspicions and guesses, Creon is a model of caution; typical of him is the statement, in answer to a question, "I do not know; and what I do not know, it is not my habit to assert" (569). In his long speech (583–615) the burden of Creon's argument is that any man of modesty would prefer to enjoy a ruler's power

without the cares of rule, as he does. All he wants is τὰ σὺν κέρδει
καλά (595). Oedipus is arrogant in his unjust charges: Creon is
"clearly" the murderer of Laius (534); he has been "caught"
plotting against the person of Oedipus (642–643). That Creon,
mild of manner, loyal, patient, should be painted such a monster
is striking proof of the stubborn reliance of Oedipus on his
own convictions. The Creon he is battling is a figment of his
imagination.[27]

In their later scene, at the end of the play, there is the
same contrast, though its emphasis is different. Creon is still
the man of complete moderation, Oedipus the extremist; but
now it is himself that Oedipus attacks, while toward Creon his
attitude is one of humility and gratitude. The change emphasizes,
of course, the completeness of Oedipus' reversal of fortune, and
it shows that he is as capable of generosity as of abuse—which
we already know, I think, without this demonstration.

Creon thus serves as a pivot about which Oedipus turns in
his contrasting phases of self-confidence and abasement. But his
usefulness as a foil for Oedipus has more depth than this. For
all his unfailing justness and moderation Creon is not a character who excites our sympathy. His virtues are a little mechanical; there is no sign of an inward fire of conviction. This aspect
of his nature is especially clear at the end of the play, but even
in his earlier self-defense his impersonal logicality fails to stir us,
especially in contrast with Oedipus' emotional intensity. To give
one small example of this difference: when Oedipus, convinced
of Creon's treachery, shouts, "My city, alas for my city" (629)!
Creon very correctly, coolly, and logically answers, "I too have
a share in the city; it is not yours alone." Oedipus is all wrong;

---

[27] The behavior of Oedipus in this scene is surely proof enough that
the Oedipus of this play is not faultless. The fact that Oedipus' suspicions
of Creon begin in the prologue (124–125) does not appreciably modify
the effect of this later attack.

his words are neither just nor logical; Creon's are both. Yet by
its fervor the unjust cry of Oedipus excites more sympathy
than the dispassionate truth of Creon.

In the final scene of the play this thread of contrast is more
apparent, and the playwright's purpose in so arranging matters
is quite clear: it is a means of ensuring continued domination
(dramatic, that is) by the tragic hero. It is striking that Creon
at no time gives a sign of emotion for the fall of Oedipus. If
he were a meaner man than he is, he would be elated; if a greater,
there would be some show of sympathy. But when Oedipus
begs to be cast forth at once from Thebes (1436–1437), Creon
answers, "I should have done so already, had I not thought it
best to consult the gods first." Creon will do nothing without
assurance that it is the right thing; but he is quite prepared to
drive out his blind and helpless kinsman without the least personal feeling. Just at the end Oedipus pleads, hopelessly of
course, that his daughters may stay with him (1522). Creon answers: πάντα μὴ βούλου κρατεῖν. The reproach is slight, and no
doubt justified; but its total want of feeling is vaguely offensive.
Creon is not malignant,[28] he is well intentioned. Of his own accord he brings Oedipus' daughters to him. But he is colorless,
without depths of good or evil. His sameness is symbolized by
his repetition, at the end, of the characteristic sentence (569)
quoted above; at the end, in answer to the impetuous questioning of Oedipus, he answers:

$$\text{ἃ μὴ φρονῶ γὰρ οὐ φιλῶ λέγειν μάτην. [1520]}$$

Were Creon a more living and attractive figure, the sympathy
and admiration of the audience would be less wholly Oedipus'.
In one important way the relationship is like that of Ajax and
Odysseus, though Odysseus is a much more attractive figure
than Creon: in both cases the distinction between the high

---

[28] The scoundrelly Creon of *OC* should not influence our view of the
Creon of *OT*. The two characters are quite separate.

spirit of the central figure and his unheroic foil is firmly drawn. The relation between Oedipus and Jocasta is mainly one of sympathy. The skepticism of Oedipus, which appears in his scene with Teiresias when in his rage he casts slurs on the ability and honesty of Teiresias, is shared by Jocasta. Indeed she serves as a temptress, at the end of Episode Two and in Episode Three, to induce Oedipus to disregard the ominous oracles and trust in his own judgment entirely. But we need not interpret Jocasta as a prototype of the free-thinking "liberated" intellectual Athenian woman of Sophocles' day;[29] her skepticism springs from her own immediate situation, from her desire to protect Oedipus and keep peace; not self-confidence, but love, governs her attitude. Three times she speaks out against the validity of oracles (707–725, 857–858, 952–953), twice drawing Oedipus after her. Of the folly of their skepticism and the ultimate vindication of the oracles it is hardly necessary to speak. But does Sophocles present their skepticism as a thing to be condemned or is his use of oracles here purely a dramaturgical convenience? We have already noticed, in Chapter II, the skill with which Sophocles uses oracles in his plays, and it was suggested there that we cannot be certain about Sophocles' own attitude toward the religious significance of oracles. This much perhaps we can say of the present instance: the skepticism of Oedipus is a symbol, not necessarily of impiety, but of confidence in the self-sufficiency of human power; and in Sophocles' view human power is inadequate armor to protect against suffering.

In any case, the skepticism of Oedipus and Jocasta creates telling dramatic suspense. Several times Jocasta is used as a parallel and prelude to the fortunes of Oedipus. First she sees that the oracles are true after all, and later he too sees it. First she finds her life ruined by the inevitable process of events, and later he comes to the same terrible knowledge. We noticed

[29] This is done by Pohlenz, *Griechische Tragödie,*[2] 219.

above how the dramatist uses the difference in their reception of the Corinthian messenger's revelation of Oedipus' origin: the knowledge and despair of Jocasta are contrasted with the blind excitement of Oedipus. The most striking case of a contrast and parallel between Jocasta and Oedipus is in their successive encounters with Τύχη. When the Corinthian has brought news of Polybus' death, news that seems to confound the oracle, that Oedipus will slay his father, Jocasta, in the excitement of her relief, cries: "Why should a man have fears? His life is under Tyche's sway; there is no certain knowledge in advance. It is best to live at random, in whatever way one can" (977–979). By the end of the episode Jocasta has realized that not Tyche but an inexorable chain of events is in command of her life and that of Oedipus; and she goes into the palace to hang herself in despair. But now Oedipus takes up the theme; baffled as to who his parents are (now that the Corinthian has told him that he is not the son of Polybus and Merope) and wildly excited by the search for truth, in the last speech of the episode Oedipus cries that he is "Fortune's child" (παῖδα τῆς Τύχης, 1080).[30] In the next short episode he arrives at the dreadful knowledge in which Jocasta has anticipated him.

A few words on the relationship between two minor figures, the Corinthian and the herdsman, will bring us to the end of our review of character relationships in this play. They are clearly differentiated. The Corinthian, who comes as the bearer of what he is confident are good tidings, has been shown in the episode before they meet to be a cheery, familiar, rather garrulous soul; the herdsman, knowing that he possesses a dreadful secret about his monarch, is trying desperately to hide it

[30] Whitman, *Sophocles*, 145, cites this speech of Oedipus as evidence of a new spirit, much enlarged upon by Sophocles in subsequent plays, the spirit of heroic endurance. The suggestion is interesting and probably correct, but the passage has also a dramatic point entirely within the play, as a parallel to Jocasta's words on Tyche.

and is therefore surly and slow to speak, just the reverse of the Corinthian. The opposite pull of these two characters brings a remarkable tension to this crucial scene. The blithe Corinthian, unaware of the horrors that he is bringing to light, is helpfully jogging the memory of the reluctant herdsman. With naïve self-satisfaction he says the terrible, irrevocable words: "Here he is, ὦ τᾶν, here before you is the babe of yore" (1145)! The Corinthian's colloquial address, his cheery delivery of the fatal message, and his obliviousness of the herdsman's desperate efforts to conceal his knowledge add enormously to the grimness of the moment. Here is a *very* brief instance of the tragic use of comedy, in the Greek style.

It would be false to suggest that these character relationships are the whole of *Oedipus Tyrannus*, or that to ponder the relationships as *disiecta membra* is the proper way to receive the play. On the contrary, the effect of the play is both unified and poetic. What I wish to suggest here is that the towering figure of Oedipus and the seemingly inevitable tension of the action are raised on a substructure of countless small but carefully designed details of characterization. There is no other play of Sophocles where the power of the drama seems to spring so naturally from the person of the tragic hero and the nature of the situation, as if scarcely any intervention by the dramatist were necessary; and there is no play of Sophocles in which the playwright's consummate genius in the manipulation of characters is more fully in operation.

vi. Electra

In its general form *Electra*, as we have seen, is like *Oedipus Tyrannus*, but its spirit is new: it is much closer to character study and less a study of the struggle of a heroic spirit against circumstances that overwhelm him. Our interest is almost entirely in Electra's reaction to events, not in her fate. The play is still one of character in situation, but Electra (unlike the

central figures of the plays we have just been discussing) is detached from the central event of the story in which she is concerned in that the event does not depend on what she is and
does. A measure of the difference between this play and *OT*,
where every scene bears on the revelations that are the fate of
Oedipus, can be seen in the fact that two-thirds of the dialogue
of *Electra* is occupied by Electra's scenes with Chrysothemis
and Clytemnestra, scenes which do not bear directly on the consummation of the revenge at all but on Electra's attitudes and
emotions.[31]

There is a frame in this play as in *Ajax*. There the frame
was for the sake of character: Odysseus, who was important
at the end, needed to be introduced. Here it is a story frame:
the accomplishment of the revenge by Orestes, Pylades, and
the paedagogus must be set in motion early so that it may proceed later without encroaching too much on the central position of Electra.

After her initial monody (86–120) Electra is joined by the
chorus, and in their kommos (121–250) the heroine is seconded,
in her expression of grief and shame, by the women of the
chorus. In the song and the following conversation in iambics
we learn Electra's attitude: bitter hatred of Clytemnestra and
Aegisthus, unshaken loyalty to her father, repugnance for her
present situation and conduct (254–255). Just at the end of
the kommos Electra makes a declaration of faith that is reminis-
cent of statements made by Ajax, Deianeira, and Antigone.
She does not at this point speak of the duty of the εὐγενής;
but the solemn conviction of her words makes us realize that
this is her credo and her fixed purpose:

---

[31] Reinhardt, *Sophokles*, 147, remarks that with *OT* Sophoclean
Schicksalstragödie comes to an end. Perhaps Reinhardt exaggerates the
difference of spirit between early and late plays, but his observations on
the new spirit, in his chapters on *Electra* and *Philoctetes*, deserve attention.

If the dead man is earth and nothing more, if the
murderers pay no answering price in blood, then
shamefastness is gone from men, and piety has van-
ished. [245–250]

This insistence on the need for revenge will be her guiding
conviction, like Ajax's martial honor, Deianeira's wifely devotion, and Antigone's family loyalty.[32]

Upon this atmosphere Chrysothemis enters. Between the following scene and the scenes between Antigone and Ismene
there are, inevitably, many similarities; but there are also important differences, as we shall see in a moment. Again there
is a contrast between heroic devotion to a single purpose and
good-natured, uninspired docility. The thing that most strikingly distinguishes this pair of sisters is the complete severance
between their whole way of thinking and even between their
use of words. Both speak of καλόν, κακόν, νοῦς, and the like, but
they do not mean the same things at all. Chrysothemis pleads
with Electra to take safe counsel before the imprisonment with
which she is threatened overtakes her and in her appeal pleads
with her to use "sense" (φρονεῖν, 384); a little later she begs her
not to fall ἀβουλίᾳ (429). Good sense to Chrysothemis is immediate practical advantage and the avoidance of trouble. Electra prays that she "may never be so devoid of sense" (νοῦ . . .
κενή, 403). To her, abandonment of her father's cause is want
of sense.

Their notions of good and bad are just as far apart. Chrysothemis never thinks with any moral implication, only of material
advantage or loss (ἐν καλῷ, 384; σὺν κακῷ, 430). Two neigh-
boring verses point this contrast clearly: in line 395 Electra

---

[32] A little later (257) Electra puts her resolve in terms of what is demanded of an εὐγενὴς γυνή. In line 989, at the end of her appeal to
Chrysothemis, she expresses the thought, familiar from *Aj.*, *Trach.*, and
Antig., that to live basely is unbecoming to one of noble nature:
ζῆν αἰσχρὸν αἰσχρῶς τοῖς καλῶς πεφυκόσιν.

says, "Do not teach me to be evil (κακήν) to my friends." Not in direct reply but in the same context Chrysothemis says: "But it is good (καλόν γε), nevertheless, not to fall through senselessness" (398). What is κακόν to Electra is to Chrysothemis the only possible καλόν in their situation. Chrysothemis can scarcely be said to have any moral perception of her own, but she is not in any sense wicked. When Electra condemns with fierce scorn her sister's errand—to pour a libation at Agamemnon's tomb on behalf of her mother—as neither θέμις nor ὅσιον, Chrysothemis is ready enough to agree, though timid about disobeying her mother; she is not ἀνόσιος, merely obedient and unimaginative.

The second encounter between the sisters opens with a contrast that is only partially expressed in words and is largely a matter of atmosphere; nevertheless it is of considerable dramatic value. While Electra stands plunged in gloomy despair—she has just heard the report of Orestes' death—Chrysothemis bursts upon her joyfully with the opening words ὑφ' ἡδονῆς (871); she brings tidings (which are only scorned by Electra) of Orestes' apparent return. Throughout the scene the same buoyancy and delicacy of spirit characterize Chrysothemis, contrasting sharply with the heaviness of spirit and the darkness of manner of Electra. Even in Electra's later transports of joy on recognizing Orestes, there is no such lightheartedness, such naïve happiness as there is in Chrysothemis' delightful description (899–906) of her feelings when she found offerings, left by Orestes as she guesses, on Agamemnon's tomb.

This contrast of personalities, to Electra's partial disadvantage, will surprise us only if we believe that Sophocles meant to draw his tragic heroes as shining perfection, a belief that can be maintained only by disregarding important aspects of the interplay between Ajax and Odysseus, Antigone and Ismene, Oedipus and Creon, Electra and Chrysothemis. Electra has even more reason than Antigone (to cite the most nearly parallel example) for a want of grace and joy. For years she has cherished one abiding, terrible ambition, the death of her mother and Aegisthus; to have lived with such a thought is not conducive to lighthearted girlishness of Chrysothemis' sort. It is a necessary part of her determination, and so of her character, for Electra to be the grim figure that she is. The contrast with Chrysothemis is not flattering, but it is true, and it reveals with poignancy the price of Electra's fortitude.

There are many points of similarity in the contrasts between the two pairs of sisters. Chrysothemis and Ismene share a distrust of the efficacy of women's strength (*El.* 997–998; *Antig.* 61–62), a like definition of wisdom (*El.* 1013–1014; *Antig.* 67–68), a readiness to obey (*El.* 396; *Antig.* 78–79), affection for their stronger sisters (*El.* 1036; *Antig.* 99). Electra and Antigone are alike in their devotion to the dead who have been wronged (*El.* 257–260; *Antig.* 74–75), their open and scornful rebelliousness (*El.* 359, 604–605; *Antig.* 450), their conception of nobility (*El.* 257, 989; *Antig.* 38). And yet, in spite of these likenesses, the two relationships are not closely similar, unless we are content to disregard everything in them except the conventional contrast between independence and timidity. Electra is no second Antigone, nor is Chrysothemis another Ismene. Electra is as determined as Antigone but less self-assured and less ready to flare into anger at her sister; she seems older, and her attitude is less one of headstrong rebellion than of desperate resistance. Electra's dissimilarity to Antigone is created, in part at least, by the difference in her relationship with her sister. Chrysothemis is more girlish and less aware of the implications of what is going on than Ismene, and she is less warmly and wholeheartedly devoted to her sister: Ismene is ready to give her life for Antigone, Chrysothemis is timid about only a slight risk. The general effect is to lessen the impression of impetuosity in the stronger sister. Antigone has a rebel's fierceness, Electra the grim determination of an avenger. The relationship in *Electra* is worked out in much greater detail, a significant fact. Sophocles' interest in the details of character relations has increased.

The relationship between Electra and her mother is one of open hostility; neither antagonist makes any real effort to persuade, and we realize from the beginning of their scene that long years have taught them the futility of it. Instead, there is accusation, defense, counteraccusation. Clytemnestra's opening defense of herself is made dramatically probable by her dream, which has already been mentioned by Chrysothemis. Troubled by the dream, Clytemnestra feels impelled to defend herself, and defense leads to debate.

Clytemnestra insists that her conduct has been just: "For it was justice that slew him, not I alone" (528); Electra's resistance is therefore unjust (550), and her conduct shameful (518). In her answer Electra concentrates on these themes of justice and shame: if Clytemnestra's killing of Agamemnon was just, then she will be the next to die, if she meets with justice (582–583); Clytemnestra's actions are "the most shameful deeds of all" (586). The theme of shame haunts this debate. At the end of her long speech Electra cries:

> Then denounce me before all, call me wicked, if you
> choose, or unbridled in speech, or filled with shame-
> lessness. If I am versed in such conduct, I do not shame
> my heritage from you. [606–609]

It is as though Electra recognizes in herself an evil inheritance from her mother, and it tortures her. The same feeling of shame for her conduct appeared earlier in Electra's words to the chorus (254, 309).

If we restrict our view of the relationship of mother and daughter to one of wickedness contrasted with rectitude, we shall of course simply forget this theme of shame; but we shall thereby be seeing only a part of the scene and only a part of the picture of Sophocles' Electra. The theme continues:

Clytemnestra answers Electra by accusing her of insolence and shameless wickedness (613–615); Electra declares that she is not without shame for what she does (616) but that her mother's wickedness drives her to shameful conduct: "Evil deeds are taught by evil deeds" (619–621). Again Clytemnestra attacks Electra's shamelessness in criticizing her mother (ὦ θρέμμ' ἀναιδές, 622), and Electra insists in reply that the words are Clytemnestra's because the deeds are hers, "and it is the deeds that find the words" (625). To Clytemnestra the shame lies in Electra's public revelation of their quarrel; Electra goes to the heart of the matter, the crimes of Clytemnestra and their consequences for the conduct of both of them.

The scene ends with the paedagogus' false report of Orestes' death. The contrast of how Electra and her mother receive this report has been noticed above (p. 93): the despair of Electra, the excitement and joyful relief (after a moment) of Clytemnestra.

Between Electra and Orestes one can hardly speak of the influence of character; their relationship depends more for its dramatic effectiveness on situation than on their characters. In the recognition this is especially true. The scene achieves its effect through the contrast between Electra's illusory despair and the happy truth that her brother stands before her; and, later, through the wild joy of Electra following her gloom. This is all Electra; it matters very little what the character of Orestes is. At the same time, though the recognition scene is in its makeup of less concern to us in our present study of character relationship than other scenes, it must be added that the scene is very powerful indeed, so powerful that more than one critic has found in it the climactic moment of the play. Must we then recognize that, for all that has been adduced in this chapter about the primary importance of character interplay, this scene, surely one of the most effective in Sophoclean drama, does not depend on it at all? Only in the most literal and immediate sense: within the confines of the scene there is no interplay of character, but the effectiveness of the scene—which as we have noticed rests almost exclusively with Electra—depends on the depth of our knowledge of Electra and of what reunion with her brother means to her. This knowledge has come chiefly (not exclusively—Electra's opening solo is poignantly revealing) through Electra's scenes with her sister and her mother.

When the recognition is over, there is some contrast of personality. Against the emotional extremes of Electra, her excitement and her transports, Orestes appears practical and unemotional. There is a dramatic purpose in this: Electra is assured the central position in the drama, even though Orestes takes the lead in the actual business of revenge, because she is the more interesting figure. The prologue has to some extent prepared us for this quiet, businesslike, unimaginative Orestes. From the beginning his attitude to what lies before him is pragmatic: it is a task, and his purpose is to reinstate himself in the position where he belongs (71–72); he gives no sign at all of possessing Electra's fervor to avenge their father and punish wickedness.[33] Again,

[33] Orestes' approach to the whole situation is almost amoral. His attitude toward the deception is summed up in line 61, οὐδὲν ῥῆμα σὺν κέρδει κακόν, a statement strikingly similar to the expression of moral indifference uttered by Odysseus in *Philoc.* 108–109, etc. It is impossible to conceive of a Sophoclean tragic hero expressing such a neutral moral outlook.

Since writing this analysis of the relationship between Electra and Orestes, I have learned, through seeing the fine performance of the play by the Cornell Dramatic Club in 1956, that my remarks need some modification. Performance of the play shows beyond question that, for the recognition scene to achieve its full effect, it does matter what kind of person Orestes is. He must have strength, and he must convey a deep personal concern for Electra. Electra, in this moment of transition from forlorn solitude and despair to triumph, must have a pillar to cling to, not a reed. An ineffectual or unconcerned Orestes at this point is dramatically impossible. Yet what has been said about Orestes' moral indifference in the prologue and about his coolness toward the business in hand is demanded by the text. Where, then, does Sophocles allow him to

after the recognition, his sober and practical nature is apparent: he constantly advises silence and expedition (1236, 1238, 1259, etc.); Electra cannot contain her alternating joy at Orestes' presence and wild hatred of her enemies (1232, 1245, etc.). We have already noticed (above, pp. 56–57) how her emotional intensity overshadows his businesslike dispatch at the end, both at Clytemnestra's death and when Aegisthus appears.

vii. Philoctetes

Philoctetes is like *Electra* in its concentration on character interaction and display; indeed this time not only the development of the action but its entire outcome depends on the interplay of characters, especially the influence of Philoctetes and Neoptolemus on each other. Lewis Campbell's comment on their relationship is not an exaggeration: "What gives to the *Philoctetes* a unique place in ancient literature, and may be said to constitute a new departure in dramatic art, is the subtle climax of emotions produced by the interaction of these two persons upon each other." [34] That Sophocles' dramatic art depends throughout largely on the interaction of characters we have

---

acquire the strength and the involvement which the recognition scene demands? The answer lies, clear to see, in the passage immediately following Electra's great speech over the urn. Only now, when he sees Electra's emotional depth and her tormented condition, does Orestes begin to realize the poignancy of the situation he is concerned in, and his awakening knowledge is shown in line 1185: "Now I see (ἄρα) that I knew nothing about my troubles." Thus the urn speech is more than the vehicle for a wonderful display of pathos. In the true Sophoclean manner it has also an active, creative force; it works on Orestes as well as on the audience. But we should not suppose that Orestes' character now changes profoundly. He remains pragmatic and businesslike. Only his attitude to Electra, in this passage, is affected. (The significance of the passage following the urn speech was made clear to me by the chapter on *Electra* in S. M. Adams, *Sophocles the Playwright* [Toronto, 1957], 74–76.)

[34] *Sophocles, Plays and Fragments*, II (Oxford, 1881), 358.

already seen; in *Philoctetes* this kind of dramatic construction reaches its peak.

The basis of the action, as we noticed earlier, is a contrast between two points of view: the authority of the Greek army embodied in Odysseus and the firm independence of the long-suffering Philoctetes. Between these opposites stands Neoptolemus, drawn by each and eventually effecting a bridge between them.

The prologue shows us Odysseus instructing Neoptolemus in the plan he has made to take Philoctetes. At least as important to the theme as the matter of their discussion are the attitudes and characteristics revealed by each of them. Odysseus is quite frankly the man of words rather than deeds, the man of clever wits: not deeds, but the tongue, is leader (99); one must have cleverness (77). Neoptolemus "must learn to be noble not alone in strength, but in giving aid even to something strange, unknown to you before" (50–53). Odysseus knows his man, and does his best to make trickery palatable to him. He is not altogether successful. Neoptolemus is very conscious of his heritage of nobility from Achilles (88–89); he has no use for anything underhand (86–87); the very manner in which he receives the idea of taking Philoctetes by guile shows his aversion to dishonesty: "What else do you bid, besides tell lies" (100)? From the beginning there is a deep rift between them. But Odysseus knows how to appeal to the young man's ambition. He assures him that by carrying out the deception he will win praise for wisdom and greatness (119); and Neoptolemus is convinced: "So be it; I shall do it, casting aside all shame" (120). But the very way in which he puts his resolve is significant: the eagerness of his words explains how he is able to continue the deception for so long in the face of growing moral misgivings; his manner of statement shows his consciousness of guilt and foreshadows his eventual change.

To Odysseus victory is worth the sacrifice of virtue (79–82);

Neoptolemus would rather fail nobly than succeed dishonestly (94–95). But Odysseus has another hold over the youth, beyond the lure of fulfilling his ambition, loyalty to the army. Though Odysseus' moral concepts are, obviously, rather casual and his methods far from admirable, he has a just cause; he represents the will and the authority of the army, and he impresses upon Neoptolemus the idea that if he fails to carry out the plan he will be failing the army (66–67). Loyalty to the army they have in common, and this alone. Otherwise they are opposites: Odysseus' indifference to honor and virtue beside Neoptolemus' devotion to idealism; clever persuasiveness beside naïveté; sophisticated knowledge of the world beside youthful inexperience.

When Odysseus appears for the second time, Neoptolemus has changed. Odysseus can no longer work on his ambition and make trickery acceptable by a rehearsal of its rewards. But he still has one weapon left, his authority as the representative of the army, and he uses it. Even before Odysseus returns, Neoptolemus, arguing with Philoctetes, has declared that obedience to the commanders is enjoined upon him "by justice and expediency" (925–926); and when Odysseus now orders him to the ship (1068) he submits without a word of opposition. There is no longer any pretense of an appeal to nobility; Odysseus' order to Neoptolemus is: "Go, and pay him [Philoctetes] no heed, *noble though you are*" (1068). Neoptolemus gives one sign of independence at this point: he leaves his sailors behind with Philoctetes.

When Odysseus and Neoptolemus return in the following episode, Odysseus' last hold is broken, for Neoptolemus has shifted his loyalty to a higher cause, as he now thinks, than that of the army. He now sees a contrast between loyalty to the army and justice, and with justice on his side he has no fear of Odysseus' threats. The breach between Odysseus and Neoptolemus is complete, and when Odysseus makes one last attempt in the name of the army to keep Neoptolemus from handing back the bow to Philoctetes, his words do not even evoke an answer (1293–1294).

As the influence of Odysseus over Neoptolemus declines, the person and the ideals of Philoctetes gain control over him. At first there is little real relation, for Neoptolemus is primed by his own ambitions and the coaching of Odysseus. But soon a change begins. The two fall to discussing the Greek heroes of the Trojan expedition, and the similarity of their attitudes toward the various men discussed soon appears and has an effect on Neoptolemus. His agreement with Philoctetes is not simply a part of the scheme of deception; his opinions are spontaneous, and there can be no doubt about this. It is not Neoptolemus, but Philoctetes, who does the echoing of thought: in lines 436–437 Neoptolemus expresses the commonplace that "war takes always the best and spares the rogue"; in lines 446–450 Philoctetes repeats the thought. Sophocles clearly wants us to see that the two men think alike; he is not trying to present this concord as an intentional deception of Philoctetes by Neoptolemus. Neoptolemus' true opinion of Odysseus comes out with equal spontaneity: Philoctetes asks about "a worthless fellow, skilled of tongue and clever" (439–440), whose name he cannot recall. Neoptolemus immediately assumes that he must mean Odysseus (441), though in fact it is not Odysseus but Thersites that Philoctetes has in mind.[35]

These first indications are followed, after the merchant scene, by a stronger suggestion of Neoptolemus' developing sentiment. We saw above that when the supposed merchant has withdrawn Neoptolemus insists that the wind is adverse, though a few minutes earlier he has said that it was favorable. This

[35] It is, I must admit, legitimate to insist that line 441 is spoken in obedience to Odysseus' instructions and therefore may not represent Neoptolemus' true opinion. But there is an air of naturalness about the words.

is slight; alone it might be doubted as evidence and be taken as fortuitous (if anything in Sophocles can be taken as fortuitous) and no part of the dramatist's revelation of Neoptolemus. But there is confirmation in the same scene. The same spontaneity as in the conversation on the warriors is present at the end of the episode, when Neoptolemus asks if he may "touch it [the bow] and reverence it like a god" (658) and when he answers Philoctetes' trust of him in words that must be heartfelt (672–673, quoted above, p. 60).[36]

Philoctetes' attack of violent pain from his sore further evokes the young man's loyalty and concern; now, when the hero is at his mercy, he realizes how hollow and worthless the success of the deception and the attainment of the arms really are. It is surely a misinterpretation of Neoptolemus' character to suppose that when he speaks of the emptiness and futility of his acquisition of the weapons (839–842) he says it merely because according to the oracle Philoctetes himself must be present at Troy for the city to be taken. The gradual development, both before and after this point, of Neoptolemus' sense of moral values and of his sympathy and admiration for Philoctetes requires us to recognize that here too the young man's disgust is not because the plan is a failure but because he is ashamed of the whole scheme of theft and deception.[37]

From here it is only a short step to complete victory for Philoctetes over Neoptolemus, who finds that he cannot go on with the trick any longer. His words in refusing to do so show the loathing which he has been feeling for it (908–909) and his recognition that it is contrary to his own nature (902–903). When, presently, Odysseus momentarily sways the youth once

[36] Cf. Weinstock, *Sophokles*, 79–82, for an excellent analysis of Neoptolemus' psychological adventures.
[37] Cf. Kieffer, *CP*, 37 (1942), 38–50, and Weinstock, *Sophokles*, 80, on this point.

more by his authority, it is significant that his brief period of domination is ended not by any outside force but by the assertion of Neoptolemus' will.[38]

Up to the point at which he returns the bow (1291–1292), Neoptolemus' attitude toward Philoctetes has been, except at the beginning when he has not yet felt his influence, wholly of sympathy and admiration. Nor has the influence been in one direction only. Philoctetes is moved by the nobility of the youth, and the depth of his trust and affection are seen when he gives into his hands the weapons that no other mortal has been permitted to touch (668–669). Even when he finds himself betrayed, Philoctetes' belief in the young man persists: "You are not base; but learning from base men you are likely to come to evil ways" (971–972). After the return of the bow, the emphasis changes, and we are aware of a distinct conflict between the youthful ambition of Neoptolemus and the cynicism of Philoctetes. When Neoptolemus appeals to him on the grounds of the glory that he will win at Troy (1344–1347), Philoctetes is moved (by the author of the arguments more than by their intrinsic persuasiveness [1350–1351]), but he cannot yield; he does not argue in return, he merely expresses an unshakable, unthinking resolve, founded on his bitter experience (e.g., 1388, 1392). Finally, on the appearance of Heracles, the youth and the mature sufferer are fully united in the sympathy of heroic spirit and common cause.

The relationship between Philoctetes and Odysseus is ex-

[38] A doubter of this picture of the gradual change of heart of Neoptolemus might ask how it is that, when at line 895 the youth cannot go on deceiving Philoctetes any longer because he has come so deeply under his influence, he does not at once return the bow. Neoptolemus himself supplies the answer in lines 925–926: he cannot return the weapons because he is loyal to the army. In other words, though in sympathy he is now wholly on Philoctetes' side, in his concept of duty he is still divided. The achievement of complete unanimity with Philoctetes comes in the next episode.

pressed more by means of the dealings of each with Neoptolemus than directly. With Neoptolemus, Odysseus represents, as we have seen, the authority of the army, and he represents also guile, cunning, and moral laxity; Philoctetes represents the demands of the high-minded individual. In words addressed to each of the others Odysseus suggests that to him moral excellence is a sort of outer dress, to be donned and doffed at will and convenience. To Neoptolemus he says, "We shall show our justice on another day" (82). To Philoctetes he declares: "When the contest is of just and noble men, you will find none holier than I" (1050–1051). But meanwhile he begs leave to forget about justice and nobility. He is the antithesis of the enduring virtue of Philoctetes, which cannot be brought to make any compromise at any price except that of obedience to the will of heaven.

The other part of the contrast between the two men must not be overlooked. As Gilbert Norwood reminds us, "It is easy, but mistaken, to label Odysseus as 'the villain.' In reality, he is the state personified." [39] He is other less attractive things too, but he is undoubtedly the symbol of the state. And along with the will of the state, he is acting for the will of heaven. Ironically enough, it is this shifty opportunist who is in accord with the will of Zeus, to which the heroic individualist eventually submits. This aspect of Odysseus' role is given striking emphasis when Odysseus insists with undeniable justice that it is the decree of Zeus that he is carrying out:

Ζεὺς ἔσθ', ἵν' εἰδῇς, Ζεύς, ὁ τῆσδε γῆς κρατῶν,
Ζεύς, ᾧ δέδοκται ταῦθ'· ὑπηρετῶ δ' ἐγώ. [989–990]

And unpalatable though it may be when Odysseus is the one to present the case, Philoctetes has eventually to recognize its truth. He does so when Heracles appears and emphasizes, just as Odysseus has done, that it is the will of Zeus that Philoctetes go to Troy (1415, 1442–1443). The protagonist's final words

[39] *Greek Tragedy*,[4] (London, 1948), 162.

are a recognition of this fact. But in his acceptance of it he rises above the cruelty and unreliability of the Greek leaders; the acceptance of his destiny is a pact between deity and the idealism that he and Neoptolemus both finally represent.[40]

viii. Oedipus at Colonus

Philoctetes is the Sophoclean play that depends more than any other for the progress of its action on the character interplay that is the object of our present examination; *Oedipus at Colonus* is the Sophoclean play in which this technique is least in evidence. It was said above that this play is different from all the others in that the theme is stated in the prologue and what follows is illustrative of this given theme rather than creative. As a result of this different dramatic approach the character relationships are less dynamic; they serve to enhance rather than to create the portrayal of Oedipus as he rises in the course of the play from powerless beggary to daemonic force, a development plainly foretold in the prologue. In general, the character interplay concerns the relations of Oedipus with two groups, those who help him and receive his grace and those who are his enemies. We shall deal very briefly with each of these groups.

"Those who receive" Oedipus are his daughters and Theseus, who represents the idealized spirit of Athens. Concerning the daughters, the first thing that strikes one is that here there is no pronounced distinction between them, except just at the end of the play, where their characterization does not directly concern Oedipus and seems designed to link this play with *Antigone*. Antigone is throughout the more prominent, but both are devoted to their father. We need not enlarge on Antigone's attendance on her father in the prologue and elsewhere; the most

[40] Heracles needs no mention in this analysis. He is no more a participating character in the customary Sophoclean sense than is Athena in *Ajax*.

important aspect of the relationship for the theme is the return made by Oedipus for this loyalty. No longer feebly dependent at the end, Oedipus leads the way from the orchestra with the words:

> This way, my children, follow me. For I, a new leader, will guide your steps, even as you have led your father. [1542–1543]

Oedipus no longer shows only the pitiful gratitude of a helpless old man; his stature at the end is such that his love is almost divine favor.

There is not, however, much real encounter of character in this relationship. That with Theseus has somewhat more. It is chiefly a relationship of sympathy; Theseus shows the magnanimity and grace of spirit necessary to make him the spiritual partner of Oedipus, worthy to enjoy the gift Oedipus has to bestow.[41] It is under the influence of Theseus that Oedipus begins to show his true stature. In his opening speech Theseus at once declares his sympathy with Oedipus: he was reared in exile, like Oedipus, and has been tried by bitter experience (562–564). They are alike too in their hatred of injustice and dishonorable action, as appears in the scene where the two of them are together with Creon and both censure in warm terms the unjust violence of Creon (911, 971, 1000, 1026). The central theme of their sympathy is expressed by the word χάρις; each generously offers the other the favor that is his to bestow; each recognizes the generosity of the other. The theme of χάρις pervades their relationship, and the word is many times repeated (586, 635, 1489, 1773, and elsewhere).

There are a few points of significant contrast between them. Theseus is a ruler, and his mind is occupied with practical politics; when Creon abducts the girls, his main reproach is for Creon's lawlessness and his apparent contempt for the power

[41] Cf. Webster, *Introduction*, 85.

of Athens. He is constantly aware of his city and his place as its ruler. Oedipus' concern is with more universal things. When Theseus asks in surprise, "Could there sometime be bitterness between me and them [the Thebans]" (606)? Oedipus' answer is his great discourse on the mutability of all things except the gods (607–628). The contrast serves to emphasize the mysterious unworldly quality that is one part of the Oedipus of this play.

Between Oedipus and Creon there is nothing but plain hostility. It has often been noticed that Creon is the one thorough villain in Sophocles. Even Polyneices has qualities that excite our sympathy; Creon has none. In the first scene between Oedipus and Creon, Creon tries, dishonestly, to lure Oedipus back to Thebes and into his power, and this transparently false attempt provides Oedipus with the setting for a powerful denunciation of his enemies. In their next meeting Theseus too is present. Each of the juxtaposed long speeches by the three men breathes a different spirit: Theseus is the politically minded just man, Creon is the man of violence and (when trapped) of flattery, Oedipus is concerned with his past ills and his coming power. His speech in this scene contains his fullest and most confident statement of his innocence and his power.

The incident with Polyneices is in some respects like Oedipus' scenes with Creon. Again there is the same clash between false claims of justice and friendship on the part of the intruder and the unerring truth and unsparing justice of Oedipus; and again the dishonesty and wrongness of the intruder give impetus for a terrible denunciation by Oedipus. The brief leave-taking between Polyneices and Antigone provides a further commentary on Polyneices' character. Antigone, ever compassionate and eager to help, pleads with him to give up the expedition against Thebes. Polyneices' answer rather pathetically reveals his utter selfishness: "I cannot. For how could I lead a second expedition, having once turned back" (1418–1419)? He is stubbornly insistent on fighting for power, even though he knows the attempt must fail. But Antigone's tender solicitude evokes from him, just at the moment of parting, a more admirable trait, an answering affection for his sisters: "I pray the gods that you two may never encounter troubles; for in all men's eyes you are unworthy of misfortune" (1444–1446). The small incident is an interesting example of Sophocles' attention to the substance of even unimportant characters, attention that is bestowed primarily for its effect on the theme of the play: the sympathy that this spark of decency in Polyneices arouses in us makes us feel more keenly the terror and power of Oedipus' curse.

Oedipus' scene with the Colonean stranger, in the prologue, needs little mention. The stranger's calm manner and his recognition of Oedipus' nobility (76) find an answering calmness and dignity in Oedipus and prepare the atmosphere for the great prayer of Oedipus to the Eumenides when the stranger has gone. The manner of the Colonean provides also a contrast to the horrified animation of the chorus on their arrival. Their cry on catching sight of Oedipus:

$$\text{δεινὸς μὲν ὁρᾶν, δεινὸς δὲ κλύειν [141]}$$

and Oedipus' answering supplication (142) are fit introduction to the scene which shows Oedipus' fortunes at their nadir. This scene too has a place in the development of the theme by its contrast with the awe that the chorus will later show for the hero.

It is no accident that this is the play in which the one Sophoclean villain appears, for the characterization in general in *Oedipus at Colonus* and the relationships between characters are drawn in black and white in comparison with the subtlety of interaction in all the other plays. As was suggested before, this difference in technique is determined by a difference in the playwright's presentation of his theme. Our recognition of

Oedipus' nature depends primarily on our knowledge, from the prologue, of what he is and only secondarily on our seeing what he is through character interaction.

Our survey of character relationships in the seven plays is now complete. It has been long—too long, perhaps, for the reader's patience—and yet it had to be long if it was to achieve the purpose that made it seem worth undertaking: to show that, whether or not we are fully aware of it when we see the plays performed or read them at a normal speed, the structure and the movement of Sophoclean drama depend on a large number of extremely intricate and complex character relationships. Too often the analysis of Sophocles' plays gives the impression that the numerous contrasts—some of which at least are recognized by all—are for the most part the sort of black-and-white sketches that we have found in *OC* alone, and there for a special reason. If we are content to think of the relationship between Antigone and Ismene as merely a contrast of independent fortitude and timid docility, that between Electra and Clytemnestra of loyalty and wickedness, that between Oedipus and Creon in *OT* of excess and moderation, we are, in these and in the many other cases that we have reviewed, doing Sophocles the injustice of reducing our view of his representation of human nature in his plays to a simplicity that his whole dramatic approach denies. If what was suggested at the outset of this study to be the essence of Sophoclean tragedy—the depiction of strong character in a crucial situation—is a correct description (and I venture to think that the evidence adduced in this chapter goes far to substantiate it), then we need to understand the whole of the leading persons in the various plays; and I doubt very much whether we can reach this understanding without a full recognition of the far-reaching and complex meaning of character interaction in Sophocles.

We are aware when we read Sophocles' plays that his major characters give the impression of power and aliveness, which increase as the drama proceeds, and that there is in the course of his dramas taken as units a remarkably dynamic quality. Part of this dynamism depends on aspects of the plays that we shall notice in the following chapters, but much of it depends on the power and fullness with which the major characters are presented to us. For example, one of the most gripping and character-revealing lines in Sophoclean drama occurs in the short central scene of revelation in *OT*, when the herdsman has exclaimed, in agonized apprehension, that he is "on the verge of speaking terror itself" (1169), and Oedipus answers:

$$κἀγὼγ' ἀκούειν· ἀλλ' ὅμως ἀκουστέον. \quad [1170]$$

The words are simple and the thought follows naturally and directly from what has gone before. What gives the line its remarkable power is our knowledge of Oedipus: the fact that we know from his scenes with Teiresias, Creon, and the others what depths of passion are being held in leash here, what an effort of self-restraint is required of the impetuous and imperious Oedipus. In *Philoctetes* the instant and joyful acceptance by Philoctetes of the divine mandate brought by Heracles is intelligible only by virtue of what we have come to know of his spirit under the influence of Neoptolemus. In *Electra* the emotional force of the recognition depends on our intimate knowledge of Electra. In *Antigone* Creon's rueful and belated realization that "it would have been better had I gone through life preserving the established laws" (1113–1114) is dramatically meaningful because of the whole complex interplay of varying concepts of law and of the emotions underlying those concepts that we have witnessed in the scenes between Creon and Antigone, Creon and Haemon, Antigone and Ismene, and indeed in every incident in the play. These are not isolated instances, but the normal development of a Sophoclean action.

Not all drama functions in this way. The Creon of Alfieri's *Antigone*, though by no means devoid of interest with his combination of deep-dyed villainy and parental softness, does not develop before us so that his reactions become charged with significance accrued through his relations with the other characters, as Sophocles' Creon does. Alfieri's Creon develops within himself only, and though we know him better at the end than at the outset of the play, we do not feel that it is through character interaction that our increased knowledge has come about. The difference is not merely between the greatness of Sophocles and the respectable but secondary talents of Alfieri; some of the world's great dramas are built in the Sophoclean fashion—though none, I think, so wholly in this way as Sophocles'—and some are not. Clytemnestra in *Agamemnon* is a figure of superlative strength, but that strength is brought home to us through the power of her own spontaneous thoughts and actions rather than through the influence or contrast of anyone else; Medea, on the other hand, certainly becomes what she becomes partly through the ineptness of Jason and the weakness of the king, though she is less dependent on this kind of revelation than any major Sophoclean character with the exception of Oedipus in *OC*. In Shakespeare the poignancy of Charmion's description of Cleopatra as "a lass unparallel'd," though it gains something from the pathos of the moment, depends very much on the bewildering intricacy of the queen as we have seen her with Antony, Octavian, and the others. Horatio's "sweet prince" likewise depends on the whole complex portrayal of Hamlet, but this portrayal has come very largely from within Hamlet himself and has not, in the Sophoclean manner, grown essentially through the relations of Hamlet with others.

Dependence on the interaction of characters for the development of the dramatic action characterizes six of the seven plays of Sophocles and is certainly present, if less vital, in the seventh. Can we speak with confidence of this as a characteristic of

Sophoclean drama? Some critics would insist that we have no right to generalize about Sophoclean, or Aeschylean, characteristics, because we have an insufficient proportion of their dramatic output to justify any comprehensive statements of this sort. No doubt it is a wise precaution to add to such generalization the recognition that we can only properly speak for the extant plays. At least we can say that this technique of building dramatic action and conveying dramatic meaning by the contrastive interplay of characters is a distinctive feature of Sophoclean drama as we know it, and it is permissible to guess that it is one aspect of the dramatic style that Sophocles described as ἠθικώτατον καὶ βέλτιστον.

ix. *Some Problems of Psychology*

In his review of Bowra's *Sophoclean Tragedy* Gilbert Norwood congratulated the author on not having once in the course of the book used the word "psychology." One can understand this aversion. There has been a tendency in recent literature and literary criticism to model efforts and judgments of literary characterization on the procedures of the psychoanalysts. Writers seek to portray and critics to unearth the influences and the background which will "explain" in a more or less scientific way the behavior of characters; and in this aetiological enthusiasm there has been a pronounced tendency to dwell on the springs of evil action more than of good. There is no denying the force of such literary pathology.[42] But we need not restrict our concept of psychology in literature to a chamber of horrors

[42] Some plays of Tennessee Williams (*The Glass Menagerie, A Streetcar Named Desire*) provide a conspicuous example, in modern drama, of the current obsession with pathological problems. As Joseph Wood Krutch points out in the last chapter of his *"Modernism" in Modern Drama* (Ithaca, 1953), Williams in one respect is "among the despairing explorers of pathological states of mind" (p. 126), though it is possible to see in Blanche Dubois some aspects of a traditional and broadly meaningful tragic hero.

or a quasi-scientific approach; in drama, as in other literary types, there can be a presentation of human personality that has little to do with clinical dissection. Disregard for strict consistency in character is a legitimate dramatic liberty, and it may even be a dramatic necessity, for the dramatist has other aims besides the achievement of an accurate and consistent portrayal of personality. He is concerned with an artistic whole, and it may sometimes be that other factors in the whole—an effect achieved through structure or through the heightening of emotion at a crucial moment or through poetic imagery—may be dominant enough to disturb the illusion of realistic personality. In Sophoclean drama, though the constructive hand of the poet is ever present, molding the characters to fit a dramatic theme that transcends them, such disturbance is rare. But there are a few passages in which the question of inconsistency arises. Tycho Wilamowitz's theory of Sophoclean dramatic technique was built on the existence of such passages, and a good deal of uncertainty about the propriety of some of these is generally felt. A brief review of four passages from the point of view of the present study may be of some use. They are the following: *Ajax* 646–692, *The Trachinian Women* 436–469, *Antigone* 904–920, and *Philoctetes* 895–920. Most of what I have to say about the passages in *Philoctetes* and *The Trachinian Women* has been said above, but it will be helpful to bring the four passages together, since they share a common problem: can we ascribe realism and consistency to Sophocles' portrayal of Ajax, Deianeira, Antigone, and Neoptolemus?

In studying character portrayal in *Philoctetes* we noticed evidence of a gradual change in the spirit and allegiance of Neoptolemus. The evidence need not be repeated here in full: Neoptolemus' unforced sympathy with Philoctetes' views about the warriors at Troy, his hesitation after the incident of the merchant, his growing devotion to Philoctetes' nobility of spirit, his disgust with the dishonesty of the stratagem. When, therefore, at line 895 he breaks down, no longer able to go on with his deception of Philoctetes, we are prepared for his open declaration of a new attitude, and there is nothing that does not arise from the character of Neoptolemus as it has long been developing under the influence of Philoctetes.

But is it possible that in seeing evidence of this preparation we are approaching the play from a twentieth-century, psychological point of view and reading into it the indications that we think ought to be there? The answer to the objection is clear. In the first place, the evidence of preparation is so extensive that it has to be accounted for in some way. In Sophocles' compressed dramatic style there are few idle words or moves; and it seems rather perverse to refuse to these indications the explanation that is most obvious and makes the best dramatic sense.[43] When we turn to the passage itself, we find ample confirmation that Neoptolemus' change of heart is not at all sudden or unpremeditated. (The consummation of the change comes when it does because this is the point when the deception will necessitate immediate and irrevocable action; the two men are starting on their way to the ship. Consummation at this point suits both the convenience of the plot and Neoptolemus' character.) Twice in this passage Neoptolemus declares that his treatment of Philoctetes has been troubling him πάλαι (906, 913; the present tense of the verb is, of course, regular Greek to express what has been and still is the case).

It is true, as Wilamowitz points out, that πάλαι need not mean "long ago." But it does indicate something established rather than something arising at the moment. That it does not refer here to the immediate present is further confirmed by still a

[43] Waldock, *Dramatist*, 204–205, sees that just after the merchant scene Neoptolemus suffers something that may be, as Waldock is candid enough to admit, a "twinge of conscience." But Waldock is not willing to follow through to the logical conclusion from his observation: that there is a relation of cause and effect between the one incident and the other.

third use of the word only a little later, where inclusion of past as well as present feeling is beyond doubt: "I am filled with a strange pity for this man, not now for the first time, but even before (οὐ νῦν πρῶτον, ἀλλὰ καὶ πάλαι)" (965–966). There can be no doubt of Sophocles' intentions; we must accept the change as a gradual one. The earlier indications are not imaginary; they are an example of careful psychological accuracy in Sophoclean characterization. Of course the psychological accuracy is not for its own sake. Psychology here subserves plot development, but that does not make it any the less real.

The other three passages are all from what I believe to be relatively early plays, and it has been suggested above that all three instances are alike in representing an abruptness of transition and hence a stiffness in character realization, a division by episodes, unlike the later Sophoclean manner. The changes do not occur before our eyes and explicitly as in *Philoctetes*.

Ajax 646–692 is the famous "speech of deception." The speech presents these problems: Is the change of heart that Ajax seems to express in it genuine, or is it a deliberate falsehood, aimed at securing Ajax an opportunity to vanish unobstructed to end his life? If it is genuine, how can we relate it to Ajax's next speech, at the end of which he commits suicide and in the course of which he gives no indication of ever having changed his resolve? If it is false, how can we reconcile this with the otherwise forthright nature of Ajax? There appears to be a question of consistency whichever way we take the speech.

There is no single answer to these questions. The first thing to notice is the position of the speech in the rhythm of the play. It follows Ajax's scene with Tecmessa, and its gentleness and philosophical tone (Ajax calls it "womanish") are the result of Tecmessa's influence. It gives rise to the following excited and optimistic ode, which is then followed by scenes of gloom—the messenger's report of Ajax's peril, the suicide, the finding of the body—and this strong contrast from scene to scene is a dramatic rhythm especially dear to Sophocles. These are the external explanations of the speech and do not justify it in terms of Ajax's character.[44]

It seems to me that Reinhardt's answer to the psychological problem is clearly right: the submissiveness of the earlier part of the speech is a recognition by Ajax that change and submission are the way of the world; but it is impossible for him to reconcile himself to the way of the world; hence, though in a theoretical way Ajax can recognize the necessity of yielding (and thus can recognize the viewpoint of Odysseus and Tecmessa), so far as his personal life is concerned there can be no change.[45] We can see in the very manner in which Ajax speaks of his submission that there is no possibility of a personal change; when he says that he will "reverence" the Atridae (666), he is obviously using hyperbolic language, and he does so because he speaks with bitterness. There is bitterness too in his reference to friendship, with the cynical conclusion that he draws—that friendship is a hollow thing (679–683). The speech is evasive, but even in the earlier part, where the only real suggestion of a change of intention occurs, the language is deliberately ambiguous. Ajax never once says outright that he will live, only that he will clear himself of the divine anger and hide his sword, digging in the earth where no one will see (656–659). At the end the meaning is so thinly veiled that except to Ajax's followers, who are ready to grasp at any straw, there can be no deception.[46] When he bids his men to ask Teucer to "take care of me and have good will toward you, for I am going whither I must" (689–690), he is scarcely practicing deception at all.

[44] Waldock (*ibid.*, 78–79) recognizes these structural reasons and insists on stopping short with them.

[45] *Sophokles*, 32–34.

[46] Bowra, who takes the whole speech to mean a change of intention (*Sophoclean Tragedy*, 39–44), is just insisting on being deceived.

He avoids direct mention of what he is going to do, presumably through a desire—very natural in the reticent Ajax (compare 319–322)—to avoid emotional display. Rather than inconsistency with the character of Ajax elsewhere in the play, there is a deepening of it. We understand more fully the extent of his bitterness and the firmness of his conviction that his life must end. In the course of the speech there is an interesting and natural progression of attitude, from the initial mood of quietness—though tinged with bitterness—to the reflection on mutability, brought on him by the thought of Hector's sword, to the final realization that he cannot after all resign himself to the flow of this "universal rhythm." [47]

Deianeira's speech to Lichas (*Trach.* 436–469) has been compared to Ajax's speech.[48] I see no need to add anything to what was said above concerning the psychological appropriateness of the speech: the inconsistency between it and Deianeira's next speech is perfectly in keeping with the irresoluteness and bewilderment that characterize Deianeira throughout. As Jebb well expresses it, in this speech Deianeira "overrates, in all sincerity, her own power of suffering." [49] To suppose that there is any intentional deception of Lichas or that the speech is inconsistent with Deianeira's character is as wrong as it is unnecessary. The similarity to the speech of Ajax is in the matter of structure; in both cases the shift of mood comes abruptly and is unlike the manner of later plays.

---

[47] Kitto, *Greek Tragedy*, 143. I have not, in discussing the passage, attempted to deal in any systematic way with the numerous interpretations of it that have been offered. Among the most substantial considerations of the problem are Jebb's, in the Introduction to his edition of *Ajax*, Schadewaldt's, in "Aias und Antigone," *Neue Wege zur Antike*, 8 (1929), 61–117, especially 70–79, the discussions in the books of Weinstock, Reinhardt, and Bowra, and I. M. Linforth's study "Three Scenes in Sophocles' *Ajax*," *Univ. of Calif. Publ. in Class. Phil.*, 15 (1954), 1–28, especially 10–20. Linforth gives some additional bibliography.

[48] Reinhardt, *Sophokles*, 32–34.   [49] Edition of *Trach.*, p. xxxv

The most celebrated problem of inconsistency in Sophocles is in Antigone's final speech, in lines 904–920. Many scholars, past and present, have rejected the lines as spurious. Only a brief discussion of the arguments need be undertaken here.[50] There are two arguments against the authenticity of the lines: the problem of fitting their content into a consistent picture of Antigone and the linguistic infelicities of lines 909–910. The stylistic argument seems to me the more telling, and it appears very likely that these two lines are not exactly what Sophocles wrote, for the obscurity of expression that characterizes them is most un-Sophoclean.[51] That the thought is borrowed from Herodotus is no argument against the passage; there are in Sophocles' plays several other such borrowings, questioned by no one.[52] Of the genuineness and the propriety of the passage in general I have not the slightest doubt. It is true that it comes as a shock and that it would be strange in a late Sophoclean play, but these are hardly relevant arguments. The speeches of Ajax and Deianeira are similar enough to quiet objection on these grounds.

The objection to the thought of the passage arises from the discrepancy between this narrow and rather wretched justification of Antigone's conduct and the magnificent confidence in the unwritten laws that she expressed in her debate with Creon. Why should Antigone turn to such a frigid argument here? Is this consistent with her previous way of thinking?

[50] Among the most noteworthy studies of the passage are Jebb's Appendix on it in his edition of *Antig.*, Schadewaldt's study mentioned above in Note 47, especially pp. 82–99, W. R. Agard's *"Antigone 904–20," CP*, 32 (1937), 263–265, and R. E. Wycherley's "Sophocles *Antigone* 904–20," *CP*, 42 (1947), 51–52.

[51] It is a curious, and perhaps significant, fact that Aristotle's citation of this passage in the *Rhetoric* (1417a) makes no direct quotation of lines 909–910, though it does quote lines 911–912.

[52] P. Masqueray has a list of these borrowings, p. 75 of Vol. I of his Budé text.

The repugnance felt toward this argument of Antigone's is largely due to a too narrow view of what Antigone is, a belief that the religious idealism of her debate with Creon is the whole Antigone. The argument of the passage under consideration springs from a frame of mind very different from that of the scene with Creon. There she was sublimely confident; here she has suffered a momentary loss of certainty about the wisdom of what she has done. It is not that she regrets it, nor that she believes that it was not demanded of her; but she is shaken, because she seems unable to make others see the matter from the same point of view as she. This is not conjecture: Sophocles shows us Antigone's developing state of mind in the preceding kommos. There for the first time she is fully struck by the magnitude of what she is giving up; she laments her untimely fate, before marriage (810–816), and the terrible nature of the living burial to which she is doomed (847–852). Most significant of all, she believes that she is utterly deserted, that no one sympathizes with her or admires her devotion. Three times in the kommos she laments that she is dying "friendless and unwept" (φίλων ἄκλαυτος, 847; ἄκλαυτος, ἄφιλος, 876; πότμον ἀδάκρυτον οὐδεὶς φίλων στενάζει, 882). She has every right to feel so, for she knows nothing of Haemon's loyalty to her; and though with Creon she stoutly maintained that the Thebans were on her side (509), the attitude of the chorus in the kommos, with their reservations and their criticisms of Antigone's "self-willed spirit" (875), very naturally inspires her with misgivings.

Such is Antigone's state of mind at the point when her speech begins: she is very much alone and desperately in need of the support and justification that the chorus have failed to give her. The opening line of the passage in question shows the intent of what follows: "Yet, to men of wisdom, the honor I paid you was well paid" (904). She is going to show the wisdom and the logic of what she has done. It is neither surprising nor inappropriate that her logic is poor. She acted in the first place from instinctive feeling rather than reasoned principles. To find logical justification for intuitions is by no means easy, and it is made much more difficult for Antigone when her first and most natural articulation of her intuition has, apparently, failed to convince. The argument here is not intended by the playwright to be convincing. Its value lies in its pathos.

Admittedly, the character of Antigone would be easier without this passage. I cannot agree with Kitto that it is "the finest borrowing in literature." [53] It is altogether too obscure in manner, too little explained in terms of clear development of mood, to be dramatically first rate. But it has a certain useful purpose in the action and is altogether appropriate to Antigone's nature; we should not reject it. Antigone's character would be more comfortable also without the second incident with Ismene. But to disregard the obvious implications of the one passage and to declare the other spurious, as Jebb and a good many others have done, is not a satisfactory critical approach. We must recognize that in the earlier of his extant plays Sophocles allows such quick and bewildering changes of attitude as we find in this speech and that of Ajax (and to a less arresting degree in that of Deianeira), not because he knew or cared nothing about psychological accuracy and consistency, but because he aimed at contrastive effects and had not yet turned to the smoothness and explicitness that mark changes of mood and thought in his later plays.

Of the four passages it may be said that none gives real evidence of a want of psychological understanding on the part of the dramatist in his portrayal of character. Two of the four— the passages in *The Trachinian Women* and *Philoctetes*—raise no problem of psychology at all, for they fit without discord into the portrayal of Deianeira and Neoptolemus elsewhere in the plays. The other two are disconcerting and are to be ascribed

[53] *Greek Tragedy*, 127.

more to Sophocles' desire for certain effects of structure and of pathos than to an effort in subtle psychological study. But they are not inconsistent with the portrayal of Ajax and Antigone.

There is a related problem which may be raised here, though it is not of quite the same sort as the others, since no specific passage is in question. I refer to the character of Electra and the closely related problem of Sophocles' attitude toward the murder of Clytemnestra. In an earlier paper [54] I accepted the view of J. T. Sheppard, according to which there are hints, in the course of the play, of doubts about the wisdom and rectitude of Orestes' act of matricide. I still believe that there are aspects of the play and ominous suggestions that fit very ill with the notion of glorious accomplishment; but there are not enough to permit us to interpret the play on the assumption that Sophocles' approach was basically the same as that of Aeschylus and Euripides. My present view has been indicated in part already. In the discussion above (pp. 66–67) of Sophocles' use of restriction it was suggested that we cannot tell what Sophocles believed about the moral consequences of Clytemnestra's murder, because this is not a part of his play; the guilt, if it is guilt, is Orestes', the play Electra's. Sophocles does not mean to give a solution to the moral problem insofar as it pertains to Orestes. What we should expect to find in the play is a clear indication of the effect of the moral question on Electra.

On the traditional view of the play no problem of consistency arises, for Electra's career is taken to be simply a change from desperate and heroic resistance to the tyrants, as shown in the scenes with Chrysothemis and Clytemnestra, to ecstatic joy at reunion with her brother and at the consummation of the revenge. No other Sophoclean leading figure is so unquestioningly self-assured as this, and such an unshaded black-and-white

[54] "Two Structural Features of Sophocles' *Electra*," *TAPA*, 73 (1942), 86–95.

sketch would be surprising.[55] Moreover, in the earlier scenes of
Electra we do not find this wholehearted, undoubting woman;
instead we find, as we should expect to find in a major
Sophoclean character, a soul tormented by the fullness of its
knowledge of what the situation means. Electra, as we have seen,
has a clear and poignantly tragic awareness that her burning desire for her mother's death leaves much to be desired in the way
of moral splendor, even though she is convinced that the demands of nobility (which to her means loyalty to her father)
compel her to hold fast to her resolve to find revenge for her
father's murder. She is in the same kind of hopeless position as
Ajax, only she is more sharply aware of the issues than he.
The emphasis in her scene with Clytemnestra on the theme of
"shame" gives clear evidence of this awareness; it is as if Electra
realizes that she has in herself something of the spirit of
Clytemnestra.

In view of this moral dilemma, either we should expect some
clear recognition later in the play that the revenge, necessary
though it was, had in it some bitterness or raised some doubts
or else we should expect some indication that the earlier dilemma
has been resolved. This is where the problem of consistency
arises. For there is no clear sign at the end that Electra has any
feelings that adequately either express or resolve her earlier
doubts and anguish. There are hints: when she shouts, at the
very moment of her mother's death, "Strike her a second blow,
if you can," and when she cries in a frenzy of hatred that
Aegisthus should be dispatched out of hand and his body cast
out for ignominious burial, she is certainly giving evidence
of something other than pure joy and exaltation of spirit at the

[55] The disconcertment of the critics is revealed by the prevalence of
the improbable view, leaving much of the play an enigma, that Sophocles
returns to the simple, Homeric spirit of the story. The most conspicuous
name connected with this view is Jebb's.

consummation of a holy deed. Neither any other major Sophoclean figure nor the Electra of the earlier part of this play would normally be capable of a fury so primitive and unreflecting. There is in these passages a strong element of unnaturalness, of loss, for the moment, of wisdom and perspective, that is grimly tragic and is an indirect continuation of the complex attitude of Electra as she is portrayed earlier in the play. But there is no clarification. Most of the end of the play, from the recognition on, is caught up in such a rush of excitement and so relentless a flood of action that there is little time for reflection.

Sophocles has—whether deliberately or not—sacrificed, at the end, subtlety and completeness of character development to the working out of an exciting dramatic tour de force. The play is simply swept along by the intensity of the immediate action at its end. This does not mean that the play is inferior; the stage effect of this ending is powerful. But it does mean that Sophocles has left his heroine partially stranded, as it were, with elements of her nature which are of the deepest tragic interest and significance unfulfilled, or fulfilled only in hints. Neither play nor tragic heroine is incomprehensible: we have a clear and intensely moving picture of Electra's constancy in the course of nobility, no matter what it costs her in happiness and well-being; we have also a bold and unsparing representation of the revenge, as it impinges on Electra, in its necessity and primitive fitness and in its disquieting savagery. What is lacking is an explicit portrayal of Electra's moral and emotional state at the end. Perhaps the nature of the plot made this incompleteness inevitable. We noticed in the preceding chapter that in this play there is a pronounced separation between the event (the revenge) and the theme (the portrayal of Electra in relation to the revenge). At the end, where the action of the event necessarily predominates, there is no opportunity for concentration on the inner life of the central figure, even though

Sophocles does contrive, as we have seen, to keep her at the center of the action.[56]

x. *The Character of the Tragic Hero*

Can we properly speak of the Sophoclean tragic hero? To do so implies that there is a uniformity in the presentation of Ajax, Deianeira, Antigone, Oedipus (in both plays), Electra, and Philoctetes that bespeaks a single attitude on the part of the playwright concerning the nature of his principal characters and their vicissitudes. Within limits, I think that we may usefully do so. There undoubtedly are important differences among the various leading persons of the plays: between, for example, the violence that brings on Ajax the punishment of deity that he is undergoing at the beginning of the play and the admirable loyalty that involves Antigone in suffering, or the touching devotion that destroys Deianeira. But for all these large differences, there are two ways, both basic, in which all Sophoclean tragic heroes exemplify the same kind of life: all of them compel our admiration by their magnanimity, and all of them are devoted to a concept of living and dying nobly. The concept varies, but the attitude and its revelation of char-

---

[56] The problem of Electra's outlook is often set aside with the feeble argument that in this play the matricide is toned down and disregarded as much as possible. But the long and bitter scene between Electra and her mother and the accomplishment of Clytemnestra's death as nearly on stage as the conventions of Greek tragedy would stand are strange ways of disregarding a theme. Electra's long speech to Chrysothemis, in which she represents the revenge as a source of glory (947–989), has been cited as a rebuttal of Electra's earlier emphasis on "shame." But it is nothing of the sort, for in this speech Electra refers only to killing Aegisthus. It is, I should now agree, an overinterpretation to suppose that Electra is here deliberately repressing any mention of murdering Clytemnestra as too terrible to think about (as I suggested in my above-mentioned paper [Note 54] and drew upon myself the just censure of Waldock, *Dramatist*, 185); but to suppose that the speech indicates, on the contrary, a belief that matricide is conducive to glory is altogether unwarranted.

acter are constant, as the evidence already adduced in this chapter shows.

The rest of this section will be an attempt to construct a synthesis out of these similarities. A critical synthesis, like a chemical synthesis, is an artificial production, lacking the authority that more modest and specific criticism commands. It is therefore well to begin such a venture in full recognition of its limitations. First, whatever we may conclude about the tragic hero in Sophocles' plays, it is exceedingly unlikely that Sophocles spent sixty years writing plays in an endeavor to point the moral or to propound the view of life and of human character that our generalization from the seven extant plays describes. The synthesis is ours, not Sophocles'. Secondly, however strongly we may believe that our generalization describes a central fact of Sophoclean thought, it must be admitted that no one generalization and no one fact is of supreme importance for Sophocles' plays; the differences and the individuality of character and dramatic spirit are more important than any similarity. Finally, it is a fortunate fact that Sophocles' plays, like all great works of art, must be interpreted a little differently by every reader and very differently by every generation of readers. The following pages will not lay down rules for the interpretation of Sophocles; their sole reason for existence is to state certain conclusions that follow from what has been said in the foregoing pages about a challenging and traditional problem of Sophoclean drama—the nature of its tragic heroes.

There is, then (returning to our argument), some basic uniformity in Sophocles' concept of noble character in the seven plays which we have. To determine the consequence of this outlook is, in brief, the problem of finding Sophocles' answer to the enigma of human suffering. All Sophoclean tragic heroes suffer. Why do they suffer? Since in *Electra, Philoctetes,* and *Oedipus at Colonus* the suffering does not end in death or disaster, we may for the time being put these plays aside and concentrate on the other four, where the protagonist's suffering is most unrelieved.

Are Ajax, Deianeira, Antigone, and Oedipus responsible for their unhappy fates, or are they the victims of circumstances, or of gods, or of men? Is theirs, in Samuel Butcher's stately phrase, the tragedy of "antagonism between a pure will and a disjointed world?" [57] I do not suppose that the question is altogether answerable. Whether we attach the responsibility to the tragic hero or to other forces is likely to depend in part on whether we are carried away by the exciting nobility of the chief figures or have more regard for the paths of moderation. Of recent years the hero-worshipers have had the ascendancy. A number of recent critics, of whom the most eloquent and thoroughgoing is Whitman, aware of qualities of excellence in the tragic heroes which are stressed by the dramatist and clearly have an abiding value—qualities which John A. Moore, followed by Opstelten (in part), Whitman, and others, summed up as *aretê*—aware of such factors in Sophoclean tragedy, these critics have rejected the notion of the tragic hero's responsibility altogether and find the basis of Sophoclean tragedy in the conflict between heroic *aretê* and the world of gods or men; the suffering springs not from faults of the hero but from the incompatibility of his excellence with the world about him; the fault lies in other men, or in the gods, or in the "irrational evil" of circumstances.[58]

Our survey of Sophoclean character relations strongly suggests that it would be unwise to accept an interpretation of character in Sophocles that oversimplifies in either direction, attributing to the leading person unmixed perfection or sup-

[57] *Aristotle's Theory of Poetry and Fine Art* [4] (New York, 1951), 325.
[58] See John A. Moore, *Sophocles and Aretê* (Cambridge, Mass., 1938), Opstelten, *Pessimism*, and Whitman, *Sophocles*.

posing that his suffering is a simple matter of punishment for guilt. Sophoclean characters are not presented with such simplicity. We must neither undervalue the importance of the nobility of Sophocles' protagonists nor dismiss the wisdom of Odysseus, the moderation of Creon, and the piety expressed in some of the choral odes as mere "framework." [59] This roundedness of vision that characterizes Sophocles' presentation of character is irksome to critics who want to find a sweeping, fully committed point of view in the playwright's judgment of human character. A firm and decided point of view is there, I think, but to understand it requires some patience. I suppose that it is the complexity of Sophocles' outlook and his refusal to take an extreme stand that constitute his "classicism." A reviewer of Whitman's book hailed the deliverance from classicism that its interpretation of Sophocles has brought us. [60] But do we really want deliverance from this attitude? And if we should want this deliverance, can we find it in Sophocles? Let us look a little further into Sophocles' presentation of the tragic hero.

The analyses made earlier in this chapter show that we cannot escape the conclusion that Sophocles means us to see that, not malevolent deity or fate, but the characters themselves are to some degree responsible for what happens to them. The case of *Oedipus Tyrannus* is quite clear. It would have been possible for Sophocles to present the story of Oedipus in such a way as to show us that the malignance of fate is alone responsible for the tragedy and that Oedipus is in all ways blameless in conduct. Instead, we have at least one long scene in the play that makes no sense whatsoever unless as a demonstration of the blinding power of Oedipus' impetuousness and self-reliance. I mean, of course, the scene with Creon. If Sophocles

[59] Whitman, *Sophocles*, tends to do the latter; cf. pp. 16–17.
[60] G. F. Else, *CP*, 48 (1953), 56–58.

means Oedipus in this play to be "a type of human ability condemned to destruction by an external insufficiency in life itself," [61] he has willfully marred the picture by this scene and by a great many other aspects of his play: the emphasis on Oedipus' anger and violence in the incident at the crossroads, his towering rage in the scene with Teiresias, and his superb self-confidence in the prologue in contrast with the priest's piety. Surely, if we are trying to understand Sophocles' play, we must read these parts of it as well as those in which Oedipus' magnificence alone is displayed. It is of course equally wrong to concentrate entirely on Oedipus' faults. We are not concerned with a question of crime and punishment but of the responsibility of Oedipus' character for his fate.[62]

In the other leading persons, too, Sophocles shows us with detailed clarity, through their relations with other persons of the plays, what aspects of their character cause the results that follow: Ajax's violence, Deianeira's unwise trust in a desperate remedy, Antigone's uncompromising stubbornness. Only with Ajax is there any question of a serious moral blemish; and even his extreme, violent pride is not mean or ignoble.[63] Sophocles is not intent on emphasizing moral shortcomings in his main characters, but he does show that some element of character in each case precipitates the catastrophe.

Are we to call this responsible element of character *hamartia?*

[61] Whitman, *Sophocles,* 122–123. Whitman virtually disregards the Creon scene (pp. 131–132).

[62] The fact of the oracle does not remove responsibility from Oedipus. (Cf. above, Chapter II, sec. v.) Bernard Knox, in his chapter on Oedipus in *Tragic Themes in Western Literature* (New Haven, 1955), edited by Cleanth Brooks, expresses the case succinctly: Oedipus' acts were "not predestined, merely predicted. An essential distinction."

[63] Cf. Linforth's study, referred to above (Note 47), which correctly observes the fact of Ajax's initial crime and its very slight place in the play. But Linforth unduly minimizes the place of Ajax's violence of spirit in the action of the play.

There is no harm in doing so, provided we do not insist that this Sophoclean *hamartia*—we are not concerned with the meaning of *hamartia* in Aristotle—necessarily suggests something reprehensible. It is in each case an imperfection of some sort, something that brings the tragic hero to life as a human being, with the standard human equipment of emotions and frailties, though possessed of a more than standard devotion to an ideal of conduct. There is in every Sophoclean tragic hero much that is heroic in the moral sense, but to equate the tragic hero with hero in the absolute is to proceed with less patience and less interest in the whole picture of a great human being than Sophocles employed.

In *Ajax* there is no question but that the hero is culpable. The fact is not stressed in the play, but it is obvious and unconcealed. When a warrior sets out to murder his fellow chieftains as a protest against what he believes to be an insult to his honor, he is displaying something else besides devotion to *aretê;* in similar circumstances Homer's Achilles, the prototype of the fiercely proud warrior, returns his sword to its sheath. In *OT* it is perverse to deny that there is a fault in the character of Oedipus, an excess of impetuousness and self-reliance. Deianeira herself recognizes the folly of her act. Even in Antigone's conduct there is an element of unwisdom, and not only from the point of view of self-protection: nothing could have been better calculated to fan the flame of Creon's wrongheaded determination to leave Polyneices' body unburied than Antigone's hostile and contemptuous disobedience.

If we are going to accept all the evidence of the plays in our interpretation, we have to find a meaningful place for both *aretê* and the kind of *hamartia* we have just been noticing. It is true that Sophoclean criticism has sometimes overstressed the tragic hero's faults and, failing to recognize the essential value of his nobility, has sometimes suggested that Sophocles wished chiefly to show that man should be modest or the gods will punish him.[64] But if in avoiding this error of criticism we proceed to the opposite extreme, disregarding as "framework" whatever points in another direction than the impeccability of the tragic hero, we shall not improve matters. The necessary compromise is not only possible but is demanded by the evidence of the plays.

When we say, as was said just above, that the violence of Ajax, the rashness of Oedipus, the folly of Deianeira, the stubbornness of Antigone, are responsible, at least in part, for the catastrophes, this is equivalent to saying that they would have fared better had they been different persons: they could not be the great figures they are without these characteristics. This is not only true but a vitally important part of great character as Sophocles presents it. For there is a further observation to be made concerning the tragic hero's responsibility; the observation has been made before (by Bowra for one), but it is worth repeating. The faults of the tragic heroes are in the closest possible connection with their strength and nobility. That Oedipus should be impetuous in word and act and strong in passion is simply a part of the whole Oedipus and is inseparable from the dauntlessness, the endurance, and the courageous insistence on truth that make him great; Deianeira's use of the poisoned robe is simply one aspect of the single-minded love she feels for Heracles; Antigone's self-affirmation and stubbornness are a part of the strength of character that makes her act in accordance with high-spirited loyalty to family in spite of opposition and in spite—at one point—of her own misgivings; Ajax's pride and violence are a part of his firm and admirable devotion to soldierly honor. Without their kind of *hamartia* they would not have their kind of heroism. Creon in *OT* has *sophrosyne* and is without *hamartia*, but he signally lacks the spiritual strength that bestows both greatness and fault on

[64] Among modern critics who have been deeply influenced by this view are Bowra and Webster.

Oedipus. It is true that "it is not necessary to be an Antigone in order not to be an Ismene," [65] and no doubt there can be a "flawless hero," but this is not the kind of tragic hero that interests Sophocles.[66] The intricate interdependence of fault and greatness is simply the culmination of the complex view of life that informs and necessitates Sophocles' whole dramatic way of contrasting character against character and idea against idea.

The playwright's view of life is far from lighthearted. He finds a large measure of cruelty in the circumstances of human life. For tragic fault is not guilt, and tragic suffering is not punishment. The catastrophic misfortunes that overwhelm the heroes (here we may include the last three plays, where, though the end is not disaster, the suffering of the tragic hero is prominent and is rooted, just as in the four plays we have been discussing, in character) are not morally deserved in terms of the leading person's character, even though it is character that precipitates suffering. This cruelty is sometimes ascribed to the gods by the sufferers, in the extremity of their anguish; but I do not think that the reader of Sophocles should succumb to the same temptation. Apart from the divinely inflicted madness of Ajax, which can scarcely be called unjust, there is no evidence in Sophocles of the willful infliction of suffering by deity on the tragic heroes.[67] It is in the nature of deity, as Sophocles portrays deity, to permit suffering; but it does not follow that deity is cruel or unjust—the attitude that demands that deity

[65] As James Hutton observed, in reviewing Bignone's *Poeti Apollonei*, *AJP*, 60 (1939), 243–245. Hutton's review is a good criticism of the hero-worshiping approach to Sophocles.

[66] It is interesting to remember that Sophocles himself became a "hero" in the usual Greek sense of a great man worshiped after his death. (Cf. *Vita Sophoclis*, 17.) Yet in his life he was—to judge from biographical information, not from his plays—a great deal closer to Odysseus of *Ajax* than to Oedipus.

[67] This is a controversial subject; what I have to say on it will be found in Chapter VI.

attend to the worldly success of the good is not the highest kind of religious thought.

If this were all, we should have to regard Sophocles' outlook on life as a pessimistic one. But the failure that springs from the tragic hero's fault, the underside of his greatness, is not the final word in Sophocles' view of the nature and meaning of human life. In all the plays, what carries the tragic hero on and makes him oblivious to the advice and common sense of his friends, firm against the threats of his enemies, is his devotion to an ideal; and in this devotion the tragic heroes of Sophocles rise without exception to the stature of moral heroes. The ideal varies from play to play, for it arises from the action, created out of the clash of heroic character and testing situation. For Ajax it is unswerving loyalty to martial honor, for Deianeira it is the purity of her devotion to Heracles; Antigone finds it in loyalty to family and intuitive religious conviction, Electra in devotion to her father; Philoctetes' idealism appears in his refusal to compromise with dishonesty in spite of his suffering and in his recognition of and response to the nobility that he finds in the character of Neoptolemus.

It was pointed out several times in the course of our examination of the character relationships in the plays that the habitual way of expressing this kind of devotion to an ideal is in terms of "nobility," the character of the εὐγενής. Ajax, Deianeira, Antigone, Electra, and Philoctetes all express their conviction that their determined course of action is right by declaring that it is what is demanded of one who is εὐγενής. This is the attitude that Moore, and after him Opstelten and Whitman, sum up as ἀρετή. It seems useful to keep to the word εὐγενής in describing this attitude, because this is the way Sophocles usually expresses it and because this word describes more exactly than any other the quality of character under discussion.

Originally, ὁ εὐγενής is the "gentleman," the man wellborn; it is a matter of inherited rank and need have no more personal

178   *A Study of Sophoclean Drama*

significance than "nobleman" need have in English usage. But as Sophocles' tragic heroes use the word, it means not only "of noble birth" but also and always "of noble nature." In *Antigone* the heroine can declare that Ismene will show, by her attitude toward the burial of Polyneices:

εἴτ᾽ εὐγενὴς πέφυκας εἴτ᾽ ἐσθλῶν κακή.[30]

To be εὐγενής, then, is not only a matter of birth, since Ismene may be base in spite of her parentage, but of one's own nature (πέφυκας).[68] In *Philoctetes*, where there is naturally a good deal said about Neoptolemus' noble inheritance from Achilles, the two sources of his nobility are distinguished at one point by Philoctetes, who says to him: "You are, my son, both noble of nature (εὐγενὴς ἡ φύσις) and descended from those of noble nature" (κἀξ εὐγενῶν, 874); not merely Neoptolemus' heritage, but his own nature is noble.[69] Sometimes, though not in a context that concerns us here, Sophocles uses the word in its original sense; thus in *Philoctetes* Helenus is referred to as a "prophet εὐγενής, son of Priam" (604–605), where εὐγενής presumably means simply "nobly born." But when the word is applied to the heroic spirit, its meaning is always the personal and moral one. It is fitting that Sophocles, with his pervasive interest in character, should use as a key word to express the essence of

[68] Sophocles never uses the word in such a way that it clearly means "noble" rather than "well born," and perhaps the concept of nobility is never fully separated by Sophocles from that of noble birth. But both Sophocles and Euripides (in contrast to Aeschylus, who uses the word seldom) sometimes clearly place far more emphasis on the suggestion of nobility than of good birth. For examples of Euripides' use, cf. *Troades* 1035 and *Phoen.* 442. Sophocles never uses the corresponding abstract εὐγένεια. On the use of the verb φύειν by Sophocles, cf. Albin Lesky's "Zwei Sophokles-Interpretationen," *Hermes*, 80 (1952), 91–105.

[69] The plays of Sophocles contain a good deal of evidence of the playwright's consciousness of the νόμος—φύσις controversy, though it is never expressed argumentatively or didactically. Especially in *Antig.* and *Philoc.* there are signs of an enlightened and refined concept of φύσις and its primary importance in human affairs.

heroism a word that suggests a quality lying deep in the nature of a hero's character.

The name of Oedipus alone was missing from the list, above, of heroes who express their devotion to an ideal by declaring it to be the duty of the εὐγενής. It is perhaps chance that this is the case; [70] if so, it is an interesting accident, since Oedipus' nobility is broader and less definable than that of any of the others. He might be said to be his own ideal, inasmuch as his nobility consists of his undeterrable and fearless insistence on knowing himself, even to the last horrifying detail. It is through the character of Oedipus that Sophocles shows most clearly his belief in the value of heroic nobility. In *OT* Oedipus has a presentiment that some strange fate is in store for him, though in his suffering he can only think of an evil fate.[71] In *OC* and *Philoctetes* alike the gods recognize and accept the worth of the noble man: Philoctetes is called, by Heracles the emissary of Zeus, to fulfill at Troy the nobility that the play has revealed in him; Oedipus is called by a divine voice and miraculously disappears from the sight of Theseus to enter the status of a ἥρως.

Even in the other plays we can hardly fail to recognize in the person of the hero, regardless of explicit vindication in life or after it, the greatness of the εὐγενὴς ἀνήρ. Sophocles' way of contrasting the heroic with the unheroic—Oedipus with Creon, Antigone with Creon and Ismene, Ajax with Odysseus, and the rest—gives us a clear answer to the question of the value of heroism. There is expressed in the greatness of their devotion to nobility the dramatist's statement that in this heroism there is an enduring value that stands firm in spite of suffering and death. Sophocles makes an implicit amendment, in each of his plays, to Oedipus' great speech in the last play:

[70] It may be that Sophocles deliberately avoids the word in *OT* because of the circumstances of Oedipus' parentage. (See Note 68 above.)
[71] *OT* 1455–1457.

Well-loved son of Aegeus, only to the gods do age and death not come.

The nobility of Oedipus and his fellows in heroism is likewise exempt from the decay wrought by "all-mastering time."

CHAPTER IV

The Role of the Chorus [1]

WHAT part does the chorus play in Sophoclean drama? Most conspicuously, it sings lyrical songs. Many of the songs are of remarkable poetic grace, and some express deeply felt religious and moral ideas with great power and beauty. The lyrics of tragedy are, along with Pindar, our main possession of Greek choral poetry.

Some of these songs can be read satisfactorily when detached from their context. The famous ode on man which is the first stasimon of *Antigone*, the second stasimon of *Oedipus Tyrannus* with its prayer that the singers may live in piety under the law of heaven, the ode in praise of Colonus and Attica in *Oedipus at Colonus*, and the song in *Antigone* on Danae, Lycurgus, and Cleopatra are self-sufficient lyric poems, complete and enjoyable in themselves. If they had been transmitted to us alone, we could barely determine that they belonged in plays, and we could not possibly say from what kind of dramatic context they had been lifted.[2] Other odes, while more extensively linked

---

[1] This chapter is based on my study "The Dramatic Role of the Chorus in Sophocles," *Phoenix*, 8 (1954), 1-22, and repeats much of the material of that article.

[2] In the fourth stasimon of *Antigone* (the Danae ode), the ode is addressed to Antigone, who is called simply παῖ (949, 987); only this and the καί of the first line make verbal connection with the context. In the

to the context, are still independent enough in content to be thoroughly intelligible alone: in *Ajax* the ode addressed to Salamis (596–645) and that on the sorrows of war (1185–1222), Stasimon Two of *Antigone* on the troubles of the house of Labdacus, and the ode on old age in *OC* (1211–1248). Even in odes that are so closely woven into their context that they form a commentary on the immediate action, Sophocles has a way of starting with a general idea or a thought removed from the immediate matter and only later circling back to the situation of the play.[3] This gives even to songs such as Stasimon One of *The Trachinian Women*, which is a description of how Heracles wrestled with Achelous for possession of Deianeira, Stasimon Four of *OT* on the fall of Oedipus, and the single stasimon of *Philoctetes* (676–729) on the suffering of Philoctetes some degree of remoteness and detachment. In kommoi, in most of the parodoi, and in only a few stasima (such as the first and third of *Electra*), the lyrics are instantly and closely connected with the action in subject matter.

The detachment that marks so many of Sophocles' choral songs raises problems when we think about the meaning of the odes in relation to the plays. If all the lyrics were as immediately and obviously concerned with the action as, for example, Stasimon Three of *The Trachinian Women* (821–850), in which the chorus reveal their recognition of what the oracle given to Heracles really meant and describe what Heracles has suffered and Deianeira done, we should have no serious trouble in assigning the lyrics their place in the action. Such an ode obviously has the simple function of providing a lyrical commentary on the events of the play. By the poetic intensity and grace of its diction and rhythm it adds a further dimension of

---

first stasimon of *Antig.* there is no verbal link at all. In *OT* Stasimon Two there are no hints of the context until the final strophe. In the "Colonus" ode of *OC* there is only the address, ξένε, in the first line.

[3] Cf. Webster, *Introduction*, 115.

meaning and dramatic force to those events. But immediacy and simplicity of reference are found in less than half the odes. There are also general reflections on the nature of man, on piety, on old age, on the beauties of Attica, on the power of love. What are we to make of these?

One way to dispose of them is to treat them simply as independent lyrics expressing Sophocles' thoughts about the various matters on which they touch. If they seem totally irrelevant, then never mind the context; their own beauty and profundity are enough to justify their presence, and convention demanded that the action of the play be broken by lyrical passages. This somewhat cavalier procedure is followed by some critics and probably many readers; we often see choral passages quoted, without context or reference to context, as examples of what Sophocles thought.[4] To quote isolated passages, whether lyric or iambic, as interesting or valuable statements or simply as attractive pieces of poetry is a time-honored and pleasurable practice. But this excerpting has nothing to do with the criticism of Sophocles' plays.

Most choral reflections—as distinguished from choral judgments, which are sometimes clearly wrong—are morally acceptable, though they may express an attitude more naïvely pious than the general tenor of the plays leads us to think Sophocles' attitude would have been. It is natural that choral reflections should be acceptable, for choral character is acceptable too. But it is a dangerous, though easy, step to assume therefore that these reflections are intended to represent Sophocles' reflections on the action in which they occur and to treat them as clues provided by the poet for the understanding of his play. This is the critical attitude underlying A. W. Schlegel's de-

---

[4] A conspicuous example of the equating of choral and Sophoclean thought may be found in Evelyn Abbott's otherwise generally admirable essay, "The Theology and Ethics of Sophocles," *Hellenica* (London, 1880), 33–66.

scription of the chorus as "a personified reflection on the action.
. . . The incorporation into the representation itself of the
sentiments of the poet. . . . In a word, the ideal spectator," [5]
and it is still the prevalent attitude among critics of Sophocles.
The ode on piety in *OT* condemns skepticism; Oedipus has
just expressed a degree of skepticism; therefore this ode is
Sophocles' condemnation of Oedipus' behavior. So the ode is
often interpreted. But is this safe? The ode on man in *Antigone*
condemns lawlessness; Antigone has just broken a law; therefore this ode condemns Antigone, and therefore, if we follow
the same logic as before, Sophocles is condemning Antigone.
But hardly anyone thinks that Sophocles meant to condemn
Antigone, and so in this case the opposite assumption is made:
the chorus is in this beautiful ode, with its tone of philosophical
seriousness, simply making a wrong judgment. [6] More will be
said below concerning the function and meaning of this ode.
For the time being, we need only notice that to accept choral
reflections as the poet's reflections with respect to the drama is
not a universally safe procedure. If we cannot accept the ode
on man as "the sentiments of the poet" concerning the act of
burial, we may well hesitate to accept the ode on piety as
Sophocles' judgment on Oedipus' skepticism.

There is another way of approach to the choral odes, an approach by which they are neither studied in a vacuum nor assumed to be Sophocles' sentiments. It is possible to assume that

[5] *Lectures on Dramatic Art and Literature,* Eng. trans. by John Black
rev. by A. J. W. Morrison (London, 1904), 69–70.

[6] There are a number of wrong judgments by choruses, as in *Aj.* 693–
718 when the chorus thinks that Ajax will not commit suicide. But there
is no other case like this ode of *Antig.,* because here the judgment, if
there is a judgment, is a moral one, made in full knowledge (except for
the identity of the doer, which does not alter the moral issue) of what
has happened. To assume that the application of the ode is morally
wrong is to mar the beauty of the ode. We can rescue it either by regarding it as irrelevant, as Waldock does, or by finding a different application for it, which will be done below, pp. 205–207.

the odes spring from the mind of the chorus, as a character or, to be more exact, a group of undifferentiated characters of the drama in a precise set of circumstances, and to see what connection they have with the action that forms their context. The context need not be only the episodes immediately preceding and following. It may involve the structure and rhythm of the play as a whole, the personality of the chorus, their relation to the other persons of the drama, the behavior of the chorus not only in the odes but also in kommoi and in iambics.

There are good reasons for using this approach. In the first place, there are some odes that quite obviously do not represent what Sophocles thought about the situation in hand but only what the group of persons forming the chorus thought, without suggesting either profundity or vacuity in their thought. In Stasimon Two of *Ajax* (693–718) the chorus joyfully and mistakenly think that Ajax will not commit suicide. The fact that the chorus are mistaken in their joy does not destroy the force of the song (in fact it helps to create its dramatic force), because it is not a mistaken moral judgment (as the ode on man in *Antigone* is, if it is a condemnation of the burial) but a mistaken view of events. Secondly, Sophoclean choral odes are quite conspicuously suited to the group of singers. Just those choral songs that seem most detached in content are sung by choruses that are most detached, grave, and self-reliant. The choral ode on old age is sung by old men; the ode in praise of Attica by Atticans. Nowhere in Sophocles' plays is there a contradiction in the attitude of the chorus between its songs and its other utterances. This adaptation of the content of choral songs to the attitude and personality of the singers does not arise by accident.

We have external evidence both from a highly reputable critic who undoubtedly knew more of Sophocles' plays than we do and from Sophocles himself that suggests that this approach is valid: in praising the Sophoclean chorus Aristotle clearly implies that it has its place in the drama as "one of the actors." [7] In describing his final style (in which most if not all of the extant plays are surely written), Sophocles called it ἠθικώτατον, and there is no reason for supposing that he meant to exclude his choral technique from this description.[8] Finally, perhaps an abstract matter but one that should never be forgotten in criticizing Sophoclean drama, there is Sophocles' capacity for remaining inside the myth and never stepping outside it to explain or to reveal to us his point of view about what is happening. If we look for the sentiments of the poet in Sophoclean odes, we are in search of what is unlikely to be presented explicitly by a playwright whose whole way of procedure is not to criticize and reshape but to work within the myth.

In the present chapter we shall, then, examine the chorus from the point of view just suggested, considering what the choruses say as utterances by characters in plays—strange characters, no doubt, with a penchant for lyrics and abstraction, but characters nevertheless, neither omniscient nor stupid, but limited like other characters by the natural limitations of their position and their interest in the action. We shall find that this approach is not altogether sufficient in itself and that there is a degree of abstraction in some odes that does not reflect the personality of the particular choral group. And we shall not, by using this approach, deny that choral thoughts may sometimes be Sophoclean thoughts.

It will be necessary to consider what the chorus is, as well as what it says or sings, and to put these two things—the personality and the words—together as often as they belong together. We begin with what the chorus is, in relation to the rest of the play.

There are two distinct types of personal relationship between the choral group and the action and persons around them. The choruses of *Ajax, The Trachinian Women, Electra,* and *Philoctetes* are closely attached each to one character: to Ajax, Deianeira,[9] Electra, and Neoptolemus, respectively. In these four plays the choruses are by no means impartial; their sympathies (in *Ajax* and *Philoctetes* their fortunes too) are with a single person, and they share his point of view. They do not echo every word of their champion, for they are not merely extensions of his personality; they have their own nature and some independence of thought. The sailors in *Ajax* warn their leader against undue boastfulness (386), and those in *Philoctetes* express their sympathy for Philoctetes before Neoptolemus has begun to feel any (169–190). But in the larger issues they stand firm with their favorite's prejudices and interests as they see them: Ajax's men are as mistakenly bitter toward Odysseus as Ajax is (148–150); Neoptolemus' men are doggedly loyal to the stratagem even after the youth himself has grown sick of it (836–838, 843–864).

In the other three plays the choruses are more independent. In *Antigone* and *Oedipus at Colonus* it is clear that, wherever their sympathies may lie, the choruses are primarily elders of Thebes and Colonus, respectively, and their attitude to what is going on is always shaped by the responsibilities and special interests of their position. In *Oedipus Tyrannus* they are devoted to Oedipus; but in the very passage in which they most firmly state their devotion (498–511), it is quite clear that they feel a civic rather than a strictly personal loyalty (unlike the chorus of *Ajax*); it is Oedipus as savior of Thebes whom they revere: "For the winged maiden came upon him, a manifest thing, and in the test he was proved wise and a blessing to the

[9] The chorus are not exclusively devoted to Deianeira. They are intensely sympathetic with her throughout, but at the end they express sympathy, though less warm sympathy, with Heracles, and in Stasimon Four they are at a loss which grief—for Deianeira or for Heracles—to yield to first.

city; therefore he shall never be judged guilty of evil by my judgment" (507–511).

If we are right in suggesting that what Sophoclean choruses say is neither irrelevant nor an inserted personal message from the poet but conveys the thoughts and emotions of a character in the play, then we should expect to find the two different types of relationship we have now observed between the choral group and the rest of the action reflected in a similar twofold division in what the various choruses say. We noticed at the beginning of this chapter that a number of Sophoclean odes are, or at least appear to be, detached from context; and it is some confirmation for our argument to find that the most separate-seeming odes are sung by the choruses that are most independent as persons, the choruses of *Antigone* (Stasima One and Four), *OT* (Stasimon Two), and *OC* (Stasimon One). Later in this chapter we shall observe that there are other reasons for the detachment of these odes and that they are not really as detached as they seem. Our argument for the role of the chorus is, therefore, by no means proved by these odes alone. But we can move on to other points with some confidence that our approach is proving useful. Before we look at other odes, however, it will be convenient to deal briefly with two slighter and much simpler choral matters: the iambic lines spoken by the coryphaeus in episodes and the kommoi, lyrical dialogues between chorus and actor.

In general, the dramatic value of the iambic lines of the chorus [10] in the episodes is slight: they call attention to newly arrived persons, ask predictable questions and make purely factual or conventional answers to questions, advise moderation in argument, grief, and action, and offer unexciting comments

[10] The fact that these lines are spoken by the coryphaeus does not make them belong any the less to the chorus as a body. There is no difference anywhere in Greek tragedy, in personality or ethos, between the speaker of choral iambics and the singers of choral lyrics.

on most of the long speeches. Their remarks nearly always simply carry on the tone of what has preceded. Perhaps, as Norwood suggested, their comments after speeches are often no more than opportunities for the audience to applaud the speeches without missing anything important.[11] Occasionally, however, there is an appreciable dramatic value in their small comments. In *The Trachinian Women* they stress the self-effacement and graciousness of Deianeira when they receive the news of Heracles' unfaithfulness with spirited indignation (383–384) and again when they urge their mistress to defend herself before the ununderstanding Hyllus (813–814). In *Antigone* there is a distinct, if slight, dramatic value in the chorus's lukewarm reception of Creon's edict (211–214) and a somewhat sharper point, because of Creon's violent reaction, to their suggestion that the burial may have been aided by the gods (278–279). What is probably the most enterprising of all these passages comes later in *Antigone*, when Creon actually turns to the chorus for advice and they promptly give it (1098–1107). A number of slighter incidents of the sort could be added, but the choral contribution to the episodes (apart from kommoi, which we shall notice separately) is very small.

In so limited a field evidence concerning the behavior of the chorus is not very impressive, but we should nevertheless take notice that in these iambic passages the distinction between devoted and independent choruses is firmly maintained. In *Ajax*, *The Trachinian Women*, and *Electra* all the nonplatitudinous comments are spoken in support and encouragement of the protagonist or in hostility to his adversaries; [12] in *Philoctetes* there are no relevant passages; in *Antigone* there is a fourth

[11] *Greek Tragedy* [4] (London, 1948), 79–80; cf. Kitto, *Greek Tragedy*, 160.

[12] In addition to the passages mentioned there are the following: *Aj.* 1091–1092; 1163–1167 (anapaestic but like the iambic passages dealt with here because in the middle of an episode, not in a kommos or stasimon); *El.* 463–464; *Trach.* 387–388.

passage (770) to add to the three already mentioned in which the chorus criticize Creon's judgment; in *OT* there is nothing fully relevant (in 284–292 the chorus give advice, but in a spirit hardly different from the chorus's advice to Deianeira, *Trach.* 387–388); in *OC* they speak with some authority in directing Oedipus to sacrifice to the Eumenides (461–506) and in ordering Creon out of Attica (824–825).[13] Thus in the three Theban plays choral contributions in the iambics are to some degree independent and authoritative, and those in the other plays express personal loyalty.

The participation of the chorus in kommoi is a much more substantial subject. There are kommoi in all seven plays, but their dramatic contribution varies in type and importance. In *The Trachinian Women* there is only one short kommos (878–895), when the nurse rushes from the house with news of Deianeira's suicide and is interrogated by the chorus. Kommoi in *Oedipus Tyrannus* are of very much the same sort: at the height of the quarrel between Oedipus and Creon (649–696) the chorus intervene to plead for peace and their intervention makes transition from the quarrel to the scene between Oedipus and Jocasta. At the appearance of Oedipus just after he has blinded himself (1297–1366), the chorus provide a background of horrified commentary to Oedipus' cries of grief and self-reproach. These kommoi achieve what might be called the basic function of the kommos—to signal and emphasize moments of great emotional stress.

In *Oedipus at Colonus* there are five kommoi.[14] Most of them contribute to the element of spectacle in addition to creating emotional effect. In the parodos, which is in kommatic form,

[13] Cf. also *OC* 726–727, 824–832.

[14] One of these passages (833–843, 876–886) is declared by Jebb in his edition of *OC*, p. 138, to be of "kommatic character" but not actually a kommos. Since its purpose and effect are exactly those of regular kommoi, whatever formal differences it has do not affect the present discussion.

Oedipus, assisted by Antigone, slowly moves from his sacrilegious place in the grove of the Eumenides. His pitiful stumbling and groping add to our impression of the physical helplessness of the old man, and the horror of the Colonean elders at the appearance and identity of Oedipus and at his transgression of the sacred grove emphasizes the battle that Oedipus must fight in order to vindicate himself and reveal his beneficent power. The passages at lines 833–843 and 876–886 (they are a unit, strophe and antistrophe) enhance the spirited action of the seizing of Oedipus' daughters; that at lines 1447–1499 increases the sense of excitement and stir when the thunder peals, summoning Oedipus: the chorus are in terror, Oedipus prepares to leave, Theseus is summoned in haste. This play, in theme the most stationary and purely illustrative, is by far the richest in physical action, and to this quality the kommoi make a large contribution.

In *Antigone* there are two kommoi, and both have great dramatic pertinence; they are the passages in which the chorus make their judgment on Antigone and Creon in turn (801–882 and 1261–1366). The lyrical nature of these two passages does more than signify emotional stress; by making the two passages a distinct pair, it emphasizes their connection; and it emphasizes also the key part played in this drama by the chorus in relation to each of the main figures, a part that has, for a chorus, an unusual degree of independence.[15]

The remaining three plays use lyrical dialogue in a somewhat different way. In all three, as we have noted above, the connection between the choral group and a principal character is very close. The kommoi of these plays enhance that closeness. In *Ajax* the anxious colloquy of the sailors with Tecmessa on the fate of their leader (201–256), their sharing of Ajax's grief (348–429), and their participation in the search for his body and in the lament over it (879–960) all strengthen the intimacy

---

[15] Cf. above, pp. 126–127.

and the personal nature of the relationship between Ajax and his men. In *Electra* the kommoi, three in number, all bear on the intensity of Electra's grief and her desire for revenge; the first two (121–250 and 823–870) stress the close sympathy that exists between the princess and these Mycenaean women; the third emphasizes an emotional crisis at the moment of Clytemnestra's death (1398–1441). In *Philoctetes* all three kommoi, two between Neoptolemus and the chorus (135–218 and 827–864) and one between the chorus and Philoctetes (1081–1217), have to do with the winning of Philoctetes by stratagem or persuasion; thus all three are concerned with the interests of Neoptolemus, to whom the chorus are devoted.

In the kommoi, too, therefore, the distinction between personally devoted and independent choruses is maintained: *Ajax*, *Electra*, and *Philoctetes* differ from *Oedipus at Colonus* and *Antigone*. Kommoi in *Oedipus Tyrannus* and *The Trachinian Women* do not affect the question.

There is another point about Sophocles' use of lyrical dialogue that should be mentioned. It has been said by Walther Kranz, in his well-known book *Stasimon*,[16] that there is no real change in the choral style of Sophocles perceptible in the extant plays— that, although there are obvious differences from play to play, we cannot speak of truly different lyrical styles in different periods. There is, however, some decline in the extent of the contribution made by the chorus alone and a corresponding increase in the use of kommoi (as well as of solos and lyrical dialogues in which the chorus have no part) in the later plays.[17] In the earlier plays down to *Oedipus Tyrannus*, the purely choral lyrics are considerably more extensive than the kommoi and actors' songs, except in *Ajax*. In the three later plays, though the proportion of lyric lines to iambic is much the same as

[16] Berlin, 1933, 174.
[17] The same tendency is apparent in Euripides. See the tables on pp. 124–125 of *Stasimon*.

before, the proportion contributed by the chorus alone is strikingly less. In part the difference arises from the kind of drama; and it is this that accounts for the high proportion of kommatic lyrics in *Ajax*. But the difference is general enough and great enough to suggest a definite tendency, late in Sophocles' career, away from the purely choral element and an endeavor to relate the chorus more closely and realistically to the stage action.

We are now ready to look at the choral songs, the parodoi and stasima, sung by the chorus alone. We shall find that the distinction between two choral relationships to the drama, which has chiefly occupied us so far in this chapter, is only a preliminary issue here and will only help a little toward clarifying this part of the chorus's role. Even in choral odes where we can clearly detect an air of independent judgment there is much more to be taken into account. But a beginning can be made with this point. We have noticed that those odes that have, beyond others, an air of detachment are sung by choruses whose measure of independence as persons is greatest: Stasimon One of *Antigone*, Stasimon Two of *Oedipus Tyrannus*, Stasimon One of *Oedipus at Colonus*. Is there a corresponding immediacy and dependence in odes sung by choruses who are personally dependent?

Let us take the parodoi as a sample. Those of *Electra*, *Philoctetes*, and *Oedipus at Colonus* are out of the question because they are kommoi. In *Ajax*, from the opening words "Telamonian Ajax," throughout the song, the chorus express their concern, devotion, and dependence. In *The Trachinian Women* the burden of the parodos is Heracles: Where is he? May he come! Zeus will protect him. But the chorus are thinking about Heracles from Deianeira's point of view; they are grieved by her grief and concern for him (103–111), and they urge her to be confident (122–140). There is not, certainly, dependence as in *Ajax*, but there is intense personal sympathy. In *Antigone* and *Oedipus Tyrannus* there is concern also, but concern for

the city of Thebes. In *Antigone* the theme of the ode is joy
and pride at the victory of Thebes over the Seven, with a
counterpoint of sorrow for the death of the two sons of Oedipus.
In *OT* the ode is a cry of distress at the plight of Thebes and
a prayer to the gods to help Thebes against the ravages of
plague.

Once again, then, we find the familiar distinction between
personal and impersonal, attached and independent choruses.
To pursue our analysis throughout the odes would be tedious
and unnecessary; we should find that the same relation between
the personality of the choral group and the nature of its songs
is steadily maintained. For example, when the chorus of *Ajax*
sing a song of joy and excitement (693–718) in the belief that
Ajax will not commit suicide, they sing of Ajax; when in
Antigone the chorus sing in joy and excitement after Creon
has left to free Antigone and bury Polyneices, they say not a
word about any of the three persons concerned but call ex-
citedly on Dionysus to help his city (1015–1052). In *Electra*,
after the report of Orestes' death when Electra's fortunes are
at lowest ebb, the chorus express sorrow for Electra, and admiration for her enduring loyalty—an ode of sympathy (1058–
1097). In *OT*, when Oedipus has learned the truth about himself, the chorus sing in horror and wonderment at the fate of
màn, of which Oedipus' is a terrifying example (1186–1222);
they are not without sympathy, but the tone is of appraisal
rather than participation, and their deepest sympathy is for man
rather than for Oedipus.

These odes and others have functions other than to express
the attitude of the choral group as such. But this attitude they
do express, beyond doubt, and therefore this is the proper starting point from which to judge their further purposes.

To see that this careful and consistent relating of choral songs
to choral personality is distinctively Sophoclean, it will be
useful to look for a moment at some aspects of the choral man-

ner of Aeschylus and Euripides. The choruses of Aeschylus are certainly dramatic, though not all of them in the same way. One type is most strikingly exemplified by *The Suppliants*, where the choral group is, of course, the protagonist; the play concerns the fate of the Danaids. In *The Eumenides*, though it is perhaps an overstatement to say that the chorus of Furies are "the most important dramatic person," [18] their role is vitally important in the same sense, though not to the same degree, as that of the chorus in *The Suppliants*. A different kind of dramatic chorus appears in *The Persians* and, with more imposing grandeur, in *Agamemnon*; here the episodes are, broadly speaking, illustrations of the theme, which finds its fullest expression and is made universal in the choral odes.[19] Euripides sometimes uses the chorus in this second Aeschylean manner. In *The Trojan Women*, as Kitto observes,[20] the lyrics are the shaping and unifying element of the play. In *The Bacchae* the chorus of Asiatic Bacchants, whose songs are the very essence of the Dionysiac spirit, have a similar role.[21] In one play, *The Suppliants*, Euripides virtually goes back to a choral protagonist in the early Aeschylean manner.

It never has been suggested, so far as I know, that any chorus of Sophocles is the protagonist; but it has often been supposed that his choruses convey the dramatic theme, more or less in the manner of *Agamemnon* or *The Bacchae*. What we have seen so far of the behavior of Sophoclean choruses points in a different direction; and we shall presently see further reasons for dissenting from the view that the Sophoclean chorus con-

[18] Kranz, *Stasimon*, 169.

[19] For the role of the chorus in *The Persians*, see the study by S. M. Adams, "Salamis Symphony: The *Persae* of Aeschylus," in *Studies in Honour of Gilbert Norwood* (Toronto, 1952), 46–54.

[20] *Greek Tragedy*, 213–214.

[21] On the choral odes of *The Trojan Women* and *The Bacchae*, cf. *Stasimon*, 248; for those of *The Bacchae* see also R. P. Winnington-Ingram, *Euripides and Dionysus* (Cambridge, 1948), *passim*.

veys the theme of the play. In a very general way the choral
style that is called by Kranz, in *Stasimon*, the "classical style"
is that of all Sophoclean choruses. Kranz describes the "classical
style" thus: "The choral odes of this period organize and give
rhythm to the action. . . . They serve as an artistic means of
amplifying and deepening the impression created by the action
on the stage; they can be a preparation for this action, or a
supplement to it." [22] Odes of this type do not primarily convey
the theme but lyrically amplify, interpret, and illustrate its
various stages.

But Kranz's description is too broad to catch the distinctive
Sophoclean manner; it is as true of most of Euripides' earlier
plays as it is of Sophocles, yet Sophoclean choruses differ from
Euripidean, sometimes profoundly. In one conspicuous way
Sophocles, though in Kranz's "classical style," is far closer to
Aeschylus than to Euripides—in the close connection that his
chorus maintains with the action of the play. Euripides' choruses
not infrequently sing odes with only a casual relation to their
dramatic context. A familiar and instructive example of this
difference between Sophocles and Euripides is provided by the
odes in praise of Athens in *Oedipus at Colonus* (668–719) and
Medea (824–865). The content is similar,[23] but the odes are
altogether different in their connection with the drama. In
Medea, Athens comes into the thoughts of the chorus because
in the preceding episode Aegeus has offered Medea a refuge

[22] *Stasimon*, 207–208; in general, Kranz's "classical style" describes the
odes of what Kitto, in *Greek Tragedy*, calls "Middle Tragedy."

[23] The comparison involves only the first system of the *Medea* ode,
lines 824–835. The second system is very different. It is a sudden outburst against Medea: how can this fair land of which we sing receive
you, the murderess of your children! This sudden shift of thought and
mood, and indeed the general effect of the ode, are not without a powerful dramatic impact. But it is of an altogether different sort from that of
the *OC* ode; its content and spirit are much less natural to the context
and to the personality of the chorus.

there. Their song on the beauties and splendors of Athens is charming, but there is no good reason why these Corinthian women should feel moved to sing so beautifully of Athens. In *Oedipus at Colonus* the connection of the ode with the action is intimate. Throughout the play the solemn beauty of the grove of the Eumenides, the charm of the surrounding neighborhood of Colonus, and the gracious and magnanimous spirit of Athens are of primary importance; for within the physically helpless, irascible old Oedipus there is a power and a nobility of spirit that become more evident as the play advances; and the concord between his qualities and those of the people and the place where he finds rest is a continuing theme through much of the drama. In the episode just before this stasimon, Theseus, the very embodiment of the idealized Athenian spirit, has welcomed Oedipus. It is completely natural and very valuable for the thought of the play when the chorus follow this scene with a song in praise of their land. Here the choral group does not lose any part of its personality, as that of *Medea* does; it is participating in the manner of an actor.[24]

There are in Euripides many odes that have a loose connection with the context; to mention just one more, the ode on the evils of parenthood, also in *Medea* (1081–1115), shows this same detachment. Kitto aptly remarks apropos of this ode that it is "a little chilling to find Euripides going off into his study";[25] and the fact that the chorus sing their grave and deliberate song in anapaests adds a good deal, as the same critic points

[24] This is not to say that this chorus of *Medea* is irrelevant. G. M. A. Grube, *The Drama of Euripides* (London, 1941), Part I, Ch. vii, "The Chorus," well defends the relevance of most Euripidean choruses. The difference between the dramatists is not, in this instance or generally, a question of relevance in contrast to irrelevance or of the presence or absence of dramatic value, but of the manner in which dramatic effect is achieved. Sophocles almost invariably works his odes into the fabric of the dramatic action; Euripides frequently does not.

[25] *Greek Tragedy*, 191–192.

out, to the impassive judiciousness of this little philosophical poem. Euripides clearly did not have the same interest as Sophocles in preserving the "character" of the chorus in the sense of carefully adapting the thought and manner of the songs to the personality and situation of the choral group. Nor is this difference just a matter of choral personality; it tells us something about the difference in attitude between Sophocles and Euripides toward dramatic structure. In the choral odes as elsewhere Euripides is the more detached and abstract playwright; with Sophocles everything is personal and immediate. It does not at all follow that Euripidean dramatic form is inferior, only that it is different and that it does not have the same kind of unbroken tension that is the hallmark of Sophoclean form.

In this comparison of Sophoclean and Euripidean manner we are, as I have said, dealing with a question of structure as well as choral personality. We must now, in order to complete our account of Sophocles' disposal of his chorus, look at several further aspects of it that bear more essentially on structure than on character drawing. There are some Sophoclean odes for which Kranz's description is adequate: the first stasimon of *Electra* (472–515), the one stasimon in *Philoctetes* (676–729) and the two brief lyrics at lines 391–402 and 507–518; most of the odes of *The Trachinian Women* (the parodos [94–140], Stasimon One [497–530], and Stasimon Four [947–970]); and the final stasimon of *Ajax* (1185–1222).

These odes need not detain us long. No one is likely to search mistakenly for the dramatist's clues to the meaning of his play, for they are simple in content and provide no more than a lyrical commentary on their context. Let us briefly examine just one of them. The odes of *Ajax* are not among Sophocles' greatest lyrics, but there is little doubt that the ode of lines 1185–1222 is the finest in the play, even though it lacks the dramatic point of Stasimon Three (693–718), which we shall notice presently. The ode lies between Teucer's scene with Menelaus and his

scene with Agamemnon and is a lament for the woes of the
common soldier in the Trojan War. In the customary Sophoclean
manner the ideas expressed fit the singers; in the final antistrophe the chorus sing: "Once my bulwark against alarms by
night and against the shafts of the foe was Ajax, the dauntless
of spirit. But now he is prey to a hateful fate. What joy, what
joy is left for me?" The ode is not intended as a philosophical
poem on the sorrows of war—that is what Euripides might
have written in such a place. Instead of philosophy we have
here a lyrical cry of distress, which springs naturally from Ajax's
sailors and intensifies the atmosphere of sorrow and of desperate
resistance that belongs to both the preceding and the following
episodes. Its contribution is not to the intellectual content but
to the spirit of this part of the play.

But for many Sophoclean odes, Kranz's description is not
definite enough. We begin with three songs whose dramatic
power of suspense and contrast has long been admired: *Ajax*
693–718, *Antigone* 1115–1154, and *OT* 1086–1109.[26] We noticed above that the *Ajax* and *Antigone* odes differ in one respect from each other because of the difference in relationship
of the chorus to the other characters. Here we are interested
in their similarity, which is more impressive and more important
for Sophoclean dramatic structure. All three are in lively dance
measures; all are joyful, with an air almost of abandon; all occur
at a crucial point in the play when the chorus have wild and
enthusiastic hopes of some happy outcome only to have those
hopes dashed by catastrophic news immediately after the song.
Thus in *Ajax*, following the celebrated speech in which Ajax
seems to have decided against suicide, the chorus, carried away

[26] Their dramatic force is noticed in *Stasimon*, 213, where they are
said to have a "delaying purpose," and by Webster, *Introduction*, 105,
184, where they are called "the cheerful choruses." Cf. the scholiast's
comment at *Aj.* 693: εὐεπίφορος δὲ ὁ ποιητὴς ἐπὶ τὰς τοιαύτας μελοποιίας
ὥστε ἐντιθέναι τι καὶ τοῦ ἡδέος.

with happiness at the apparent turn of events, sing ἔφριξ' ἔρωτι, περιχαρὴς δ' ἀνεπτάμαν: "I thrill with desire, my joy takes wing." As soon as their song is over, news comes which indicates only too clearly that Ajax has gone from his tent to take his life. In *Antigone* at the moment when Creon, yielding at last, has rushed away to free Antigone and bury Polyneices, the chorus invoke the aid of Dionysus in an excited and hopeful song. Then at once the messenger enters with his story of failure and death. Most powerful of all is the song in *Oedipus Tyrannus*. At the end of the preceding episode Oedipus is still pressing for discovery; calling himself the child of Τύχη, with feverish optimism he declares his determination to discover his origins, however lowly. Catching his spirit, the chorus prophesy that he will prove to be their compatriot, the son of mountain-ranging Pan perhaps, or of the Loxian, or Cyllene's lord, or Theban Bacchus. Immediately after the ode there is the taut, harrowing scene of final revelation.

To these three odes two slighter examples of the same kind of song may be added, both in *The Trachinian Women*. One is a little song of triumph (205–224) following the good news of Heracles' approach and followed at once by the arrival of Lichas and the captives, including the fateful Iole.[27] The other is the lighthearted ode (633–662) anticipating the happy arrival of Heracles. Directly after it Deianeira discovers that her use of the supposed philter has been, in all likelihood, a terrible mistake, and before the episode is over Hyllus has returned to tell of Heracles' agony.[28]

None of these odes contributes any thought or any element of story that in a tangible, material way advances the play; in each case the content of the ode is very simple. But by their continuation, in a somewhat frantic tone, of the spirit of hope

[27] Cf. Christian Muff, *Die chorische Technik des Sophokles* (Halle, 1877), 39.
[28] Cf. Kranz, *Stasimon*, 213.

that precedes and, even more, by the contrast between their happy excitement and the somber events that follow, they have the strongest effect on the rhythm of the play. They are integral and contributing parts of the dramatic structure, and they achieve the same kind of contrastive effect that we have seen Sophocles creating in other elements of his plays, between one character and another and between one scene and another. Furthermore, as we shall presently see, these odes are not isolated phenomena but simply the most striking examples of a customary Sophoclean technique in which the choral odes influence the rhythm of the play by a contrast or some similar structural effect.

Of course the other dramatists, too, use their choruses structurally, but not at all with the same immediacy as Sophocles. In *Prometheus Bound*, the one play of Aeschylus in which the choral technique resembles Sophocles' at all closely, there is no comparable effect of contrast through a choral ode. In Euripides' plays there are some comparable examples, but a comparison of two superficially similar examples of the relation between chorus and action will show how profound the difference really is. In *Oedipus at Colonus*, just before the powerful scenes in which Oedipus denounces Polyneices and then makes an inspired and triumphant departure, the chorus sing a pessimistic ode (1211–1248) on the sorrows and the loneliness of old age. The difference between their despairing gloom and the vigor and power of spirit displayed by Oedipus in what follows has a dramatic force of the sort we have just noticed. In *Alcestis*, immediately before Heracles brings Alcestis back from the grave, the chorus sing an ode (962–1005) of sorrowful resignation, telling Admetus that he must bow to Necessity, that Alcestis is beyond recall. The relation of the stasimon to what follows is formally much the same here as in *Oedipus at Colonus*. Yet the *Alcestis* ode does not have anything like the same effect on the dramatic rhythm, because it is detached, philosophical, even a little bookish. It begins with a reference to literature and study, from which the chorus declare that they have learned that there is nothing stronger than Necessity (962–966). This learned approach breaks the dramatic flow; we realize that we are being addressed, not by a group of Thessalian elders, but by Euripides.[29] In *Oedipus at Colonus* the ode belongs in spirit to the immediate situation and to the ethos of the elders of Colonus. Instead of breaking, it intensifies, the dramatic atmosphere.

Let us look at some further Sophoclean odes that create or emphasize an effect of contrast. They will not be as striking as the three we began with; our purpose here is not to pick out what is most choice but to see, if we can, what procedures dictate the form and spirit of Sophoclean odes. In the parodos of *Antigone* (100–154) the chorus tell of the defeat of the Argive army and the triumph of Thebes. Immediately after it Creon enters and makes his specious inaugural address. In *Antigone*, as we noticed above (p. 85), the prologue and the first episode introduce two different elements of the theme. The parodos is accommodated to this structure; the Theban elders know nothing of Antigone's anger or her determination to flout the edict of the new monarch, and their song of victory is in complete contrast to the passion and excitement of the prologue. Its connection with the following scene is just the reverse of this relationship of contrast. With its dominant theme of victory it provides exactly the right tone for the introduction of the scene. It also, of course, gives information about the repulse of the invading army, but what is dramatically important is its spirit, which blends perfectly with the proud

[29] Grube, *The Drama of Euripides*, 124, argues that we should not have the impression that it is the poet speaking, because the thought is commonplace and hence appropriate to the choral group. It is, however, the manner of the opening lines rather than the content of the ode that breaks the dramatic illusion.

and confident tone of Creon's opening address and thus contributes to the ultimate irony of the contrast between this lofty beginning and the tumultuous and undignified incident after the guard's arrival. Thus the tone of the ode, by its contrast with what goes before and its adaptation to the mood that follows, is structurally valuable.

The parodos of *Oedipus Tyrannus* (151–215) adapts the same principle to different circumstances. In the prologue Creon returns from Delphi to announce that the plague will end only if the murderer of Laius is driven from Thebes. The first episode begins with Oedipus' proclamation to the people, commanding them to reveal the murderer if they can. There is no contrast, in the spirit or content, between the two scenes; *Oedipus* is a play of continuous dramatic development. There might therefore seem to be no dramatic use for the parodos beyond linking prologue to episode by lyrical repetition of key ideas in the prologue, "amplifying and deepening the impression created," as Kranz expresses it. Certainly the parodos does perform this service, but it also does more, and its additional role is typically Sophoclean. The song has three themes: inquiry about the meaning of the oracle (151–158), lament for the ravages of the plague (168–187), and prayer invoking the aid of Athena, Artemis, Apollo, Zeus, and Dionysus (159–167, 188–215). All three are continuations of themes begun in the prologue, but that of prayer, which is dominant in the ode, has an additional force. When Oedipus comes out at the end of the ode to address the people, he begins with the single word αἰτεῖς, "You pray." [30] He then declares, in effect, that he will provide the answer to their prayer. A close connection is thus established between parodos and episode; but what counts for far more in the dramatic structure is the ironical contrast of solemn prayer addressed to all the gods and the immediate answer with which

[30] The verb is singular because Oedipus addresses the coryphaeus, but this is dramatically the same as addressing the chorus.

Oedipus takes upon himself the terrible burden of fulfilling that prayer.[31]

The ode in *Oedipus at Colonus* in praise of Colonus and Athens arises naturally, as we have seen, from the dramatic context and from the character of the chorus. It also contributes to a contrast, for the following episode brings the arrival of Creon and a sharp disturbance of the graceful tranquillity that characterized the preceding episode and reached its height in the ode. The parodos of this play (117–253) has the same effect of creating a sharp contrast of emotions, in this case with what precedes. For the excitement and horror of the elders of Colonus in this first meeting with Oedipus contrast markedly with the impressive serenity of the prologue.

In the second stasimon of *Electra* the chorus express their grief and sympathy for Electra (1058–1097). The dramatic force of the song arises from its contrast with the joyful recog-

[31] Bernard M. W. Knox, "The Date of the *Oedipus Tyrannus* of Sophocles," *AJP*, 77 (1956), 133–147, believes that the reference to Ares, lines 190–202, is out of character for the Theban elders since Ares was a patron deity of Thebes, while in this passage Ares is represented as the enemy of Thebes, personifying the plague. Knox asserts that "the Theban origin of the chorus has clearly been forgotten" and "the words of this strophe cannot be considered appropriate to anything in the play." The point is an interesting one, but I doubt its validity. Only if the Ares of this passage were clearly Ares, god of war, would the unfriendly references to him be out of character. (Even the war god is only intermittently linked with Thebes; he is often Thracian, as at *Antig.* 970.) By referring to him as ἄχαλκος ἀσπίδων (191) the poet clearly differentiates this Ares from the war god. This is not unique in Sophocles: Ares loses his usual personality of mythology also at *Aj.* 612–613 and 1196 and at *OC* 1047; he represents violence other than the violence of war at *Aj.* 254 (λιθόλευστον ῎Αρη). Furthermore, the imagery of this passage, in which the plague is represented by Ares, the personification of violence and strife, is readily understandable. The plague came about as a result of an act of violence, the murder of Laius; the plague can only be ended by the "driving out" (ἐλαύνειν, 98) of the murderer of Laius, just as the chorus here pray that the "bronzeless Ares," the plague, may be driven out.

nition scene, which follows at once; as soon as the song ends, Orestes enters.

The final stasimon of *Oedipus at Colonus* (1556–1578) is a prayer to the nether gods that Oedipus' passing may be painless and tranquil. It sustains the atmosphere of wonder that began in the preceding episode with Oedipus' thrilling departure. Appropriately, the prayer is offered for the aged Oedipus by men who are his fellows in old age and have therefore a deep feeling for the mystery of what follows life. But more telling, dramatically, is the contrast between the gloom and apprehension and submission of its tone and the sublime tranquillity and triumph of the actual passing of Oedipus as it is reported by the messenger in the next episode.

Contrast is not the only dramatic element that Sophoclean choral odes contribute. The first three stasima of *Antigone* are excellent examples of songs that contribute to an atmosphere of suspense through ambiguity. All three odes are to some degree of the "detached" sort and for that reason are especially liable to interpretation as comments by Sophocles on the action of the play. Let us see whether a consideration of their structural function can help in their interpretation.

The first stasimon, the ode on man (332–375), is perhaps the most famous lyric in Sophocles. No one questions the intrinsic poetic merit of the ode, but its dramatic point, as was mentioned above, has been variously interpreted.[32] At the beginning

---

[32] Waldock, *Dramatist*, 112–114, finds it irrelevant and contends that the final antistrophe is "a rather hasty attempt at relevance before the song has quite run its course." But this view disregards the strikingly formalized repetition in ὑψίπολις· ἄπολις (370) of παντοπόρος· ἄπορος (360), which in turn is inextricable from the thought and mood of the first system. There could hardly be a more patent example of thought development emphasized by the pattern of meter and words. Bowra, *Sophoclean Tragedy*, 84–86 (cf. Kitto, *Greek Tragedy*, 158), regards it as an indictment of the burial of Polyneices and hence, unconsciously, of Antigone's conduct.

the chorus declare that nothing is more wonderful than man. What is the wonderful thing, the δεινόν, that motivates their song? The daring act of burial, many critics would answer. Δεινόν can mean "daring"; but it clearly does not mean it here; what the chorus go on to talk about is not the boldness of man, primarily, but his wonderful accomplishments, his skills. Others would say that the reference is to the burial not as a daring act but as a marvelous act, inspiring a sense of awe. There is indeed a note of mystery and awe in the report of the guard about the manner of the burial, which is strengthened by the chorus's answering suggestion that the gods may have had a hand in the deed (278–279). But again we must notice that the ode has no further suggestion of awe or mystery but rather of the orderly and clever accomplishments of civilization. The same kind of problem arises at the end, when the song closes on an ominous note, casting a shadow of doubt over the whole proud statement of man's greatness and sufficiency: sometimes man's cleverness leads to good, sometimes to ill;

> when he [man] observes the laws of the land, and the justice of the gods to which he has sworn, high stands his city; no city has he whom presumption leads to evil ways. May the doer of such deeds never be by my hearth, or share my thoughts. [368–375]

Who in the play is the evildoer? Is it the burier of the body? Since the chorus have already expressed a measure of disapproval of Creon's edict and have suggested that the gods had a hand in the burial, it seems impossible that they are now, only a little later, condemning the act in solemn and unequivocal tones. Such inconsistency in choral attitude would contradict the procedure that we have seen Sophocles following regularly, and I do not think that this chorus need be taken to be an exception.

The purpose of the ode is something quite other than to pass moral judgment on the act of burial. Neither the beginning nor the end of the ode has any precise reference to the act. The ode arises from the spirit of the preceding episode. The episode begins with a calm and orderly speech of Creon, apparently portending law and well-being for Thebes; Creon's attitude is, on the surface, an example of the achievement of civilized man. At the end of the episode there is anger and disturbance. The impression left by the whole is of stability and order suddenly jarred into confusion, doubt, and disorder. The ode reflects this change; its relevance to the context lies precisely in its repetition of the emotional development of the episode.[33] The end of the ode is meant to reintroduce and to amplify this spirit of disquiet and confusion. Just who is the disturber of order and right, who it is that has been led "to evil ways"—Creon or the burier of the body—is deliberately left in doubt. The most important dramatic contribution of the ode is its introduction of serious and unresolved doubts.

In the next stasimon (582–625) the same problem arises, and, in my opinion, the same answer applies. Of its two lyrical systems, the first is a lament for the house of Labdacus, springing very naturally from the unhappy events of the scene before; the second is a deeply religious warning against the false hopes and transgressions of mankind. Again the chorus speak with earnestness, but it is hard to settle on the object of their warning. Is it Antigone who is so sternly reproached in the second lyrical system? Nowhere do the chorus directly accuse her of worse faults than stubbornness, offense against Dike (the natural balance of things), and lack of wisdom. The sins they are inveighing against here are clearly of a more heinous kind;

---

[33] Kitto is right in objecting (*Greek Tragedy*, 158) to Jebb's statement that choral comment "must" reflect, in order, the developments of the preceding episode. There is no evidence for any such convention in the choral odes of Sophocles. In this instance the juxtaposition of events in the episode has a marked dramatic significance, and its reflection in the ode is also for a dramatic purpose. It is not a matter of convention.

surely no one (except possibly Creon) would call Antigone's conduct ὑπερβασία, challenging the power of Zeus. But it is just as difficult to suppose that a direct and conscious indictment of Creon is intended, even though the words are "suggestive and ominous," [34] for at this point the chorus are still loyal to him. Again we must conclude that the ambiguity is intended. The chorus, having heard the quarrel between Antigone and Creon, are convinced that someone is going against the will of heaven; but in their lyrical musing on the problem they do not point directly at the sinner, because they do not know precisely who the sinner is. Later on, in the final kommos, they will turn on Creon with precision enough. But at this early point in the drama they are expressing only an intuition of evil. In dialogue such ambiguity would be intolerable, if not impossible; but in lyrics, where references can be indirect and general, the ambiguity is not only acceptable but dramatically valuable. It maintains and expands a feeling of impending calamity for wrongdoing without constituting a direct moral indictment which would weaken the tension of the plot.

The third stasimon is a short ode to Eros. It has a certain effect of shock, this little song to the god of love following hard on the scene of shouting and hatred between Creon and his son. It has also, like the songs that precede, the purpose of maintaining tension.[35] Here, not long before the turning point of the play, when Creon's guilt will be clear, the chorus are permitted to appear more than ever to be censuring Antigone's cause: "You [Eros] have drawn the minds of just men into injustice, to their ruin" (791–792). Do they mean Haemon? We may think so if we wish, but they do not ever say that Haemon is guilty of injustice; only that his love for Antigone rivals in

---

[34] Jebb, *Antigone* [3] (Cambridge, 1900), p. xii.

[35] S. M. Adams, "The *Antigone* of Sophocles," *Phoenix*, 9 (1955), 47–62, has an excellent paragraph (p. 57) on the relevance of the theme of Eros to several aspects of the play.

power "mighty laws." Once again there is ambiguity, and it can hardly be by chance.

All three stasima convey an impression of ominous doubt and suggest present and impending evil and disaster. Their dramatic contribution is to some degree separate from the action of the episodes.

The first stasimon of *Oedipus Tyrannus* (463–512) is similar in effect to these three odes of *Antigone*, though here the creation of doubt and the building up of tension do not depend so much on ambiguity as on the bewilderment and excitement of the elders. The first system develops in mood and subject out of the foregoing scene between Oedipus and Teiresias and tells in excited tones of the pursuit of Laius' murderer. The second system does not have the superb lyrical brilliance of the first but is more pointedly dramatic, and its metrical form, in which choriambs and ionics predominate, has a stateliness and solemnity (in contrast to the trochaic staccato of the first system) that enhance the thought. How, ponder the chorus, can the terrible words of the prophet be right, how can it be Oedipus who killed Laius? It cannot be; Zeus and Apollo know all, but there is no certainty that any mortal can surpass his fellows in mantic skill; I shall remain faithful to Oedipus, the savior of Thebes (483–511). The earnestness of their deliberation and the solemn gravity of their affirmation of faith in Oedipus make a dramatic contribution that does not depend on anything in the episodes; the questions and emotions of the Theban elders, presented in lyrics that are deeply impressive in tone, add greatly to the atmosphere of doubt and fear and search that keeps gathering all through the first part of the play.

There is one more kind of structural effect achieved by Sophoclean choral odes that deserves mention, although it is essentially a negative effect: while the odes we have been noticing have, by contrast or suspense or ambiguity, created or enhanced dramatic tension, these odes to some degree relax the

intensity of a situation. Perhaps they are no more than instances
of songs in the "classical style," but two of them in particular,
Oedipus Tyrannus 1186–1222 and *Antigone* 944–987, have so
pronounced an effect on the rhythm of the dramatic action that
they require separate mention.[36]

The *Oedipus* ode begins with an agonized lament for the
fate of mankind:

> Woe for the generations of man! Your lives are equal
> to nothingness in my reckoning. What man ever has
> more of prosperity than its mere seeming, and after
> the seeming, a decline?

Then, in a lyrical review of Oedipus' greatness and suffering,
the chorus give voice to the emotional stress that has been
built up almost beyond endurance in the terrible incident that
precedes, and by giving voice to it they bring a measure of relief. Gloomy and despairing though their cry is, it yet calms
and brings a lull in the action; there is a relaxing of tension before the excitement of the report of the *exangelos*. Structurally
the function of the ode is modest, but its fine emotional consummation of the catastrophe makes it at once lyrically great and
dramatically appropriate.

In *Antigone* the corresponding ode is sung just after Antigone
has been led off to be imprisoned. It tells of three imprisonments: of Danae, Lycurgus, and Cleopatra. It is a striking poem;
but as dramatic material, with relevance to the play, it has often
seemed intransigent, because critics have tried to extract from
it a kind of relevance that it does not have. Each imprisonment
seems to have a different moral atmosphere: Danae's brought
her glorious motherhood; Lycurgus' was a dismal punishment
for impiety; Cleopatra's was a case of pitiful and undeserved
suffering. Which are we to liken to Antigone's case? It is dif-

[36] Kitto links these two odes and notices their relief value (*Greek Tragedy*, 165).

ficult to believe, with Bowra, that the three stories are offered
as different ways of interpreting what happens to Antigone.[37]
This is too complex and distracting. Here, as generally, the
contribution of the ode is very simple: instead of moral pro-
nouncement we have a poetic elaboration, very moving and
vivid, of the single theme of imprisonment, forming a kind of
lyrical finale to the foregoing scene. It is the emotion of the
chorus, and the imaginative reach of their song, not their intellectual prowess, that count here.[38] After the stirring kommos and
the departure of Antigone there is no place for further dramatic development of this theme. The ode is a transformation
of the pathos of events into lyrical terms that fulfill and give
respite from the tragic action. Then the plot is renewed with
the Teiresias scene.

Finally, something should be said about the second stasimon
of *Oedipus Tyrannus* (863–910). Of its two lyrical systems,
the first contains a prayer for piety and reverence and a condemnation of *hybris;* the second expresses the hope that evil
practices may be punished and ends with the fervent wish that
Apollo's oracles may be fulfilled and the fear that religion is
vanishing from the earth. Because of its devoutly religious tone
the ode creates a very strong impression. It is frequently made
to bear an interpretative weight in relation to the play as a
whole that it does not deserve. To one critic this is one of
just two passages "where we feel certain that Sophocles is

[37] *Sophoclean Tragedy*, 105; criticized cogently and wittily by Waldock, *Dramatist*, 117–119.

[38] When Waldock says of this chorus (*Dramatist*, 117) that its relevance is a "loose formality," he underestimates the importance of lyrical, as distinct from intellectual, relevance. A completely different relevance is seen in this ode by I. Errandonea, "El estasimo cuarto de
Antigona," *Emerita*, 20 (1952), 108–121, reprinted as "Das 4. Stasimon
des "Antigone" von Sophokles," *Symbolae Osloenses*, 30 (1953), 16–26.
Errandonea believes that the ode looks ahead and that the imprisonments
all symbolize aspects of the punishment which will befall Creon. The
argument is ingenious but unconvincing.

preaching."[39] But if Sophocles is preaching here, what is the point of the sermon in relation to the play? Does it charge Oedipus with *hybris?* Is he the man Δίκας ἀφόβητος κτλ? It is extremely difficult to find confirmation in the rest of the play for this judgment, and therefore we may well hesitate to regard it as such. To suppose, on the other hand, that the ode proves that the Sophoclean chorus "represents the somewhat confused morality of the bourgeoisie"[40] is no better; for though we may not agree with all the religious and ethical views in this ode, it is a straightforward and admirably clear statement of a reasonable set of beliefs. Let us see if what we have noticed in many odes of Sophocles—the harmonizing of the odes with the personality of the chorus and the use of odes to contribute specific dramatic effects to the rhythm of the play—will help in our assessment of this ode too.

The ode follows the tense and disquieting scene in which Jocasta, aiming to calm Oedipus' fears, sets out to show the folly of believing in oracles. At first she fails. She refers to the old oracle according to which Laius will die at the hands of his son and her "proof" of its error leads to Oedipus' strong suspicion that it was he who killed Laius. But she persists, and at the end of the episode she has finally won a half-hearted agreement from Oedipus. The feeling of the scene is one of doubt, questioning, ambiguity; it leaves one with a profound sense of uneasiness. At this point the ode is sung. Immediately after it

[39] D. W. Lucas, *The Greek Tragic Poets* (London, 1950), 150. (The other "sermon" is Antigone's speech on the Unwritten Laws.) Max Pohlenz's account of the ode (*Griechische Tragödie*,[2] 219–220) is more extreme: "We are listening here not to the elders of Thebes, but to the poet Sophocles, who expostulates with his people and with deity itself, and makes his own poetic confession of faith." It was, Pohlenz continues, the moral consequences of the plague of 430–428 B.C. that roused Sophocles to this earnestness. Kitto's brief remarks on the ode (*Greek Tragedy*, 158, 165, 178) in some respects anticipate the view expressed in this chapter.

[40] Whitman, *Sophocles*, 135.

Jocasta enters and prays to Apollo. As she prays, the Corinthian messenger appears to tell of Polybus' death—news that is cheering at first but that soon leads to calamitous revelations. It is easy to see how the ode, with its lyrical expression of uneasiness and fear, of desire for the security of some stable refuge, continues and amplifies the spirit of the preceding episode. But its relevance to what follows is even closer and more peculiarly Sophoclean. As the stasimon ends with the words, "Nowhere does Apollo retain his honors; religion is passing away," Jocasta, whose doubts were the source of the chorus's disquietude, appears on the scene. She is intent on sacrificing at all the shrines of the gods; and it is Apollo to whom she prays especially: "To thee, Lycaean Apollo, I come as suppliant, for thou art nearest." Apollo is indeed nearest, nearest in the thought of the chorus and nearest to Jocasta, though not in the way she hopes. The irony thus begun continues throughout the episode. As if in answer to her prayer, the man from Corinth arrives to bring her a momentary relief from her worries; but by the end of the scene the whole terrible truth is clear to Jocasta.

What, then, are the dramatic qualities of the ode? First, it is revelant to the context—not just because it discusses topics that have a place in the episodes before and after, but also, and mainly, because the manner in which the chorus make their reflections is fitting both to the personality of the elders and to the dramatic atmosphere in which the ode is set. Secondly, instead of interrupting the course of the drama with a sermon by Sophocles, settling moral and religious problems, the words of this ode simply express, in language of vigor and beauty, the religious thoughts of the chorus, evoked by their doubts and anxiety. The ode settles nothing.[41] But as in the *Antigone* odes the very ambiguity and inconclusiveness of the song in-

[41] As Kitto points out (*Greek Tragedy*, 165), the moral comments in this ode quite clearly do not refer to Oedipus and Jocasta, even though they are motivated by the king and queen.

crease dramatic tension, where a sermon would break it. Finally, there is a distinctively Sophoclean touch in the ironical interplay between the ode, Jocasta's prayer, and the appearance of the Corinthian.

The above sketch of how the chorus fits into Sophoclean drama is frankly incomplete. An attempt to give an exhaustive account would necessitate discussion of imagery and meter and study of the thought of the odes at some length. But the aim of this chapter was simpler—to offer only a preliminary step toward understanding the chorus. As such, it is, I think, both correct and essential. We have seen that, consistently and effectively, Sophocles keeps the spirit and the thought of his choral songs in line with the personality and the immediate position and attitude of the group of singers. And we have seen also that he often goes beyond this kind of dramatic relevance to create various effects of contrast, suspense, relief, irony, and ambiguity, which contribute to the effectiveness of the action. The present chapter has thus been, for the most part, a long postscript to the preceding two chapters: the choral group is a character, and its personality and its relation to other characters are worked out with the same skill that Sophocles expends on the rest of his character portrayal; and the choral songs are integral parts of the dramatic structure, contributing, like the other parts, to the compact shape and the subtle rhythm of the whole.

CHAPTER V

Some Notes on Diction

SOPHOCLEAN language is everywhere dramatic. There is a quality of urgency and compression about it: in terse, interlocked passages of stichomythic argument between Antigone and Ismene in the second episode of *Antigone*, between Electra and her mother deadlocked in controversy over "justice" and "shame," and between the straining insistence of Oedipus and the helpless resistance of the old herdsman; in such linked speeches as those of Ajax and Tecmessa in the first episode of *Ajax*, and of Oedipus, Theseus, and Creon in their scene together in *Oedipus at Colonus*; even in monologues or set speeches like those of Ajax to himself, of Deianeira to the chorus, and of Creon discoursing on government to the elders of Thebes. In every situation and in every type of speech Sophocles' diction maintains close dramatic relevance and immediacy. How is this done? Dramatic relevance is a matter of thought, structure, and characterization; but these are in Sophoclean drama constantly supported and emphasized by many effects of diction, some of them quite incidental and scarcely noticeable, others far-ranging and conspicuous.

A comprehensive study of Sophoclean diction has yet to be written. Some prolegomena have appeared,[1] and studies of cer-

[1] J. C. F. Nuchelmanns, *Die Nomina des Sophokleischen Wortschatzes: Vorarbeiten zu einer sprachgeschichtlichen und stylistischen Analyse* (Utrecht, 1949).

tain aspects of this difficult subject have been written.[2] But the subject as a whole is very complex and very large, involving aspects of vocabulary, syntax, and imagery and requiring examination of these aspects in relation to one another and to the other facets of Sophoclean style.

The present chapter will do little toward filling this large gap in Sophoclean studies. We are concerned only with diction in its most obvious relations to dramatic method. But "dramatic diction" would be hard to separate, as an area, from the poet's diction in general. That is why it is necessary to call this chapter "Notes"; it is an incomplete set of comments bearing on some aspects of Sophoclean diction. What is proposed is (*a*) to review very briefly certain general characteristics of Sophoclean diction which have dramatic force; (*b*) to deal a little more extensively with one area in which diction and other aspects of dramatic method are interrelated—the subject of repeated themes; (*c*) within this subject of theme recurrence to treat with some fullness representative examples in which recurrence of themes is most clearly dependent on specific points of diction.

To examine with thoroughness the incidental points of diction that in some way contribute to the dramatic quality of Sophoclean style would involve a complete review of all instances of such rhetorical features as anaphora, alliteration, and other assonances, polarity of expression, enjambment, and colloquialism. There is no point at which "dramatic" usage ends and merely "poetic" usage remains. All that can be done in a reasonable space is to look at a few examples of each of these features wherein a perceptible dramatic effect is produced.

Of all these minor techniques of diction the most conspicuous in Sophocles is anaphora. Like most of these rhetorical usages, anaphora is basically a means of emphasis, bringing two succes-

[2] F. R. Earp, *The Style of Sophocles* (Cambridge, 1944), analyzes Sophoclean diction; R. F. Goheen, *The Imagery of Sophocles'* Antigone (Princeton, 1951), studies the relationship between imagery and dramatic themes in *Antigone*.

sive clauses or statements into close relationship. Where such pairing has a dramatic point, anaphora obviously has a dramatic purpose, and this purpose is most conspicuously served in successive stichomythic lines.[3] The passage that comes to mind first is the celebrated one in *Antigone:*

> Κρ. οὔτοι ποθ᾽ οὑχθρός, οὐδ᾽ ὅταν θάνῃ, φίλος.
> Αν. οὔτοι συνέχθειν ἀλλὰ συμφιλεῖν ἔφυν. [522–523]

Here, of course, the pairing effect of the anaphora underlines the contrast between Creon and Antigone. Less striking but similar in technique and effect is the anaphora of *Electra* 945–946 (ὅρα—ὁρῶ). Anaphora is frequently used, also, where no contrastive or argumentative effect is produced, the word being repeated by a single speaker. Sometimes dramatic force is clear: when the paedagogus in *Electra* urgently summons Orestes to enter the house to kill Clytemnestra, the thrice-repeated νῦν (1368–1369) is dramatic; and in the same play so is the triple σέ in Aegisthus' contemptuous and malevolent words to Electra (1445). But what are we to say of the repeated φθίνει of *OC* 610? That anaphora adds power to this great statement of Oedipus is clear. But is it a dramatic power? To conclude that it is (and probably it is right so to conclude) illustrates the impossibility of firm distinction between dramatic and poetic diction.

Alliteration, too, and other similar assonances, may have direct, tangible dramatic force through their emphasis of the emotion of the speaker. In the angry scene between Oedipus and Teiresias when Oedipus bursts out in abuse:

> σοὶ δὲ τοῦτ᾽ οὐκ ἔστ᾽, ἐπεὶ
> τυφλὸς τά τ᾽ ὦτα τόν τε νοῦν τά τ᾽ ὄμματ᾽ εἶ. [*OT* 370–371]

[3] Omitted, for the moment, are repetitions of words that have, in themselves, an argumentative, characterizing, or other dramatic force. This too is anaphora, of course, but it is also something more. Repetitions of this kind will be considered below, pp. 223–229.

the violent hammering of the *t*-sounds emphasizes the rage of
Oedipus and so sharpens the dramatic point of the speech.
Analogously, Electra's prayer for revenge on the murderers
gains in vehemence from alliterated *p*-sounds:

ποίνιμα πάθεα παθεῖν πόροι. [*Electra* 210]

But more often than not alliteration has no readily identifiable
single effect except the general effect of emphasis. In *Ajax* near
the end of the speech of deception Ajax says:

ὑμεῖς θ', ἑταῖροι, ταὐτὰ τῇδέ μοι τάδε
τιμᾶτε, Τεύκρῳ τ', ἢν μόλῃ, σημήνατε
μέλειν μὲν ἡμῶν, εὐνοεῖν δ' ὑμῖν ἅμα. [687–689]

Here are alliteration and assonance in abundance, first of dentals,
then of nasals. Precisely what effect is achieved it is hard to define,
though there clearly is an effect; and certainly not the same—in
spite of the *t*-sounds—as at *OT* 370–371. It is similarly difficult
to assign a precise emotional force, though again the emphasis
is clear, at *Ajax* 528 (τὸ ταχθὲν εὖ τολμᾷ τελεῖν).

A standard method of achieving emphasis in ancient Greek
is by polarity of expression. Sophocles uses it often. Sometimes
there is no specific dramatic force, as when Neoptolemus says:

χἠ ναῦς γὰρ ἄξει κοὐκ ἀπαρνηθήσεται. [*Philoctetes* 527]

Sometimes this simple rhetorical form can be dramatic, as when
it underlines Antigone's proud "confession" that she has broken
Creon's law:

καὶ φημὶ δρᾶσαι κοὐκ ἀπαρνοῦμαι τὸ μή. [*Antigone* 443]

and in Ajax's mad insistence on flogging "Odysseus" (*Ajax*
113). A particularly striking piece of rhetorical structure serving
a dramatic purpose is the combination of polarity and enjambment when Oedipus wrongheadedly refuses to listen to Creon's
argument:

Skilled are you in speaking, poor am I in learning
From you.

λέγειν σὺ δεινός, μανθάνειν δ' ἐγὼ κακὸς
σοῦ. [*OT* 545–546]

Sometimes a minor feature of diction such as a colloquialism
or an unexpected manner of address can have strong dramatic
impact. Probably the most striking example of dramatic capital
produced out of a colloquial word is in *OT* when the Corinthian
happily addresses the Theban herdsman ὢ τᾶν (1145) at that
moment of excruciating tension, the denouement of the plot.
The abrupt address οὗτος is unusual in the stately diction of
tragedy; in this it is like a colloquialism, whether or not it can
be quite properly so called. Usually it will suggest only the
rudeness of an unpolished and spirited person, as when the
messenger in *The Trachinian Women* accosts Lichas with οὗτος,
βλέφ' ὧδε (402). But on one memorable occasion this form of
address takes on a conspicuous dramatic value, when the divine
voice summons Oedipus:

ὢ οὗτος οὗτος, Οἰδίπους, τί μέλλομεν
χωρεῖν; [*OC* 1627]

Here the abruptness and familiarity underline the combination
of impersonality and intimacy of divine power toward Oedipus.

Examples of these small rhetorical effects and others like
them could be multiplied. The incessant maxims of Creon in
Antigone and the hearty familiarity of Ajax's words to Athena
in the prologue of *Ajax* are examples of a like suiting of diction
to dramatic purpose.

The topic of recurrent themes is complex, and only partially
germane to our inquiry in this chapter. Sometimes themes such
as "justice," "gain," "wisdom," and "piety" dominate a scene,
or a series of scenes, and are marked by a corresponding recurrence of words or word groups. Such recurrent themes clearly
involve questions of dramatic diction, and we shall return to

some theme recurrences of this sort below. Sometimes, on the other hand, recurrence of theme does not involve diction, or involves it only incidentally and in such a way that the reader does not feel that the playwright means to emphasize recurrence of theme by repetitive patterns of words. This kind of recurrence is not primarily a matter of diction and does not concern us here.[4]

One particular branch of this topic of theme recurrence calls for some attention, the kind of theme recurrence that is conveyed by patterns of imagery or by such lyrical means as universalizing statements (e.g., on the power of Eros in Stasimon Three of *Antigone*) or mythological examples (e.g., the examples of imprisonment in Stasimon Four of *Antigone*). This aspect of diction has been given careful and valuable study for just one play in Goheen's *The Imagery of Sophocles'* Antigone. Goheen has examined the main patterns of imagery and related them to the ideas of the play. While such study is almost bound, by the somewhat elusive character of its subject matter, to be inconclusive and to some degree subjective, Goheen's study shows that patterns of imagery can be usefully and substantially related to other questions of dramatic interpretation. To study the plays as Goheen has studied *Antigone* is obviously out of the question here, but it may be useful just to mention very briefly some themes in the plays in which imagery is closely related to the development of dramatic themes.[5]

[4] Cf. Webster, *Introduction*, 107: "Certain ideas run through the plays like coloured threads and hold them together." On pp. 185–186 Webster has lists of recurrent themes in the plays. I am inclined to think that other lists, of equal validity, might be composed for some of the plays. The thematic importance of some of Webster's themes ("Philoctetes' cries," for instance) and the existence of some of them as specific themes ("The gods" in *Trach.* and *Philoc.* but not in the other plays) seem questionable.

[5] Bernard Knox's chapter "Oedipus," in *Tragic Themes in Western Literature*, ed. by Cleanth Brooks (New Haven, 1955), examines some of the imagery of *OT*.

In *Antigone* there are many ideas and events that are related to the key theme of "burial." The pivotal incident of the play is the burial of Polyneices. Antigone's punishment for this act is burial alive. One of the most striking and extensive lyrical passages in the play, Stasimon Four, elaborates on the closely related theme of "imprisonment"; it has a direct connection with Antigone's punishment and hence an indirect connection with the other aspect of the theme of burial. (It may well be that this imagistic link deserves more attention with regard to the relevance of the ode than it generally gets.) The theme of burial, furthermore, is intertwined with another important theme of *Antigone*, that of love.[6] Love for her brother Polyneices lies behind both "burials" of Antigone. In connection with her punishment the image of the "bride of death" is used (e.g., ὦ τύμβος, ὦ νυμφεῖον, 891). The contrast between the intended marriage with Haemon and the marriage with death is pointed; it is in the tomb that Antigone and Haemon are finally united, in death, but with the image of marriage still kept prominent.[7] Thus through the connection of these two themes a kind of metaphorical connection exists between Stasimon Four, on imprisonment, and Stasimon Three, on the power of Eros, and this ode, because of its position, involves the scene between Creon and Haemon as well as the love of Haemon and Antigone. And finally, the Creon-Teiresias scene, with its stress on impious burial and nonburial (1068–1076), is a part of this far-reaching complex of themes and images. The dramatic effect of this linking is hard to gauge and should not, I think, be pressed interpretatively, but that it contributes to unity and tautness of dramatic form is scarcely disputable.

This feature of construction, wherein imagery and theme recurrence are combined, is not peculiar to *Antigone*. In *The*

---

[6] Cf. Goheen, *Imagery*, 37–41.

[7] The messenger says, of the dying Haemon embracing Antigone's corpse: τὰ νυμφικὰ / τέλη λαχὼν δείλαιος εἰν Ἅιδου δόμοις (1240–1241).

Trachinian Women the idea of "the dangers of beauty" is a recurrent theme, involving Deianeira and Iole.[8] There is another theme related to this one by contrast, a "monster" theme. Deianeira was rescued by Heracles from the monstrous bridegroom Achelous. She was tricked and ruined and Heracles was ruined by the monster Nessus. Heracles was constantly involved with monsters (cf. 1089–1102). And there is in Heracles himself, as depicted in this play, a certain bestial, monstrous element. In *OC* the double power of Oedipus to bless and to curse is emphasized by a stress throughout the play on χάρις (of which more below, p. 244) and on the Erinyes, who are present in the background throughout since Oedipus is in their sacred grove.[9] A similar dramatic combination of imagery, theme, and stage circumstances is found in *Philoctetes*, where the high-minded Neoptolemus gradually comes to see that the heroism of Philoctetes is inextricably linked not only with the bow (as at first appeared), but also with the hero's festering, wounded foot.[10]

In *Ajax* the theme of "the sword" is a particularly clear example of this technique, with language, physical properties, and dramatic themes linked and dramatically exploited. Ajax takes his life with the sword of an enemy, with Hector's sword, that "gift that is no gift." It is interesting to see how the sword comes gradually and ominously into greater and greater prominence. At first the references are only metaphorical and indirect: Ajax orders Tecmessa to stop wailing and go into the hut, for "a wise physician does not moan charms over a wound that needs the knife" (πρὸς τομῶντι πήματι, 582); and the chorus

[8] Cf. Webster, *Introduction*, 185, and Linforth, "The Pyre on Mount Oeta in Sophocles' *Trachiniae*," 260
[9] They are recalled when Oedipus curses his sons (1391): καλῶ δὲ τάσδε δαίμονας, and in the chorus's final ode (cf. 1570).
[10] Cf. J. C. Kamerbeek, "Sophoclea II," *Mnemosyne*, 4. 1 (1948), 198–204, for an interesting discussion of the connection between the hero's wound and his daemon.

reinforce the figure in their answer when they express uneasiness at Ajax's "whetted tongue" (γλῶσσα τεθηγμένη, 584). In the next scene the sword appears as a physical reality (τόδ' ἔγχος, 658), and there are dark words about "burying" it. Ajax's language continues the metaphor of the preceding scene: "I, who was firm like dipped steel (βαφῇ σίδηρος ὥς, 651), have grown womanly soft." When we next see Ajax, in the scene of suicide, the sword appears, dramatically, in the opening words, as it does on the stage, fixed and ready to kill:

$$\text{ὁ μὲν σφαγεὺς ἕστηκεν. [815]}$$

There are many more such combinations of imagery and theme, but it would not serve our purpose to multiply examples, particularly in a realm where the dramatic purpose is not always demonstrable beyond question. We turn now to matters of theme recurrence more purely dictional and more certainly a part of the poet's intended scheme.

There are a number of instances in which a repeated verbal pattern, from ode to episode or the reverse, clearly has a dramatic point. In *OT* the ironical involvement of Oedipus in the prayer theme of the parodos has been noticed (above, p. 203). In *Ajax*, as Kamerbeek points out, the excitement of Stasimon Three gains from the fact that in the antistrophe of this song the lyrics repeat a number of themes from Ajax's preceding speech;[11] and Stasimon Two of the same play, by recalling in its second strophe words earlier spoken by Tecmessa, keeps before our minds certain important ideas.[12] Less obvious in its dramatic purpose is Sophocles' occasional way of repeating a word, or echoing a word by using another very similar to it, within an ode. Thus in the parodos of *The Trachinian Women* the first verse of the first strophe and the first verse of the final

[11] Cf. J. C. Kamerbeek, "Sophoclea III," *Mnemosyne*, 4. 3 (1950), 18–20.

[12] Lines 625–626 echo Tecmessa's words in lines 506–507.

epode both have the phrase αἰόλα νύξ; and in *Ajax* the word πτηνῆς near the beginning of the opening choral anapaests is echoed by πτηνῶν near the end of this passage; in *Antigone* the phrase ἐκτὸς ἄτας ends both strophe and antistrophe of the second system of Stasimon Two. While there is not, so far as I can see, any precise dramatic purpose served by these repetitions, the words have a binding effect that increases the feeling of unity in the passages concerned. Dramatic value is clearer in a somewhat similar repetition in *Electra*, Stasimon One, of χαλκό-πλακτος . . . γένυς (484–485) and χαλκόπους Ἐρινύς (491). Here there is the same binding effect, and here the bond between the bronze inexorability of the axe with which Clytemnestra killed Agamemnon and the inexorable pursuit of the Fury has obvious point.

Repetition of themes is not purely a matter of diction, as we have seen in some of the preceding examples. It is primarily an element of structure, and it is often concerned very closely with character portrayal too. Thus it is one part of the σύστασις πράξεως, of "structure" in the broad sense, which is our concern throughout this study. In the rest of this chapter, we shall be concerned with instances where theme repetition is supported by significant word repetition and where, therefore, the element of diction plays a conspicuous part. There is a difference between the repetition of a theme and its repetition in words that are clearly chosen to bring the repetition into sharp emphasis. In *Ajax*, for example, the conflicting ideas of nobility held by Ajax and Tecmessa are, as we have seen, important for the thought of the play; and the continuation of the theme of nobility from one speech to the next would be significant no matter how expressed. But when we find that Sophocles underlines the repetition and the conflict that it conveys by making Tecmessa repeat in a conspicuous place a key word of Ajax's speech (εὐγενής) in order to recall to our minds Ajax's use of that very word, we recognize that the playwright is deliberately strengthening the thematic repetition by a device of diction.

This is the kind of theme repetition that will occupy us in the following pages, but of course the repetition need not be so direct and immediate as it is in this passage in *Ajax*. In *OT*, for example, all through the scene between Oedipus and Teiresias the play on sight and blindness is used to the full by Sophocles. When, later in the action, Oedipus begins to suspect that he is after all the murderer of Laius, it is natural for him to recall the prophet's charges, and, such being the honesty and mag-nanimity of his nature, to acknowledge the likelihood that Teiresias was right and himself wrong. It is therefore a natural consequence of his character for him to express this thought and thus remind us of their dispute. But when he uses, in reference to the earlier scene, a word that instantly recalls the contrast of sight and blindness, "I have a terrible fear that the priest *saw* indeed" (747), we realize again that the playwright is using word repetition to strengthen dramatic effect.

Patterns of word echoes of this sort are a common dramatic device and have often been noticed in Aeschylus and Euripides.[13] They are by no means foreign to Shakespeare: for example, in Act One of *Macbeth* Macbeth's first words, "So foul and fair a day I have not seen," unconsciously echo the Witches' "Fair is foul and foul is fair." That they are both common and of great dramatic force in Sophocles will, I think, be clear from the evidence presented in this chapter;[14] and in Sophocles, con-

[13] Webster, *Introduction*, 184–186, has references to studies of theme repetition in Aeschylus and Euripides. To the references given there, add, for Aeschylus, Eugene O'Neill, Jr., "The Prologue of the *Troades*," *TAPA*, 72 (1941), 294, Note 9; for Euripides, R. P. Winnington-Ingram, *Euripides and Dionysus* (Cambridge, 1948), *passim*.

[14] It is a difficult, and to some degree a subjective, matter to decide what constitutes significant repetition and what does not. It is well known that ancient Greek poets did not seek to avoid repetition even

sonant with the tendency of his dramatic art in other respects, these repetitions often stress an inherent conflict.

Such patterns of repetition, though some effect of contrast is often created by them, are not essentially of an argumentative nature, and the repetition may even be quite unconscious so far as the speaker is concerned, as in the above example from *OT*. There are in Sophocles, however, a great many instances of linguistic usages in which there is a deliberate and effective repetition of words in order to stress some point of argument. This kind of repetition is a regular and characteristic feature of stichomythia in all three tragic poets and need not occupy us for long. But it may be worth while to notice a few Sophoclean examples of this device and some related instances where conflicting views are stressed by other techniques of diction.

In *The Trachinian Women*, when Hyllus has managed to break in on Heracles' wrathful monologue, he tries to defend his mother by insisting on the innocence of her intentions. Heracles' answer rejects Hyllus' defense and makes the rejection by repeating one key word of Hyllus' sentence but substituting a different word for a second key word:

Υλ. ἅπαν τὸ χρῆμ' ἥμαρτε χρηστὰ μωμένη.

Ηρ. χρήστ', ὦ κάκιστε, πατέρα σὸν κτείνασα δρᾷ; [1136–1137]

The repetition of χρηστά is in the usual manner of stichomythia, but it stresses with more than routine effectiveness the contrast between intention and act (μωμένη—δρᾷ); to Hyllus the important fact is Deianeira's intention; to Heracles only the actuality matters, for it alone affects him.

---

when there was no specific point in the repetition. (For an impressive list of unconscious repetitions in Sophocles' plays, see John Jackson, *Marginalia Scaenica* [Oxford, 1955], 220–222.) The reader will probably question the validity of some examples adduced in this chapter; but I have tried to avoid instances wherein the likelihood of adventitious repetition is great.

In Teucer's debate with Menelaus and Agamemnon in *Ajax* there is a good deal of argumentative stichomythia, and the conflict of thought is often expressed by an interlocking pattern of word repetition, one short example of which is worth noticing. In line 1125 Teucer declares:

With *justice* on one's side, it is right to speak with pride.

Menelaus echoes the word "justice" in his reply:

Is it *justice* for Ajax to be honored, who *killed* me?

The new theme introduced by Menelaus is at once repeated, argumentatively, by Teucer:

Killed you? A marvel, if you live though dead.

In the following pair of lines a new argumentative repetition occurs (θεός—θεούς), and so on. There is nothing remarkable in these lines, in thought or diction, but they demonstrate clearly this technique of interlocking repetition to emphasize conflicts. I add one example, not stichomythic, from the scene between Teucer and Agamemnon: Agamemnon in his long opening speech refers to Ajax as a "nothing" (τοῦ μηδέν, 1231; cf. ἀνδρὸς οὐκέτ' ὄντος, 1257); in his answer, Teucer echoes this rather striking phrase and turns it back upon all the Greeks except Ajax:

When in the rout of battle, you were nothing

(τὸ μηδὲν ὄντας). [1275]

The conflict of personality and of outlook between the two sisters in *Antigone* in the prologue and in their meeting at the end of the second episode is couched everywhere in verbal antitheses, and the following group of examples is only one aspect of the contrast. Toward the end of the prologue, when Antigone knows that her sister will not join her in disobeying Creon, she wants to separate herself completely from Ismene;

Ismene on the other hand, gentle and sympathetic, still would feel some spiritual union with her sister, even though she cannot bring herself to act with her. To this theme of conflicting attitudes there is a marked verbal contribution, related to the aspects of diction that we are now concerned with, though in this case it is not a question of repetition. Ismene repeatedly expresses a wish for association with Antigone: "I fear *for you*" (82), "Hide the deed, and I shall, *with you*" (85). Antigone constantly insists on separation: "*Don't* feel fear *for me*; attend to *your own* fortunes" (83); "Speak it aloud" (86; in answer to "Hide," in 85). This is perhaps not yet more than the mere conveyance of their thoughts necessitates; but in their second meeting the language used by each of the sisters is markedly adapted in its very form to their opposing desires. Ismene's words are in form associative: συμμετίσχω (537), ξύμπλουν (541), σὺν σοί (545), ἴση νῷν (558). Antigone speaks in antitheses: οὔτ᾽ ἠθέλησας οὔτ᾽ ἐγὼ ᾽κοινωσάμην (539), σὺ μέν . . . ἐγὼ δέ (555), σὺ μὲν τοῖς, τοῖς δ᾽ ἐγώ (557), σὺ μὲν ζῇς, ἡ δ᾽ ἐμὴ ψυχή . . . (559). There is no virtuosity about the selection of words, but the cumulative effect of the opposing word patterns is striking.

A favorite polar expression in ancient Greek literature is that between word and deed. It is no stranger to Sophoclean diction: Antigone uses it in censuring Ismene's unwillingness to act (*Antigone* 542–543); it occurs in Odysseus' lessons in falsehood to Neoptolemus in the prologue of *Philoctetes* (99); there is a particularly extended and meaningful use of it in *Electra*, in the scene between the heroine and her mother where it serves to emphasize the theme of "shame" that we have noticed before. Defending her conduct, Electra declares that her mother's deeds (ἔργα, 620) force her to behave as she does. Clytemnestra exclaims, "I and my words and my deeds bring too many words from you" (622–623)! Electra's reply is a remarkable example of the linking and emphasizing effect of word repetition:

σύ τοι λέγεις νιν, οὐκ ἐγώ. σὺ γὰρ ποεῖς
<u>τοὔργον</u>· τὰ δ' <u>ἔργα</u> τοὺς <u>λόγους</u> εὑρίσκεται. [624–625]

One other passage in *Electra* is especially worthy of quotation:

Ηλ. ἄπελθε· σοὶ γὰρ ὠφέλησις οὐκ ἔνι.
Χρ. ἔνεστιν· ἀλλὰ σοὶ μάθησις οὐ πάρα. [1031–1032]

The whole shape of these two contrasted lines contributes to the antithesis; they are parallel at beginning and end, and the key words, ὠφέλησις—μάθησις, are as nearly as possible in identical position both grammatically and metrically. The two words are a summary of the basic difference in outlook between Electra and Chrysothemis: Electra's emphasis is on her sister's unwillingness to help; to Chrysothemis, Electra's proposal of action is sheer folly.

Many more examples of this method of stressing opposing points of view by means of word repetitions and related linguistic effects could be adduced. But let us turn now to the point of diction that mainly concerns us in this chapter, the emphasis of dramatic themes by means of words or phrases that strikingly recall significant previous occurrences of the word or word group. The importance of such repetitions varies from simply providing a minor dramatic thrill by incidentally recalling a situation, attitude, or characteristic to serving as the vehicle for a major theme of the play.

Let us notice first a few relatively slight examples from *Ajax*. In the "speech of deception" Ajax declares that he will "bury" his sword (κρύψω τόδ' ἔγχος, 658). Later events show that the word here had the hidden meaning of burial in Ajax's body. When the hero commits suicide, the audience might recall this striking phrase even without a reminiscence. To ensure that it is recalled the playwright echoes it in Tecmessa's words at the moment when Ajax's body is discovered:

Here Ajax lies newly slain, folded around his buried sword (κρυφαίῳ φασγάνῳ περιπτυχής). [898–899]

Tecmessa's verse on "grace,"

$$\chi \acute{a} \rho \iota \varsigma \ \chi \acute{a} \rho \iota \nu \ \gamma \acute{a} \rho \ \dot{\epsilon} \sigma \tau \iota \nu \ \dot{\eta} \ \tau \acute{\iota} \kappa \tau o \upsilon \sigma' \ \dot{a} \epsilon \acute{\iota}, \quad [522]$$

is unforgettably and hauntingly beautiful. I do not think that it is fanciful to suppose that her later words, when she learns that Ajax has probably left his tent to commit suicide, are meant to recall this theme. She says that she has been "cast forth from the grace of old" ($\tau \hat{\eta} \varsigma \ \pi a \lambda a \iota \hat{a} \varsigma \ \chi \acute{a} \rho \iota \tau o \varsigma \ \dot{\epsilon} \kappa \beta \epsilon \beta \lambda \eta \mu \acute{\epsilon} \nu \eta$, 808). She is referring to the fact that Ajax has now deserted her. It was suggested above that the reference to "grace" in this later passage hints at a former relationship of intimate affection and trust between Ajax and Tecmessa, for all the harshness of the warrior. This line, then, adds a new luster to the earlier one: when Tecmessa spoke of "grace that brings forth grace," she meant, at least in part, the $\chi \acute{a} \rho \iota \varsigma$ that existed between her and Ajax.

In the second part of *Ajax*, concerned as it is with the question of Ajax's burial, it is only natural that the theme of "justice" should be prominent; but the marked reiteration of words of the root δικ-, especially in the mouth of Odysseus at the end, goes beyond the bare necessity of expressing the theme. Teucer begins the theme of justice when he declares that he will justly ($\delta \iota \kappa a \acute{\iota} \omega \varsigma$) bury Ajax (1109–1110) in spite of Menelaus; the theme enters into the debate between Teucer and Menelaus ($\xi \grave{\upsilon} \nu \ \tau \hat{\omega} \ \delta \iota \kappa a \acute{\iota} \omega$—$\delta \acute{\iota} \kappa a \iota a$, 1125–1126); it comes again in the Teucer-Agamemnon scene ($\tau o \grave{\upsilon} \varsigma \ \delta \acute{\iota} \kappa \eta \ \nu \iota \kappa \hat{\omega} \nu \tau a \varsigma$, 1248, and Teucer's reply, $\mathring{a} \rho' \ \dot{\upsilon} \mu \hat{\iota} \nu \ o \mathring{\upsilon} \tau o \varsigma \ \tau a \hat{\upsilon} \tau' \ \ddot{\epsilon} \delta \rho a \sigma \epsilon \nu \ \ddot{\epsilon} \nu \delta \iota \kappa a$; 1282). When Odysseus enters at the end, there can be no question of an argumentative intention on his part in the repetition of the theme, since he was not present in the scenes which his words recall: "Never let violence of spirit so master you that you trample justice underfoot" ($\ddot{\omega} \sigma \tau \epsilon \ \tau \grave{\eta} \nu \ \delta \acute{\iota} \kappa \eta \nu \ \pi a \tau \epsilon \hat{\iota} \nu$, 1334–1335); "it would not be just for him to be dishonored by you" (1342); "it is not just to injure a good man when he has fallen" (1344–1345).

The theme of justice is not the only one that Odysseus' words echo. In the debate between Menelaus and Teucer, Menelaus is reduced, under the insistent thrusts of Teucer, to admitting that his hostility to Ajax is a simple matter of hatred: μισοῦντ' ἐμίσει, "I hated him and he hated me" (1134). In the remarkable summing-up by Odysseus, the verb μισεῖν is three times repeated: τοσόνδε μισεῖν, 1335; οὐδ' ἐὰν μισῶν κυρῇς, 1345; ἐμίσουν, 1347. The verbal echo reinforces the difference of attitude between Odysseus and the sons of Atreus. Odysseus too hated Ajax, "when it was fair to hate him" (1347); but when the hero is dead, Odysseus has the breadth of vision to see beyond personal hostility. Menelaus and Agamemnon lack this vision.[15]

In *The Trachinian Women* there are several effective minor reinforcements of theme by word echoes. In making her declaration of devotion to Heracles and her refusal to go on living if he dies, Deianeira puts her resolve in these words:

ταύτῃ σὺν ὁρμῇ κἀμὲ συνθανεῖν ἅμα. [720]
By that same impact I too shall die.

The passage is a memorable one, and it may be supposed that even a slight reminiscence of it has intentional force. When, not much later, Hyllus quotes his father as urging him to approach and help him, even if it means that he must die with him (εἰ χρὴ . . . συνθανεῖν ἐμοί, 798), the repetition quietly provides ironical commentary on the difference of outlook between Deianeira and Heracles.[16] Deianeira in her speech to Lichas refers to Iole as τῇ μεταιτίᾳ / τοῦ μηδὲν αἰσχροῦ (447–448). This preliminary reference lends added force and pathos to the later similarly worded but very different designation of Iole by Hyllus when he recoils in horror from his father's demand that he marry her (ἥ μοι μητρὶ μὲν θανεῖν μόνη / μεταίτιος, 1233–1234).

[15] It is worth recalling that there is a strong element of verbal reminiscence in Odysseus' words at line 1359, echoing Ajax at lines 682–683. Cf. p. 109 above.

[16] The contrast between their verbally similar final apostrophes provides a similar commentary. Cf. p. 117 above.

When Deianeira at the conclusion of Hyllus' description of the suffering of Heracles silently withdraws to take her own life, the chorus exclaim τί σῖγ' ἀφέρπεις (813)? They are appalled at her refusal to justify herself and thus they emphasize her selflessness. Hyllus, on the other hand, infuriated by what seems to him an act of treacherous revenge on Heracles, wants no explanation and is glad to see her gone (ἐᾶτ' ἀφέρπειν, 815). When later, having meanwhile learned the truth about the robe, he tries to explain matters to Heracles, his words echo those of the chorus and thus emphasize his change of feeling toward Deianeira:

> ἔχει γὰρ οὕτως ὥστε μὴ σιγᾶν πρέπειν. [1126] [17]
> The case is such that silence is not right

A more extensive verbal theme than any of these is a series of passages hinging on words for "secrecy." The first passages have to do with Iole and the stealth of her introduction into the house. Deianeira, on hearing that the beautiful girl before her was the real reason for Heracles' latest exploit, exclaims, "What is this secret bane (πημονὴν λαθραῖον) that I have received into my house" (376–377)? A few lines below the chorus burst out in anger at what Heracles has done:

> May doers of evil perish, or such of them as practice
> secret evils (λαθραῖα κακά). [383–384]

The words foreshadow the secret deed that Deianeira is soon to perform with such lamentable results. There is much talk by Deianeira about the "secrecy" of her plan: when she announces it to the chorus she tells them that she has come to them "in secret" (λάθρᾳ, 533); a little later, in an attempt to bolster her own confidence about an undertaking that she clearly feels to be of a dubious nature, she says:

---

[17] Possibly Heracles' subsequent silence about Deianeira is a continuation of this theme of silence.

If in darkness (σκότῳ) you practice evils, you will not suffer shame. [596–597] [18]

As soon as she discovers her error, she declares (669–670) that she "would never advise anyone to be caught with enthusiasm for a hidden deed" (προθυμίαν ἄδηλον ἔργου).

The use of word echoes is more pervasive and more striking in *Antigone* and *Electra* than in any of the other plays. Several of the themes of *Electra* that are emphasized in this way have been discussed at some length in our study of the characters in Chapter III. Our attention in the rest of this chapter will be mainly upon *Antigone*, with a few briefly noticed examples from *Electra*, *Philoctetes*, and *OC*. There are three major examples in *Antigone*, all involving themes of cardinal importance for the action.

Conflicting definitions and implied definitions of "good sense," "good counsel," "wisdom," and the like run through much of the play. In the prologue Ismene several times defends her refusal to join in the plan to bury Polyneices on the grounds that the act is contrary to good sense. Her one long speech (49–68) begins with a demand that Antigone "take thought" (φρόνησον, 49) and ends with the declaration that to engage in matters "outside one's scope" (περισσά, 68) is not sensible (οὐκ ἔχει νοῦν οὐδένα, 68). Antigone reacts to this declaration but does not exactly counter it; instead, she sarcastically bids Ismene leave her to her "folly" (τὴν ἐξ ἐμοῦ δυσβουλίαν, 95). Just at the end of the prologue Ismene, in declaring her affection for her sister, reverts once more to the theme (ἄνους, 99).

The notion of wisdom or the lack of it is thus introduced in relation to Antigone's conduct, but this contrast in attitude between the two sisters is not developed; we have noticed in Chap-

---

[18] The interpretation of the passage to mean "suffer evils" was mentioned above (p. 114n.) but not accepted. The strong verbal emphasis on the secrecy of Deianeira's deed is a further reason for taking αἰσχρὰ πράσσειν here in its usual sense of "practice evils."

ter III how Sophocles capitalizes on the same theme in *Electra*. In *Antigone* it is with Creon that the theme of "sense" is developed. In the scene between father and son Haemon's first long speech takes up the theme. Haemon tries to change his father's will by diplomacy and reasonable argument. The youth begins with a generalization on the importance of wisdom:

> Father, the gods endow mankind with sense (φρένας),
> and this is the best of all our possessions. [683–684]

Not, he hastens to add, that he would say that his father is wrong—and yet no man can of himself know all things, and in the present case there are many in Thebes who think that Antigone deserves reward rather than punishment; it is for Creon's own good to consider the strength of this opposing thought. Such is the tenor of Haemon's opening paragraph, and it culminates with another rather pointed generalization: the man who thinks that he alone has wisdom (φρονεῖν, 707) is likely to be proved a fool. The next part of the speech is entirely devoted to the notion of wisdom, prudence, and the acceptance of good advice: it is no discredit, even to a wise man, to learn much (μανθάνειν πολλά, 710–711); if I, young man though I am, can offer wise counsel (γνώμη, 719), it is best to accept it; and finally (ending with a generalization as he began), since no man is likely to know all,

> καὶ τῶν λεγόντων εὖ καλὸν τὸ μανθάνειν. [723]
> It is wise to learn also from those who counsel well.

The chorus repeat the theme in their mild way (εἰκός . . . μαθεῖν, 724–725), and Creon seizes on it angrily: at my age to be taught wisdom (διδαξόμεσθα δὴ φρονεῖν) by a youth! The following stichomythia returns, after other matters, to this discussion of "sense" when Haemon, now speaking more directly though still with emotions controlled, refers to his father's plans as "empty" (753), and in angry retort Creon calls his son "empty

of wits" (φρενῶν κενός, 754); in return Haemon, with dignity
and exemplary restraint, declares: "Were you not my father,
I should say that you lack wisdom" (οὐκ εὖ φρονεῖν, 755).

Within this scene the repetitions are, of course, argumentative and therefore not quite identical with unconscious echoes
like those at the end of *Ajax*. But when the same pattern of
terms recurs in the scene with Teiresias and again in the final
kommos, we see that the playwright is deliberately echoing the
theme for a broader purpose than just the immediate argument
of one scene. When Teiresias solemnly avers that good counsel
(εὐβουλία, 1050) is the chief of all possessions, we cannot fail
to hear echoes of Haemon's opening words. And here again
Creon angrily takes up the challenge, though his retort (that
lack of wisdom [μὴ φρονεῖν, 1051] is the greatest evil) is no
more than abuse. (The argumentative nature of his reply is
marked by anaphora: ὅσῳ [1050] answered by ὅσῳπερ [1051]).
When Teiresias launches his terrible prophecy of disaster against
Creon, he concludes it with another reference to the theme of
wisdom, bidding Creon learn to "nourish better wits than he
now bears" (νοῦν ἀμείνω . . . τῶν φρενῶν ὧν νῦν φέρει, 1090).
When Teiresias has left, Creon begins to weaken, and the chorus
dare offer him advice. Their advice echoes the solemn declaration of Teiresias (and the urging of Haemon), for they say,
εὐβουλίας δεῖ (1098). The theme of "sense" is beginning to recoil
on Creon. In the kommos with which the play ends, the theme
is heard repeatedly, and the reversal suffered by Creon is under-
lined by the verbal echoes. Three times Creon laments his lack
of sense: ἰὼ φρενῶν δυσφρόνων ἁμαρτήματα (1261); ὤμοι ἐμῶν
ἄνολβα βουλευμάτων (1265); ἐμαῖς . . . δυσβουλίαις (1269).
At the very end, in their final words, the chorus twice go back
to the theme; they generalize, but the direct application of their
words to Creon is beyond question—these final anapaests are
not the colorless generalities that final choral tags usually are,
and the close verbal link with the theme of sense shows this

clearly: "The first part of happiness by far is wisdom" (τὸ φρονεῖν). Their last words, and the last words of the play, are

γήρᾳ τὸ φρονεῖν ἐδίδαξαν.

The theme has recoiled in full on Creon.

A similar thread of terms concerning "piety" runs through the play. If the theme of wisdom involves chiefly the ideas and attitude of Creon, that of piety involves both principals equally. The theme is first significantly voiced in the scene between Creon and the unhappy guard who has had to report the burial of Polyneices' body. Creon, who is at this point and for long after convinced that he is at one with the will of the gods, lectures the guard mercilessly, and, assuming that the watchmen have been bribed by a hostile faction in the city to do the deed, he holds forth on the evils of bribery, culminating with the thought that money teaches men "to know every kind of impious deed" (παντὸς ἔργου δυσσέβειαν, 301). This is a generalization, but that he has the burial in mind (and hence is in effect calling that deed an act of impiety) is obvious; from the general statement he turns at once to a reference to that act (302–303). A few lines later when he threatens dire punishment to the perpetrators, he makes his revenge a matter of piety ("If Zeus still has reverence [σέβας] from me" [304]). The words are echoed in the scene between Antigone and Creon. To Antigone with her forthright and simple attitude the issue is clear: it is right to have reverence for (σέβειν) one's kin (511). But to Creon politics and religious feeling are all one: Polyneices was a traitor and hence impious (τῷ δυσσεβεῖ, 516); therefore, a mark of respect for him is a mark of disrespect toward Eteocles (ἐκείνῳ δυσσεβῆ, 514). The completely alien channels of thought of Antigone and Creon have been noticed above; here we can observe how their contrasted use of these key words fits and enhances the general contrast between them.

In the debate between Creon and Haemon the theme is further

developed. Creon seems haunted by the notion of "piety," and when Haemon argues on Antigone's behalf Creon sarcastically inquires whether he is to "reverence (εὐσεβεῖν) those who are lawless" (731); a little later, without a trace of sarcasm, he makes the same shortsighted identification of politics and religion as he did earlier when he asks if he is wrong "in revering my own power as king" (τὰς ἐμὰς ἀρχὰς σέβων, 744). Haemon's answer points out precisely the confusion in Creon's thinking, and the precision is sharpened by repetition of the key word:

οὐ γὰρ σέβεις, τιμάς γε τὰς θεῶν πατῶν. [745]
It is not reverent to trample on divine prerogatives.

But Creon is not able to focus on this simple logic as yet and takes refuge in abuse. At the end of the episode, when Haemon has left, Creon (though he is weakening: he decides to spare Ismene and technically to avoid guilt for Antigone's death, 771, 775–776) continues with the theme of "reverence," shouting that he will send Antigone to Hades, "whom alone of the gods she reveres" (ὃν μόνον σέβει θεῶν, 777), that she may learn that it is "inordinate toil to revere (σέβειν) the realm of Hades" (780). Creon is close, here, to meaningless tirade; but it is far from meaningless that the concept that preys on him is "reverence." And we can see that he is still, though confusedly, working on the assumption that divine power—some divine power, at any rate—supports his edict.

After this repeated emphasis on "piety" in relation to Creon's outlook, we next come upon three very striking instances of the same word pattern in application to Antigone, in her kommos, her last iambic speech, and her anapaestic lines as she finally leaves the scene. In the kommos it is the chorus who introduce the theme in their cautious judgment of Antigone's case (872–875); they cannot endorse her disobedience, but one great merit they hesitantly allow her:

σέβειν μὲν εὐσέβειά τις. [872]

The phrase is not perfectly clear; I take it (with Masqueray, as against Jebb [19]) to mean "your reverence for Polyneices is an act of piety." The basic intent of what the chorus are expressing is clear: they find a contrast between Antigone's piety (which is good) and her disobedience (which must lead to punishment). Thus they compromise between the point of view of Creon, to whom piety and obedience to his edict are the same (cf. 744), and Haemon, who asserts that piety is right and law that conflicts with it wrong (cf. 745). In her following iambic speech Antigone declares that she has gained "through piety the name of impious" (τὴν δυσσέβειαν εὐσεβοῦσ' ἐκτησάμην, 924).[20] It is interesting to notice that she is here echoing not so much Creon's direct attack on her in their scene, nor the chorus's judgment, as she is the intervening development of the theme in the scene between Creon and Haemon, of which she is unaware. Antigone's last words are a further echo of the same theme, this time couched in self-confident and challenging terms: "Behold, Thebans, the punishment I win,

$$\text{τὴν εὐσεβίαν σεβίσασα. [943]}$$

This theme too, like that of "wisdom," is repeated in the final words of the chorus:

$$\text{χρὴ δὲ τά γ' ἐς θεοὺς}$$
$$\text{μηδὲν ἀσεπτεῖν. [1349–1350]}$$

Here there is no distribution of praise for piety and blame for disobedience; the unmistakable meaning of the chorus's words is that Creon's actions were impious. Antigone is cleared.

---

[19] The new Budé text of *Antigone* by Dain and Mazon (1955) interprets the phrase as Masqueray did.

[20] Schadewaldt, "Aias und Antigone," 86, takes Antigone's words to mean that her reverence has literally brought her to impiety, not only to the reputation for impiety. This improbable interpretation springs from Schadewaldt's supposition that the whole speech is meant to suggest that Antigone has changed her point of view and now sees a conflict between her personal piety and the piety that is her duty as a member of society.

No less important for the meaning of the play, though less frequently repeated, is a word pattern concerning the issue of "law." The main moment of discussion is, naturally enough, the scene between Antigone and Creon. When Creon challenges Antigone on her disobedience: "And did you then presume to go beyond my laws (τούσδε νόμους)?" (449), the very word νόμους is like a cue for which Antigone has been waiting, and she proceeds to give her famous speech on "law." Echoing Creon's words (τοιούσδε . . . νόμους, 452), she then declares her allegiance to the ἄγραπτα κἀσφαλῆ θεῶν νόμιμα (454–455). Creon is, of course, deaf to this thought and presently equates the breaking of his law with *hybris* (480–481). Creon has already, earlier in the play, shown that to him the law of the gods and the law of Creon are identical (ἐκείνων . . . νόμους διασκεδῶν, 287), and to this idea he stubbornly clings. In his speech on "eunomia" (639–680) he castigates "the man who violates the laws" (663); it is a generalization, but it arises from Antigone's disobedience. Finally, the regenerate Creon, just as he recanted about "wisdom," has a change of heart about "law" also and fully accepts the concept of law expressed by Antigone in lines 454–455. As he speeds vainly on his way to try to undo the damage which his law has wrought, he declares ruefully:

> It is best, I fear, to go through life observing the estab-
> lished laws (τοὺς καθεστῶτας νόμους). [1113–1114]

The established laws, as the context clearly shows, are the ἄγραπτα νόμιμα of Antigone.[21]

21 Cf. Jebb's note *ad loc.* in his edition of *Antig.*
Other themes given prominence by repetition in *Antig.* include discussions of κέρδος (especially in the Creon-Teiresias scene) and of περισσός (in relation to Antigone's character and conduct). One slight but very fine word echo involves lines 79 and 907. In the prologue Ismene declares that she cannot act βίᾳ πολιτῶν. In her famous speech of "explanation" Antigone says that she has acted βίᾳ πολιτῶν, though earlier she was sure that the citizens sympathized with her. The repetition has sometimes been used as evidence that the passage is spurious. In view of Sophocles' subtle and careful use of such repetitions it seems more rea-

240   *A Study of Sophoclean Drama*

In *OT* we have already dealt in some detail with the contrast between the blindness and vision of Oedipus and Teiresias in their scene together and the recurrence of the theme at line 747; we have mentioned also the significant repetition of τύχη by Jocasta and Oedipus in the third episode. There are other patterns of repetition that we might notice, but instead of amassing all available evidence let us pass on to *Electra*, which ranks with *Antigone* in the abundance and the importance of its word echoes.

In discussing character portrayal we noticed that the contrast between Electra and Chrysothemis is supported by striking differences of concept about good and evil and about wisdom and folly. Here it will suffice to analyze just one of these themes from the point of view of its realization in a pattern of word echoes. We noticed above that to Chrysothemis "good" and "bad" have only a material, never a moral, meaning: "good" means comfort and well-being, "bad" means suffering and disadvantage. Electra thinks primarily, almost exclusively, of the moral connotations. Before her encounter with her sister, Electra has said what she thinks good and bad mean in her situation: loyalty to her father is good (237); and in line 308 the phrase ἐν τοῖς κακοῖς means, as the context clearly shows, the spiritual intolerableness of the present state. Later she tells Chrysothemis that she will "appear evil in the sight of the many" (πλείστοις κακή, 367) if she does not avenge her father; she calls Chrysothemis' efforts to dissuade her from thoughts of revenge an attempt to "teach me to be evil (κακήν) to my friends" (395). Chrysothemis never once attaches a moral meaning to the words: Electra's threatened imprisonment is κακὸν μέγιστον (374); the

sonable to regard it as a proof of genuineness. The phrase is one indication, among others in the speech, of a loss of confidence on Antigone's part. (Cf. also above, pp. 163–165.) Schadewaldt, "Aias und Antigone," 84, notices the repetition but goes too far, I think, in supposing that it means that Antigone's whole attitude toward what she has done has changed.

avoidance of trouble is καλόν (398); the suffering that Electra is likely to undergo for her rebelliousness is evil (σὺν κακῷ μέτει, 430).

These examples are from their first meeting; in the second the contrast continues. Urging Chrysothemis to co-operate, Electra insists further on equating good conduct with carrying out the revenge (989), while Chrysothemis is still morally unconscious. When rejoicing because she thinks that Orestes has returned, she exclaims that "the present day will perhaps provide πολλῶν καλῶν" (919); she clearly means not the moral triumph of revenge but its material advantages. When she hears that Orestes is dead, she laments that she nows finds ἄλλα κακά "further sorrows" or "troubles" (937). In arguing the folly of Electra's desperate plan for revenge without Orestes' help, she warns:

> Take care lest, faring ill, we bring upon ourselves still greater evils (μείζω κακά) [1003–1004]

—not the evil of failing to take revenge but the troubles that will follow an unsuccessful attempt. And at the end of the episode she warns her sister that through her folly she will be involved "in evils" (ἐν κακοῖς, 1056); once again the context shows that the evils are those of disadvantage, not moral evils.[22]

[22] There is a further most striking and puzzling use of "good" as a theme in *Electra* in the phrase καλῶς ἔχει and similar phrases. In view of Sophocles' attentiveness to such matters it is tempting to agree with Sheppard's view that there is an ironical force in the repeated phrase (cf. J. T. Sheppard, "*Electra*: A Defence of Sophocles," *CR*, 41 [1927], 2–9). Just before the murder of Clytemnestra is committed, Orestes asks the paedagogus, "How is it within the house?" (1339); the reply is καλῶς. A few lines later the paedagogus darkly says: καλῶς τὰ κείνων πάντα, καὶ τὰ μὴ καλῶς (1345). The same faintly ominous note is heard again just after the murder. Electra asks, "Orestes, how do you fare" (1424)? and Orestes answers: καλῶς, 'Απόλλων εἰ καλῶς ἐθέσπισεν. Once again at the very end the same theme is touched on, and again there is a suggestion of doubt. When Orestes drives Aegisthus into the house to kill him, Aegisthus asks: "Why, if the deed is good (καλόν), does it need

The patterns of word repetition supporting the themes of "sense" and of "shame" in this play, no less distinct and emphatic, have been noticed above in our discussion of the characters. One small point concerning the linguistic emphasis on the theme of "sense" should be added, because it is a very revealing example of Sophocles' procedure in this matter. As we have seen, all through the play, "sense" (νοῦς) means to Chrysothemis self-protection and submission; to Electra it means awareness of moral duty. At one point Chrysothemis bids her sister to "get sense" (νοῦν σχές) and not fight with those who are stronger (1013–1014). Just at the end of the play, when Aegisthus enters, Electra phrases her ironical "submission" in words that strikingly recall, not only the typical attitude of Chrysothemis, but her exact words at line 1013; Electra says: τῷ γὰρ χρόνῳ νοῦν ἔσχον (1464–1465). The force of these ironical words is considerably increased by the fact that they form part of a pattern.

The fundamental conflict of *Philoctetes*, though it is outwardly embodied in the persons of Philoctetes and Odysseus, resides also within Neoptolemus. There is a moral conflict centered in his "nobility" and his "nature" as he is influenced by the two older men. Odysseus is acutely aware of Neoptolemus' pride in his natural nobility and does what he can to relate "nobility" to his plans. Philoctetes is just as aware of Neoptolemus' nobility, and in his very different way he too tries to turn it to his advantage. The two words that embody this conflict

darkness" (1493–1494)? And just a moment later Aegisthus refers (prophetically?) to the μέλλοντα Πελοπιδῶν κακά (1488). I think there can be no doubt that Sophocles means to create an atmosphere of shadow and questioning by this play on καλόν and κακόν. It is one more element in the enigmatic emotional and moral situation at the end of this play.

There is the same questioning air about recurrent uses of the phrase καλῶς ἔχει by Electra, after the report of Orestes' death. Cf. lines 790, 791, 793, 816.

are γενναῖος and φύσις. In the prologue Odysseus insists that Neoptolemus must be noble (δεῖ γενναῖον εἶναι, 50–51) but in a strange way (52); and this strange nobility presently turns out to be the accomplishment of their purpose on Lemnos by means of trickery. Philoctetes' attitude toward nobility is summed up in words that are in complete contrast to those of Odysseus; Philoctetes insists that

> to men of noble nature (τοῖσι γενναίοισι) a base act seems hateful, a worthy act seems glorious. [475–476]

Odysseus, in later recognizing the conflict between Neoptolemus' nobility and his obedience to him, uses this same word; ordering the young man back to the ship, he tells him to pay no attention to Philoctetes, "noble though you are" (γενναῖός περ ὤν, 1068). The theme of "nature" (φύσις) also begins in the prologue, when Odysseus, with unwonted frankness, recognizes that stealth is not likely to appeal to Neoptolemus:

> I know well, my son, that you are not by nature fit (φύσει μὴ πεφυκότα) to speak or to contrive such base matters. [79–80]

Neoptolemus himself echoes the theme of nature in his pathetic words when he knows that he cannot go on with the deception of Philoctetes: "Everything is bitter when a man deserts his own nature (τὴν αὐτοῦ φύσιν)" (902–903). Before this, Philoctetes has recalled the theme: "You are noble by nature (εὐγενὴς γὰρ ἡ φύσις) and descended of noble men" (874). Finally, when at the end Neoptolemus is entirely won over to him and has returned the bow and rejected Odysseus, Philoctetes declares: "You have revealed the nature (φύσιν), my son, from which you are sprung" (1310).[23]

[23] There are two passages in *Philoc.* (79–85 and 473–481) which sum up very strikingly the two opposing influences at work on Neoptolemus. The phraseology of the two passages is so similar that the playwright seems to have intended to stress the contrast by verbal reminiscence. Both

We have already noticed that the theme of "grace" plays a conspicuous part in *Oedipus at Colonus*. The word χάρις recurs all through the play. It describes the relationship between Oedipus and Theseus (and with him Athens). At line 586, for example, it refers to the favor that Oedipus asks of Athens (τήνδε χάριν); at lines 636–637 it refers to the still undefined benefit that Oedipus is to bring to Athens (χάριν τὴν τοῦδε), as it does also in lines 1489–1490 (τελεσφόρον χάριν δοῦναι) and in the words of the chorus at line 1498 (δικαίαν χάριν παρασχεῖν παθών—here the notion of mutual grace is present). The same word describes the love between Oedipus and his daughters (σὺν πόθῳ γὰρ ἡ χάρις, 1106); the hatred between Oedipus and Creon is described as a lack of χάρις (767, 779). Just at the end of the play the word occurs in a context that suggests that the earthly χάρις that has existed between Oedipus and Theseus, Athens, and his daughters, has now been transcended by a divine, "chthonic grace":

ἐν οἷς γὰρ

χάρις ἡ χθονία ξύν᾽ ἀπόκειται [24]

πενθεῖν οὐ χρή. [1751–1752]

Odysseus and Philoctetes begin their pleas by recognizing the "difficulty" they are presenting to Neoptolemus, and both use the same word (ἔξοιδα, 79, 474) to introduce the comment. Both imply recognition of Neoptolemus' nobility (φύσει κτλ., 79; τοῖσι γενναίοισι, 475); both bid him "dare" (τόλμα, 82; τόλμησον, 481), and the echo emphasizes the antithesis between what each bids him dare; both ask his help for just a part of a day (ἡμέρας μέρος βραχύ, 83; ἡμέρας . . . οὐχ ὅλης μιᾶς, 480); both speak of the reward that will follow (κτῆμα τῆς νίκης, 81; εὐκλείας γέρας, 478). (The repetitions in the final choral words of *Antig.* and in Odysseus' words near the end of *Aj.* are similar in effect.)

[24] The MSS have ξυναπόκειται (or συν-); the meter requires long -ᴗ-, which is easily obtained by Reisig's slight change: ξύν᾽ ἀπόκειται. Pearson prints Martin's conjecture νὺξ ἀπόκειται. This weakens the concept of Oedipus' "grace," which has now become a "chthonic" gift. In view of the theme of χάρις in close connection with Oedipus throughout the play, I think that there can be no doubt that Reisig's reading is the right one. Jebb so reads, and interprets correctly, in his note *ad loc.* in his edition of *OC*.

The word acts as a binding device, giving unity to the feeling that exists between Oedipus and those who deserve his favor.

A curious minor word echo in *OC* is our last example of this feature of Sophoclean drama. Several times in the play there is a mysterious emphasis on the value of "a word." [25] In his first great denunciation of his sons Oedipus tells how he was sent by them from Thebes as a beggar and an exile, "for the sake of one small word" (ἔπους σμικροῦ χάριν, 443)—because they were not willing to say the word of defense that would have allowed him to stay in Thebes. In the messenger's speech we are told that Oedipus, just before his disappearance, spoke to his daughters of the toil that they had endured and must still endure; then he told them that "one word alone" (ἓν μόνον ἔπος) assuages all these hardships (1615–1616). The word is "love" (τὸ φιλεῖν, 1617). Similar phrases are found twice elsewhere: ἐν σμικρῷ λόγῳ (569) and ἐκ σμικροῦ λόγου (620). Each time the phrase is Oedipus'; what precise point the repetition has I do not profess to understand, but it is in harmony with the stress in this play on simple and fundamental moral values. And there is a pleasantly paradoxical touch in the emphasis on a "little word" in this most ample of Sophoclean plays.

Not much need be said in conclusion about the importance of these instances of the reinforcement of themes by patterns of word echoes. That they contribute significantly to Sophocles' dramatic art is surely beyond doubt, though their contribution is seldom obvious, because it is always part of a larger unity: the verbal theme of χάρις in *OC*, though it clearly exists and can be spoken about as a separate entity, is entirely subordinate to the wider theme of the blessing and the curse that Oedipus brings; the echoing, conflicting meanings of νοῦς and καλόν in *Electra* subserve the wider contrast between the two sisters. And so it is with all these themes; the patterns of verbal echoes

[25] This theme is commented on by J. A. Mackail in his essay entitled "Sophocles," in *Lectures on Greek Poetry* (London, 1910), 141–173. See especially p. 150.

constitute one means, among several, whereby interplay of character and basic themes in the development of the action are infused with ever-increasing force. These word patterns play no small part in fashioning and maintaining the dynamic aliveness of a Sophoclean dramatic action.

CHAPTER VI

The Irony of Sophocles

"DRAMATIC IRONY" is a concept that is dangerous to define too closely. In two of the best studies of irony in literature the authors have overcome this hazard by the prudent expedient of not defining the term[1] or by defining it with a protean flexibility: "The whole attitude of the interested spectator."[2] But assuming, as I think we properly can, that tragedy and irony are not conterminous, we shall in the present chapter try to see to what extent Sophoclean tragedy is ironic and what bearing irony has on the structure and meaning of Sophoclean drama.

"Sophoclean irony" is a well-worn term, often used to mean that kind of verbal irony wherein the speaker's words have one meaning for him and another, significantly different and in some way contrasting, for the audience. Familiar above all from *Oedipus Tyrannus*, this irony might almost better be called Oedipodean than Sophoclean, so exclusively is it applied to the verbal irony of this one drama. But word play is the lowest level of dramatic irony. It is on the whole unfortunate that it should be accepted as the irony characteristic of Sophocles, for

[1] J. A. K. Thomson, *Irony* (Cambridge, Mass., 1927).
[2] G. G. Sedgewick, *Of Irony, Especially in Drama* (Toronto, 1948), 33.

taken by itself it is, though dramatically useful and sometimes even exciting, comparatively slight.

There is a further reach of irony that is a common feature of most tragedy. It is based on the "irony of fate" which has been called "the contradiction between 'is' and 'seems' in the working of destiny and circumstances." [3] Dramatic irony exists when the playwright exploits this "practical irony" (as Thirlwall termed it [4]) in the presentation of his play or creates, by means of artificial contrasts between "is" and "seems," situations to be exploited. The whole framework of *OT* is dramatic irony of this sort—not only when the irony of the situation is verbally emphasized but just as much when, without a word of "Sophoclean irony," Sophocles exploits a discrepancy between what is and what seems. The short scene in which Oedipus, the Corinthian messenger, and the herdsman are involved is (as Sedgewick observes [5]) a superb example of dramatic irony, without a word of verbal irony: all three men have different approaches to the central issue, the identity of Oedipus. We are aware of these differences from the beginning of the scene and are therefore alert to their consequence for the behavior of the persons and for the tension of the scene. The old herdsman, the only one of the three who shares knowledge of the truth with the audience (we know in advance that he knows [6]), speaks with terrified reluctance; the Corinthian, with his affable, talkative "helpfulness," is the reverse of reluctance; watching both, in grim determination to know the truth, stands Oedipus. The audience, in full knowledge, sees error and awareness moving irresistibly to a clash and to catastrophic resolution.

[3] *Ibid.*, 21.

[4] Connop Thirlwall, "On the Irony of Sophocles," *Philological Museum*, 2 (1833), 483–537. For the term "practical irony," see p. 485.

[5] *Of Irony*, 39–41.

[6] We have been told (758–762) that "as soon as he saw" Oedipus in power, "he begged to be sent into the fields . . . as far from the sight of the city as he could be."

The type of irony wherein the playwright devises artificial contrasts through the deception of one character by another provides the setting for some of the most theatrically rousing scenes in Greek tragedy: the deception of Aegisthus by Electra and Orestes in Sophocles' *Electra*, Clytemnestra's heartless blandishment of Agamemnon in *Agamemnon*, and the inhuman luring of Pentheus to destruction by Dionysus in *The Bacchae*. The situation is not quite the same as in the exploitation of a "natural" irony such as that of *Oedipus*; in the irony of deception there must always be someone who shares the audience's attitude, and the victim may be the only one deceived, as in the final scene of *Electra* and in *The Bacchae*. There is not, moreover, the same sense of inevitability about a contrived situation. But both are ironies of situation, distinct from verbal irony and not dependent on it.

To summarize the types of irony mentioned, we could say that dramatic irony is the exploitation by the playwright of situations, natural or artificial, in which one or more characters are unaware of the true state of things; the exploitation may, but need not, involve the use of language with double meaning.[7]

Perhaps this statement is too lacking in precision to give any real form to the concept of dramatic irony. But it is difficult to be more precise without becoming involved in distinctions that are very hard to justify. One writer on irony, dissatisfied with the definitions (or indefinitenesses) of Thomson and Sedgewick, adds the qualification that "an ironical state of mind . . . is in part a comic point of view."[8] This comic element (the argument proceeds) depends on a sense of detachment; thus an audience does not "feel irony in the catastrophe of *Othello*"

[7] This definition agrees substantially with that of S. K. Johnson, "Some Aspects of Dramatic Irony in Sophoclean Tragedy," *CR*, 42 (1928), 209–214.

[8] Alan Reynolds Thompson, *The Dry Mock* (Berkeley, 1948), 33.

because "we are not *detached* from Othello and Desdemona," and "if we are not detached from painful things we cannot be amused by them." *Oedipus*, on the other hand, is regarded as ironic: "Shakespeare was not making game of the Moor," whereas "in a limited sense Sophocles was making game of Oedipus by letting Fate make game of him; and therefore we think of the Greek play as ironical, but not Shakespeare's." It is difficult to see in what way Shakespeare was not allowing Iago to make game of Othello, if we say that Sophocles was making game of Oedipus. It is true that in *Othello* there is not so much emphatic verbal irony as in *Oedipus*, but verbal irony is not essential, nor does the proposer of this distinction suggest that it is. It is true also that there is a difference between the natural situation of *Oedipus* and the artificial situation of *Othello;* but elsewhere the same critic finds the equally artificial situation of *The Bacchae* highly ironical.[9]

It is hard to see wherein lies any decisive difference other than a subjective difference of response: the critic whom I have quoted does not feel detached from Othello and Desdemona; by implication he indicates that he does feel detached from Oedipus. If my reaction is the opposite—and since there is in the circumstances of the two plays no basic difference to prevent this from being the case, it may well happen—I might declare *Othello* ironical and *Oedipus* not. It is presumably to fill this loophole of subjectivity of response that Sedgewick in his definition stipulated that irony depends on the reaction of an "*interested* spectator." Given that two playwrights both utilize in some meaningful way the latent possibilities of irony, it is better to allow for different types of irony than to try to make distinctions that are necessarily subjective.

To return to Sophocles' ways of exploiting and creating ironies: Our ultimate aim is to assess the value of irony for his

[9] *Ibid.*, 183.

drama; but first it will help to make some further analysis of the various types of irony used by him.[10]

We have distinguished between the "naturally ironical" situation—Oedipus unknowingly in pursuit of himself, Deianeira unwittingly destroying what she seeks to keep—and the contrived irony wherein a conscious deception is practiced: the deception of Philoctetes by Neoptolemus, of Clytemnestra by the henchman of Orestes, of Aegisthus by Electra and Orestes. In either type, the irony of situation may make its effect simply by its existence in the dramatic action, or it may be marked by verbal irony. For example, the action at the end of *Electra*, when Aegisthus approaches the corpse of Clytemnestra supposing that it is Orestes who lies there dead, is ironical: Aegisthus, unaware of the true situation, joyfully walks toward his death. We know at the beginning of the incident what will happen, and so Sophocles is exploiting the irony dramatically, quite apart from such verbal ironies as Orestes' assurance that Clytemnestra "is near you" (1474) as Aegisthus steps forward to remove the shroud.

In the deception of Philoctetes there is almost no verbal irony in the words of Neoptolemus until just before the appearance of the "merchant," and yet the irony of the situation is exploited throughout, simply by our awareness of it—an awareness which the playwright has ensured by preparation for it in the prologue. The same dual possibility applies also, of course, to situations of natural irony. In *Antigone*, after Creon's inaugural address to the chorus, the guard enters, and in the

[10] One type of irony need only be mentioned: the everyday irony, the commonest type of all, in which a person says one thing and quite consciously and without any intention of deceit means another. I give one example from Sophocles: Electra says to Chrysothemis, *El.* 393, "A good life is this of mine—wonderfully so!" This is a purely verbal irony, without dramatic point unless made dramatically meaningful by an irony of circumstance.

following scene Creon inveighs against the burial of Polyneices' body on the assumption that the guards have done the deed, bribed by disaffected citizens of Thebes. From the prologue we know who buried the body; in the present scene there is a play on Creon's ignorance, which is exploited as a means of illustrating his suspicious and tyrannical nature. The situation itself provides the irony, without the reinforcement of ambiguous language.

It may be said that in general Sophocles' irony depends less on the effect of two-edged words than on the effect of the ironical situation itself. Perhaps most of the ironical situations in Sophocles are emphasized by verbal ironies, but it is incorrect to suppose that these are the essence of Sophocles' irony.

Oedipus Tyrannus is only partially an exception. We cannot think of the irony of this play without thinking of its verbal ambiguities, and many of them are of great dramatic value. The speech at the beginning of the first episode (216–275), in which Oedipus offers his aid to the stricken city and calls upon the citizens to help, is the *locus classicus* of "Sophoclean irony"; from the beginning, when he calls himself "stranger to the story . . . and stranger to the deed," through the solemn curse that he so pointedly lays upon himself ("if he shares my hearth," 249), to the harrowing double meanings in his references to Laius' offspring and his own (260–262), the speech is alive with this kind of word play.[11] Verbal irony is common elsewhere in the play too. For example, on the entrance of the Corinthian

---

[11] A good deal of the irony, especially the verbal irony, of the earlier part of *OT* seems to require for its effectiveness some prior knowledge of the story by the audience. The same could be said of some of the irony of *Trach.* (cf. below, pp. 256–258). Yet in view of Aristotle's remark (*Poetics* 1451 b 25–26) that "even the well-known stories are well-known only to a few, and yet give pleasure to all," one hesitates to rely much on the assumption of prior knowledge. Did Sophocles have in mind the pleasure of those who would read his plays, as well as the "few" in the audience who could appreciate the more learned ironies?

messenger in search of Oedipus, the chorus say that the king is within but (indicating Jocasta) that "this woman is his wife and mother—of his children" (928).[12] Yet, though we may rightly admire the skill and force with which Sophocles has exploited the ironical theme verbally, it is a mistake to let our appreciation of his irony end with that. More potent irony resides in the mere fact of Oedipus: at once the protector of his people and the source of their destruction; the keen-eyed solver of riddles and the deluded blind man; the hunter and the hunted; the tower of rectitude and the repository of sin.

As a matter of fact, as later dramatists who have used the story have discovered, Sophocles did not press very far, let alone exhaust the verbal ironies provided by his plot, especially in the relationship of Oedipus and Jocasta. Critics have pointed out that Sophocles' Jocasta, in her role as peacemaker and then as would-be comforter, acts like a mother to Oedipus; the irony of this is never expressed in ambiguous words. It remained for others to exploit in full the possibilities of this motif for verbal irony, not only the post-Freudian Gide and Cocteau but Dryden and Voltaire too. To appreciate the moderation of Sophocles' touch in verbal irony, it is instructive to compare Dryden's *Oedipus*, where the mother-son relationship is exploited to the full.

> OEDIPUS: No pious son e'er lov'd his Mother more
> Than I my dear Jocasta.

Jocasta's reply is an eight-line broadside of irony, culminating with

> when I have you in my arms, methinks
> I lull my child asleep.

---

[12] The dash which I have used seems a legitimate way of representing the pause made by ἥδε between γυνὴ δὲ μήτηρ and τῶν κείνου τέκνων. The irony is helped, as Masqueray points out (note *ad loc.* in his Budé edition), by the fact that the natural pause of the line is after ἥδε.

There are almost identical passages, perhaps influenced by Dryden, in Voltaire and Gide. In the same scene Dryden indulges in other equally heavy ironies. Jocasta enters just as Oedipus finishes his curse on the murderer of Laius (borrowed from Sophocles but laid on with a much heavier hand), which ends:

> And the same Fate or worse, than Laius met,
> Let be his lot: his children be accurst;
> His Wife and kindred, all of his be curs'd.

Jocasta's first words are:

> At your Devotions! Heav'n succeed your wishes;
> And bring th' effect of these your pious pray'rs
> On you, on me, and all.[13]

Almost as if afraid that the audience might not appreciate the fact that this is irony, Dryden has Oedipus rather prosaically point out Jocasta's error to her:

> Why, we were cursing.

A little later Jocasta unfortunately says:

> Be thou like my Lajus.

Again Dryden runs the irony into the ground:

> OEDIPUS: This imprecation was for Lajus death,
> And thou hast wish'd me like him.

There are more of these "touches" in the same scene.

The verbal irony of *Oedipus Tyrannus* is never so unrestrained as this, and some of the most telling effects of irony come about with no verbal irony. When, for example, Jocasta's prayer to Apollo (911–923) is seemingly answered immediately by the arrival of the Corinthian, the effect of the prayer is, in

[13] Possibly the irony of prayer in this passage is borrowed from the prayers of Jocasta (*OT* 911–923) and Clytemnestra (*El.* 634–659).

retrospect, ironical in the extreme; the full irony is not apparent until we (along with Jocasta) realize that the Corinthian's news about the origins of Oedipus means the revelation of the hidden truth. In the development of this irony there is no two-edged language at all, but rather a two-edged event—an answer to Jocasta's prayer that seems favorable but is adverse. It was pointed out above (p. 213), moreover, that the irony of the prayer is introduced by the spirit of the preceding choral ode. Similarly, in the irony of Oedipus' address to the Thebans, one element springs simply from the ironic contrast of the choral prayer to the gods and the acceptance of the burden of that prayer by Oedipus (216); [14] here again the irony is of situation rather than of words, even though in the rest of the speech verbal irony is much used.

No one questions the prevalence of irony in *OT*. But in the other plays how important for Sophocles' presentation of his tragedies is irony? Provided we grant that dramatic irony need not be chock-full of pungent verbal effects, we may answer that it is conspicuous in all the plays and is integral to the life of four others beside *OT*: *Ajax*, *The Trachinian Women*, *Electra*, and *Philoctetes*.

The plot of *Ajax*, as we have seen, depends on a contrast between the heroic single-mindedness of Ajax and the non-heroic, broad-minded wisdom of Odysseus. No doubt the contrast could have been developed without irony; significantly Sophocles makes it an essentially ironic contrast: Odysseus, the enemy of Ajax, is the one man with the good sense to recognize the worth of Ajax and to ensure that proper tribute is paid to him. There is no doubt that Sophocles intends this irony. From the prologue on, the hostility of the two men is kept before us: in the prologue Odysseus refers to Ajax as "my foe" (78); it is Odysseus above all (even more than the Atridae) who is the imagined victim of Ajax's mad violence (101–113); the Salamin-

[14] Cf. above, p. 203, and Sheppard's edition of *OT*, pp. xx–xxi.

ian sailors at their first entrance assume that Odysseus is working against their leader (148–150); Ajax supposes that Odysseus
is gloating over his downfall (379–382); Tecmessa assumes
that Odysseus is somehow responsible for the death of Ajax
(952–953); in the final scene Odysseus again reminds us that he
and Ajax were enemies (1347); and at the end Teucer again
brings the matter to prominence when he declines Odysseus'
help in burying Ajax. There is a structural advantage in the
sheer unexpectedness of a man's bitterest enemy turning out
to be his only preserver.

The Trachinian Women is rich in implicit ironies: that
Heracles, mightiest of heroes, is brought low by a woman; that
the dead Nessus should destroy the living Heracles; that the
"rest" promised to Heracles should be death; that the maiden
for whom Deianeira's tenderest sympathy is felt is the cause
of disaster to Deianeira. One irony is at the very center of the
action: that Deianeira, whose whole life is devoted to Heracles
and whose admiration and love for him are unbounded, should,
just because of her love, bring about his destruction.

Here is a play, then, that is no less involved in ironies than
OT, and yet we hear very little from critics about its ironies.
This is partly, no doubt, because it is read less and thought
about a great deal less often than *Oedipus;* but it may also be
because there are not so many strong verbal ironies as in
Oedipus. Some of these are in no way inferior in subtlety to
those of *OT*, if less compelling. When Deianeira first speaks,
quite vaguely, of sending "gifts" to Heracles, she bids Lichas
enter the house in order that he may take "what gifts may fittingly be sent in return for gifts" (494)—in return, that is, for
the "gifts" that Heracles has sent, i.e., the spoils of Oechalia,
including Iole. The word here paraphrased "fittingly be sent"
(προσαρμόσαι) is a strange word in this use; its literal meaning
is "to fit closely," and, of course, the audience is expected to

detect (in retrospect, at least) its secondary reference to the clinging of the poisoned robe. The slight oddness of the word and the fact that it does not fit quite comfortably in its context help to mark this subtle verbal irony. (Jebb in his note *ad loc.* thinks that there is a third meaning in the word, a reference to the robe, of which Deianeira is conscious—not, of course, to its fatal clinging to Heracles' body, but only to its fitting as a garment. This would explain Deianeira's choice of the word.)

Deianeira makes a further unconscious reference to the deadly nature of her gift to Heracles just before Lichas leaves. She has just told Lichas how the robe is to be handled and goes on to explain why she sends such a garment:

> For I made a vow that if I ever saw him safe at home,
> or heard of his approach, in all justice I would deck
> him in this tunic and show him to the gods, a sacrificer
> of novel aspect, clad in a novel garment. [610–613]

"In all justice" (πανδίκως) means to Deianeira "in consequence of my vow," and perhaps also because of "a wife's natural sympathy." [15] To the audience it means also the unintended justice of Deianeira's gift in return for Heracles' wretched treatment of her. "Novel" does not adequately render the double meaning of καινός, both "new" and "strange." Deianeira (as Jebb explains [16]) calls Heracles a "novel sacrificer" only as an extension to the wearer of the "new radiance" of the garment; the adjective belongs in sense only to "garment." In the unconscious meaning (Heracles will be a grimly novel sacrificer) the application of the adjective to the wearer is of primary importance.

The main irony of the play depends not on a trick but on the failure of a trick. It is thus the product of a naturally ironical situation rather than of a deception, and so it is closer to the irony

---

[15] Jebb, note *ad loc.* in his edition of the play.   [16] Note *ad loc.*

of *Ajax* and *OT* than to that of *Electra*. It is a case of circumstances working a trick on a character rather than of one character deceiving another.

Antigone has no such well-marked irony of situation. It is true that Creon, a selfish man, himself loses everything through his selfishness. But this self-destruction through the attempt at self-aggrandizement is only a variant of a basic theme of popular morality, the fall of the man of pride and violence. There is, in *Antigone*, no sufficiently sharp pointing of the theme of selfishness to allow us to speak of a precise irony. We have already referred to the irony of Creon's accusation of the guards, to which the pomp of his solemn address just before adds force, and there are other incidental ironies in the play, but nothing so pervasive or central to the theme as in *Ajax* and *The Trachinian Women*.[17]

Electra and *Philoctetes*—and these plays alone—are marked by instances of ironical situations deliberately contrived by persons in the plays. In *Electra* there are two such situations, the deception of Clytemnestra, and incidentally of Electra, by the speech reporting Orestes' death in the Pythian games, and the deception of Aegisthus at the end. The second of these is

---

[17] There may be intentional irony in the fact that Creon, when he sets out to undo the wrongs he has done, loses his chance to rescue Antigone (and thus also Haemon and himself) because he takes time first to make amends to the gods by burying Polyneices. But the irony is uncertain. We cannot assume that Creon would have been in time to save Antigone if he had gone directly to the cave. Also, there is no direct explanation in the play of why the order of activities suggested by the chorus (1100–1101, to rescue Antigone first and then to bury Polyneices) was not followed. Moreover, there is a good dramatic reason, quite unconnected with irony, for having the events reported in the present order, as Jebb points out (his edition of *Antig.*, pp. xviii–xx): to have the burial reported after the events at the cave would be wretchedly anticlimactic. On the whole, then, it seems doubtful whether irony is intended. But see Reinhardt, who thinks that the "Zu-Spät" of Creon is part of his *daimon* (*Sophokles*, 100–101).

the vehicle for an extraordinarily rousing finale. The earlier deception is less theatrically thrilling, but it is of more importance to the play as a whole, because it sets the course for Electra's moods and actions until the recognition is achieved. In the recognition scene the original deception is reinforced by Orestes' deception in delaying to reveal his identity. Here again is a situation of contrived irony.

There is a further irony in *Electra*, more essential to the tragedy than these two acts of deliberate deception: the irony of the situation of the sternly moral Electra, who is driven by her unflinching loyalty to the moral course of action into conduct which she herself recognizes as immoral. Here again is a "natural irony" lying close to the main theme of the play, as in *Ajax, The Trachinian Women,* and *Oedipus Tyrannus.*[18]

In *Philoctetes* there are other ironies besides the hero's deception by Neoptolemus. Of the deception little need be said. We noticed above that there is not much conspicuous verbal irony throughout most of it; but just after Philoctetes' long and pathetic appeal to Neoptolemus to rescue him (468–506), when the chorus have announced their willingness to endure the presence of the hero on board ship (522–523), Neoptolemus replies with words that are intentionally and pointedly ambiguous: "It would be disgraceful for me to be shown more grudging than you in advantageous service for this stranger" (524–525). "Advantageous" (πρὸς τὸ καίριον) is ambiguous: to Philoctetes it means his advantage—to be taken home; Neoptolemus and the chorus realize that it refers to the advantage of the Greek army at Troy and to the military ambitions of the youth himself. The speech ends with "May the gods carry us safely from this

---

[18] Another important instance of irony in *Electra* is the incident of Clytemnestra's prayer, which, exactly like Jocasta's, is answered by news seemingly favorable to the suppliant but in reality deadly. There is also the contrived irony of Electra's pathetic speech as she holds "Orestes' ashes" in an urn, while Orestes stands before her. As we saw above (Chapter III, Note 33), this passage has a force additional to its pathos.

land to wheresoever we wish to sail" (528–529). Again the vagueness is intentional (emphasized by the optative βουλοίμεσθα, even if it is optative by attraction [19]). Neoptolemus of course intends their voyage to be to Troy, but Philoctetes can naturally suppose that he means Skyros or Euboea, where he has suggested that he might be taken.

A more telling irony lies in the fact that Neoptolemus, even as he succeeds in his deception of Philoctetes, falls more and more under his influence until he is unable, just at the point of complete success (with Philoctetes urging that they leave at once), to go on with the deception. We have traced the course of this contrapuntal irony above in discussing the interaction of characters in the play: the very quality of Neoptolemus that makes Philoctetes an easy victim for him, the nobility of outlook which Philoctetes perceives and responds to, ultimately makes it impossible for Neoptolemus to succeed in the deception. We are prepared for this development by the prologue, where we learn very clearly that Neoptolemus regards his role of deceiver with profound distaste. We can scarcely fail to watch for signs of his weakening under the pressure of his obvious spiritual kinship with Philoctetes.

In discussing the interaction of character between Philoctetes and Odysseus above (pp. 148–150), we mentioned in passing the irony that is implicit in the fact that it is the morally questionable Odysseus who is on the side of deity ("It is *Zeus*, know well, *Zeus*, ruler of this land, yes, *Zeus* who has decided thus [that Philoctetes is to go to Troy]; I serve his will" 989–990), and that Philoctetes, though at the moment his reply is a rejection ("You make a pretext of the gods," 992), in the long run submits when at the end Heracles substantiates the claim of Odysseus, making clear beyond all doubt that it is the will of Zeus that Philoctetes go to Troy. Here once more as in *The*

[19] As Jebb says, note *ad loc.* in his edition of the play.

Trachinian Women, OT, and *Electra* there is an irony of situation in the very nature of Sophocles' theme.

Oedipus at Colonus, just as it differs in spirit from the other plays in many respects, is less ironical in theme than any of the others. There is, of course, one irony inseparable from the person of Oedipus: the outwardly helpless Oedipus is the possessor of a mighty inward strength. It is the irony of sight and blindness repeated from *OT* and reversed. The irony is apparent to the audience throughout; for before the incident in which Oedipus' physical helplessness is most stressed—the encounter with the chorus in the parodos—we have already in the prologue been given a clear indication of Oedipus' power to bless and curse (87–93). This irony is important for the progress of the action. The final resolution of the irony, symbolized by the inspired departure of Oedipus (1540–1555),[20] is the dramatic climax of the play; yet as irony it is much less gripping than many other instances of slighter thematic significance. For the most telling kind of irony is that in which somebody is threatened by disaster—tragic irony as opposed to merely dramatic irony. The irony of *OC* is without this tragic force, just as the play as a whole lacks the grimness of most of Sophocles' extant plays.

This incomplete summary of ironies in the seven plays is enough to show that irony pervades Sophoclean drama. A question of some importance for the understanding of Sophoclean dramatic method arises from this fact. Granted that Sophocles uses ironies in abundance, is irony essential to Sophoclean tragedy, an integral part of the poet's portrayal of life, or is it a method of procedure, a device of structure that is in the last analysis external? It is pertinent to remember that there is a very close connection between irony and another important

[20] The choral ode of 1211–1248, its spirit in strong contrast to the following behavior of Oedipus, contributes to this irony. Cf. above, pp. 201f.

element in the plays of Sophocles—contrast. That irony is essentially a species of contrast was pointed out by Lewis Campbell in his note on the dramatic irony of Sophocles, which he wrote as a protest against the use of the term "dramatic irony," maintaining that what Thirlwall had so designated could more properly be termed "pathetic contrast." [21] The term dramatic irony has persisted in spite of Campbell's objection; but there is no question that he is right in insisting that irony is a type of contrast, for the soul of dramatic irony is contrast between what seems and what is. Irony, then, is simply one important aspect of that technique of contrast that underlies a good deal of Sophoclean dramatic style.

It is doubtful whether it is ever possible to differentiate between an artist's thought and a technique of presentation so pervasive and all-embracing as contrast—including irony—is in Sophocles. The artificial ironies of *Electra* and *Philoctetes*, since they are not essential to the themes of the plays, are perhaps to be ascribed to theatrical utility. But with the natural ironies of the plays the case is surely different. In the story of Oedipus the thing that struck Sophocles above all was the element of contrast implicit in the theme. Another dramatist might have concentrated on the notion—also implicit in the traditional theme—of inherited guilt (Aeschylus probably did so); or he might have made the story one of sin and its punishment or of the pathetic downfall of a martyrlike innocent. But to Sophocles the theme meant an Oedipus who was at once the most magnificent of men and yet blind, the most intelligent of men and yet ruined by his own actions. So in *Philoctetes* Sophocles was struck by the contrast of the high-minded rebel against the will of deity and the tricky servant of deity; in the story of Ajax, by the ironical interplay between the enemies, Ajax and Odysseus; in *Electra*, by the dilemma of a morality that neces-

[21] Lewis Campbell, "Note on the So-called Irony of Sophocles," I, 126–133, of his second edition of the plays (Oxford, 1879).

sitates immorality. If we try to describe the outlook of Sophocles we cannot omit irony. Sophoclean drama is stated largely in terms of contrast because Sophocles saw things in terms of contrast and was deeply aware of the ironies of human experience. The shape of Sophoclean drama is the expression of the playwright's view of life, and an integral part of that view is contrast, not least that contrast between "seems" and "is" that is called irony.

Is Sophocles' outlook, then, primarily a bitter one? If the kind of irony that pervades *Oedipus Tyrannus*, *Ajax*, and *The Trachinian Women* is the basis of Sophocles' view of life, then that view is bitter, for the irony of these plays is bitter: the annihilation of the most magnificent of rulers, the humiliation of the greatest of warriors, the confounding and destruction of the gentlest and most devoted of women. At the end of Chapter III in our discussion of the character of Sophocles' tragic heroes, the point was made that, for all the differences in the leading persons of the seven plays, they are alike in that they suffer partly because they are endowed with qualities at once admirably heroic and humanly imperfect; the notion of man as the plaything of fate is foreign to Sophoclean tragedy. But we noticed too that there is, in addition to the characters' responsibility for suffering, cruelty in the very terms of life as Sophocles presents them. This cruelty is largely identical with the irony we are concerned with now—irony that is a part of Sophocles' tragic view of life and goes beyond dramatic technique, though it is inseparable from it. Sophocles' dramatic technique is not just an artificially contrived structure, produced by the playwright's stagecraft. It is also an artistic representation of human life, resulting from the poet's intuition of its circumstances. In Chapter III we found that the portrayal of the tragic hero is the culmination both of an intricate and profound understanding of human character and of a complex and patient technique.

Sophoclean irony of situation, also, is a combination of dramatic system and poetic view.

It is not a view that is readily understood. It is subtle and mysterious rather than luminous and rational, and any attempt to define the whence and why of this irony of situation must be conjectural. At the same time irony is an essential problem in Sophoclean drama, and it is therefore worth while to suggest even a tentative answer to these questions Whence and Why.

It is usual to regard deity as responsible for human suffering. But as soon as we look with some care at the presentation of deity in the plays we find that this is anything but a satisfactory answer. There are several different religious outlooks in the plays, and it will not do to seize on the attitude in some one group of passages, as is often done, and call it the Sophoclean view. From all sides we get conflicting views: the morality and justice of the gods are sometimes asserted and sometimes denied; the gods are declared to be capricious and cruel and yet their help is regularly expected and invoked for human aspirations; sometimes the gods are thought of as beings who are jealous of their prerogatives, but at other times divine will is equated with the impersonal action of fate. Although it is difficult to find any satisfying pattern in this bewildering variety, we can reduce the seeming chaos to a few conspicuous and largely traditional religious attitudes.

In the parodos of *Ajax* the sailors fear that Ajax's madness may have been inflicted on him by Artemis in anger at some slight offered, on a hunting expedition, to her prerogatives (172–178). This is a Homeric outlook, with deity jealous of its honor (τιμή) and ready to take umbrage at any injury to it. A less naïve and more sinister note, of unpredictable and unexplained cruelty, is sounded in many passages: Ajax complains that Athena is torturing him (*Aj.* 401–403; cf. 455–456); Oedipus cries that Apollo brought on his sufferings ('Απόλλων τάδ' ἦν, *OT* 1329); Hyllus rails against the injustice and cruelty of the gods (*Trach.* 1266–1274); Philoctetes avers that the gods protect the base (*Philoc.* 447) and "finds the gods evil" (452). Similarly, Oedipus and Philoctetes declare that they are hated by the gods (*OT* 1345–1346, *Philoc.* 1020); and Ajax rejects the gods (*Aj.* 590). All these attitudes, though differently shaded, form a coherent kind of thought: deity is hostile to human endeavor, and if it takes account of man at all it does so only to knock him down, for no moral reason.

A commoner attitude or group of attitudes states that the gods are dispensers of all things good and bad: "At god's will all men laugh and sorrow," sing the chorus of *Ajax* (383); and Teucer later in the play declares that gods "contrive" everything that comes to men (1036–1037). Creon in *Antigone* declares that it is the gods who have shaken Thebes and righted Thebes (162–163). In the parodos of *The Trachinian Women* the chorus sing that Zeus brings a cycle of joys and sorrows to all men (126–131); and the closing lines of the play ascribe all that has happened—for good or ill—to Zeus: κοὐδὲν τούτων ὅ τι μὴ Ζεύς.[22] No man can escape the power of deity (*Aj.* 455–456, *El.* 496–497, *OC* 252–254); the gods alone have full knowledge (*OT* 498–499); the gods alone are steadfast and unchanging (*OC* 607–609). To this notion of the control, power, and knowledge of the gods answers the oft-heard advice that unquestioning piety is best: χρὴ δὲ τά γ' ἐς θεοὺς μηδὲν ἀσεπτεῖν (*Antig.* 1349–1350); that, as Neoptolemus says, "men must bear the fortunes sent to them by the gods" (*Philoc.* 1316–1317); that one must trust in the gods (*Philoc.* 1374); that εὐσέβεια is of highest importance (*Philoc.* 1440–1443). From this idea of

[22] The last four lines of *Trach.* are ascribed to Hyllus in some MSS, by an ancient commentator, and by many editors. But the recent work on Sophoclean text history by Turyn, De Marco, and others indicates that the MS tradition for ascription to the chorus is much stronger; ascription to Hyllus seems to be an ancient variant from the standard tradition. The new Budé edition (1955) ascribes the words to the chorus.

the unlimited power of deity and the consequent need for reverence and for an acceptance of what the gods send, it is not a long step to the concept of deity that merges with the impersonal notion of that which must be: fate, chance, and the like. Hence there occur phrases like πρὸς θεῶν εἱμαρμένα (*Trach.* 169), πότμος δαιμόνων (*Philoc.* 1116), θεία τύχη (*Philoc.* 1326), θεῶν ἐπὶ συντυχίαις (*Antig.* 157). In this second area of religious attitudes the basic concept is unmoved, impersonal deity, whose main attribute is power, to whom terms of morality do not apply, and who is neither hostile nor friendly to humanity. Man must obey and trust but cannot hope to comprehend.

There is still a third set of religious feelings, in which the interest of the gods in the affairs of men is asserted or assumed —not the hostile, jealous, and selfish interest implicit in the first group of passages above, but a helpfulness or a sponsoring of moral rectitude. The help of the gods is prayed for, or is assumed, in every kind of activity. Even Ajax, who at times regards himself as hated and rejected of heaven, in his final speech (815–865) calls upon Zeus, Hermes, Helius, and the Erinyes to carry out his will, and even earlier he bids Tecmessa pray to the gods to bring about "what my heart desires" (685–686);[23] and Calchas, as reported by the messenger, hopes that Ajax can yet be saved, σὺν θεῷ (779). There is scarcely one important figure in any of the plays who does not at some time assume that deity, or some specific deity, will help him.

Such invocations need not and often do not have any moral implication. But almost as numerous are the statements or assumptions that divinity supports what is morally good and punishes evil. In *Ajax* we have the word of Athena that the gods

---

[23] Perhaps these words are spoken in bitter irony, inasmuch as Ajax has said before that he owes nothing to the gods (590). But since in his next speech he calls on the gods in a way that cannot be ironical, it is as reasonable to take the present passage as spoken in earnest as to take it to be ironical.

"love the modest man and hate the wicked" (132–133). In *Electra* the sympathetic chorus bid Electra entrust her anger to Zeus (173–176); the implication is clear that Zeus will support her righteous cause. Later the chorus equate loyalty to moral rectitude with devotion to Zeus (1095–1097), and Electra herself regards the crimes of Aegisthus and Clytemnestra as "impiety" and assumes that the gods punish such deeds (1382–1383). In *Antigone* both Antigone and Creon think that what they take to be morally right has divine sanction (e.g., *Antig.* 77, 282–287, 450–460). The chorus of *Antigone* assure us that Zeus hates men of boastful words (128–129). Lichas in *The Trachinian Women* is sure that the gods do not tolerate *hybris* (280). Philoctetes, embittered though he is, "knows" that the gods have a care for justice (1035–1039). Finally, the old Oedipus declares that

> the gods look late, but earnestly, on a man who forsakes their ways and turns to madness. [*OC* 1536–1537]

Before we go on to consider the implications for Sophoclean drama of this variety of attitudes, there are two long choral passages that call for notice. The second stasimon of *OT* (863–910) is a remarkably full and dignified statement of an attitude of religious piety. In the opening strophe the chorus pray for "purity in word and action" and know that guidance for such conduct is in "laws that walk on high, sired in the expanse of heaven," and that in these laws there is "a mighty god, who does not grow old." The combination of divine power and divine goodness is unmistakable here, and the same religious attitude appears clearly in the corollary statement in the second strophe: if a man lives evilly, how will he protect himself from "the shafts of the gods"? We are not concerned now with the application of the thought of the ode to its context, and it is obviously wrong to assume that this announcement of divine punishment for wickedness is aimed against Oedipus or Jocasta, for neither of them is recognizable in the description of sinners in the second strophe. We need not be disturbed when the up-shot of the ode, in the second antistrophe, is an appeal to Zeus and Apollo to vindicate their oracles. This, in the usual Sopho-clean manner, brings the ode, hitherto general, into the partic-ular realm of the plot, but it does not particularize the entire thought of the choral song. Because of their piety, the chorus believe in the morality of the gods and the truth of oracles, but these are parallel features of their piety, not linked as in a logical proposition. The ode is of the detached type, very much like the first stasimon of *Antigone*, and its bearing on what precedes it is similarly a matter of feeling rather than of logical sequence. Its importance for our present question is that it sets forth, posi-tively and clearly, the justice, morality, and interest of the gods.

In *Antigone*, Stasimon Two (582–625), the path of thought is less clear. The first system (582–603) presents no problems. It contains a straightforward statement of the idea that deity brings suffering to most men: "Blessed are they whose life tastes no bitterness." The house of the Labdacids is shaken by the powers of heaven, a god presses upon it: ἐρείπει θεῶν τις. There is some suggestion of human responsibility for sorrow in the case of Antigone (603), and thus perhaps, by implica-tion, of the whole family; but there is an impression also, and more strongly, of suffering inflicted mysteriously from above.

The second system (604–625) is harder to understand. It be-gins, in the spirit of Stasimon Two of *OT*, with an impressive note of divine punishment for wickedness:

Thy power, O Zeus, what human transgression can overwhelm?

But at the end of the strophe the law of life is enunciated that "nothing supremely great enters the life of men without disaster." [24] With this we seem to be in another realm, that of the jealousy of divinity for human greatness, be it pure or wicked, the traditional notion of φθόνος θεῶν. But the chain of thought is not yet complete; antistrophe is linked to strophe with "for." "For hope . . . deceives many men with foolish desires . . . and evil seems good to him whose wits deity is leading on to destruction." It is extremely difficult in this final antistrophe to determine whether the ode has to do with the divine punishment of human wickedness or the deliberate corruption, and then destruction, of man by god. There are dramatic reasons for this obscurity. As Jebb saw,[25] there is an oblique reference here to the coming ruin of Creon, but Sophocles does not care to have his chorus, at this stage, openly condemn Creon or charge him or anyone else in the play with evil behavior. In the end, of course, we know that it is by Creon's own weakness of character that "evil seems good," and so the ode is, retrospectively, a statement of human wickedness punished. But taken by itself the second system of this ode is open to interpretation as a statement either of divine jealousy or of divine justice.

In these two great lyric statements concerning divinity, then, we find no single unambiguous religious conviction that we can ascribe to the poet. The belief in gods of justice is crossed by a belief in gods of power who check the power of man.

We found the same plurality of attitude in the assembled religious statements in the plays, a plurality that can, however, be reduced to three main concepts: repressive gods of cruelty, gods of power who are indifferent to men and hardly unlike impersonal fate, and gods of justice. Which of these is the

[24] The text of lines 613–614 is uncertain. My translation is based on Pearson's text, which, like most editions, has Heath's conjecture πάμπολύ γ' in place of the reading of the MSS, πάμπολις, in line 614. For the thought, cf. *Trach.* 126–131.

[25] Jebb, note *ad loc.* in his edition of the play.

"Sophoclean" view? No matter how we sort the specific passages, we cannot pick out any one concept that claims peculiar authority. We cannot even determine an attitude typical of the chorus or of the major characters. The chorus expresses the idea of jealous gods (in the parodos of *Ajax*), of gods of power dispensing a measure of woe to all men (e.g., *Trach.* 126–131), and of gods of justice (in *OT*, Stasimon Two). The same variety of views is found among minor characters: in the messenger speech of *Electra* the familiar note of trouble brought upon man by gods is sounded (696–697); Teucer declares that all things that come to men are wrought by the gods (*Aj.* 1036–1037); Lichas in *The Trachinian Women* declares the hostility of the gods to wickedness (280); Calchas counts on divine help to aid Ajax (*Aj.* 779). So also with the principal figures. Philoctetes, though he accuses the gods of injustice and cruelty (*Philoc.* 452, 1020), calls upon them for help (315–316) and believes in their justice (1036–1039). It is true that leading figures ascribe cruelty and hatred to the gods oftener than others do, but this is patently because they are the sufferers in the plays and have reason to cry out; it would be unwise to take their anguished complaints for Sophoclean theology. Furthermore, passages in which leading persons assume or expect the help of the gods, or speak of the justice of the gods, far outnumber the passages of complaint.

Nor can we make any meaningful division of attitudes, as expressed in specific passages, from play to play. All seven plays exhibit the three leading concepts, except that in *Oedipus at Colonus*, which is to the least degree of the seven a play of suffering, there is no outcry against divine cruelty. What statistical differences there may be in the distribution of types of reference to deity have no value for differentiating religious attitudes. In *OC* there are far more references to divine aid than in any other play, because Oedipus in this play is clearly in league with deity and calls upon the gods many times when pronouncing blessings and maledictions. This is not a difference from the other plays in religious outlook but marks the closeness and constancy of Oedipus' relation to the gods.

So far as specific passages are concerned, then, there are no very enlightening conclusions to be drawn about the Sophoclean religious attitude. Is this not quite what we should expect of Sophocles? Surely this is just one further aspect of Sophoclean "mythical thinking"—concentration on the story as it is without editorial guidance or digressive philosophizing. Sophocles has no theological pronouncements to make and no points of criticism to score. What he presents to us in the mouths of his characters—the chorus by all means included—is, by and large, the inconclusive and heterogeneous group of attitudes characteristic of the archaic age, and still widely held in fifth-century Athens, which Dodds has described with an expressive term borrowed from Murray, "the inherited conglomerate." [26] It is a religious outlook in which the constant attribute of the gods is power. Whether that power is exercised for the maintenance of justice and the punishment of wickedness among men or is simply a rebuke and a check imposed on man for overstepping the bounds of humanity and inspiring divine jealousy is not in this religious approach firmly established.

What is demanded of man is humility in the face of divine power; the anger of god, whether just or jealous, is to be feared. The same mixture of concepts features the poetry of the archaic period; in the Theognidean collection, above all, we find these notions.[27] This archaic attitude is often taken to be Sophocles'

[26] Gilbert Murray, *Greek Studies* (Oxford, 1946), 67. The term is used by Dodds in his chapter "Rationalism and Reaction in the Classical Age," in *The Greeks and the Irrational.*

[27] In the Theognidean collection, see lines 133–134, 141–142, 157–158, 171–172, 443–446, 591–594, 659–668, 1033–1034, 1162c–f, for the gods as dispensers of good and evil and the wielders of all power; lines 373–380, 741–742, 743–752, for moral indifference, cruelty, and power as characteristics of deity; lines 143–144, 201–202, 1181–1182, 1195–1196, for

religious thought.[28] The dominant feeling in this religion is one of fear: divine power, though we may hope that it is just, is mysterious and unpredictable, and it may strike down the prosperous for no apparent reason. It need hardly be said that this attitude is a regression—if it is the attitude of Sophocles—from the Aeschylean theodicy, above all from the concept of *Agamemnon* 750–762, where the old notion of the punishment of guiltless prosperity is firmly rejected. It is pertinent to notice, however, that the archaic concept, with its insecurity and kaleidoscopic changes, is eminently suited to tragic drama.

If, however, we abandon the search for precise statements of Sophocles' attitude to the gods and permit ourselves to be guided instead by what is revealed concerning the relations of gods and men in the plays taken as entities, we perceive a much more purposeful and single-natured concept. Let us begin at the chronological end, where the situation is clearest.

In *Oedipus at Colonus* deity recognizes and accepts the worth of Oedipus, and the power that he will have as a ἥρως becomes manifest as the play advances. There is no tenderness in the divine attitude; the summons at the end is, though intimate, peremptory and impersonal. The "grace" that marks the play is human grace and, at the end, the "chthonic" grace of Oedipus himself. But the divine recognition is nonetheless clear, and it is a recognition, not of humility, but of moral endurance and strength of spirit: in the old Oedipus, for all his years of suffering, there is still more of the αὐθάδης than of the σώφρων. There can be no doubt here of the interest of deity in human worth or of its justness to it. Nor is it only some daemonic or chthonic power that accepts Oedipus; it is deity at large, deity above and

---

deity as the punisher of evil; lines 757–760, 773–776, 851–852, 1178a–b, for the assumption of divine help for men and divine interest in human morality.

[28] Cf. Webster, *Introduction*, 18–37; Dodds, *The Greeks and the Irrational*, 49.

below: when Oedipus has mysteriously disappeared, Theseus does obeisance both to the earth and to "Olympus of the gods" (1656).[29]

The situation is just as clear and more typical in *Philoctetes*. Divinity is more personally remote in this play in spite of Heracles' epiphany at the end because Philoctetes is not a ἥρως; he does not have the personal kinship to deity that Oedipus has. Moreover, Philoctetes suffers, inveighs against the gods, and finds cruelty in his situation. But behind the ironic cruelty, in *Philoctetes* the justice of the gods is absolutely clear, and again it is justice done to human strength and heroism, not a reward for human humility. It is Zeus's will that the heroism of Philoctetes be crowned by victory at Troy, and Philoctetes, for all his suffering and anger, knows that divine justice is on his side, that "the spur of divinity" (1040) has pricked the army on to seek him. (Cf. also 1466–1468.) Neoptolemus' divination in the parodos that Philoctetes' suffering is imposed by a divine plan, not by chance or cruelty, is correct, and the play shows that the divine will, though indifferent to Philoctetes' human feelings, is alive and just to his human worth. It is impersonal, remote, long-range justice, but it is unmistakable, and it is imposed by deity.

In *Electra* the question of divine justice or injustice scarcely enters because the play has to do with Electra's human will and feelings, operating in a human context. But what evidence there is in the play indicates that deity is united with justice in that the punishment of wickedness has divine sanction.[30] The relationship of human revenge and divine justice is not worked out

[29] On the combination of Olympian and chthonic deity in *OC*, see Winnington-Ingram, *JHS*, 74 (1954), 16–24.

[30] Sophocles' attitude toward the consequences for Orestes of the act of matricide is, for dramatic reasons, deliberately suppressed (see above, pp. 66–67), and there is a recurrent atmosphere of doubt (cf. Chapter V, Note 22). But Sophocles' depiction of the divine attitude toward Clytemnestra and Aegisthus is not thereby altered.

with exactness in this play, because divine justice is not at the center of the dramatic theme as it is in *OC* and in *Philoctetes*.

Of the earlier plays, *Ajax* and *Antigone* need raise no doubts concerning divine rectitude. It is hard to argue that Ajax is unfairly dealt with. He suffers the anger of the gods for as clear a demonstration of *hybris* as one could imagine; driven on by the injury which his excessive pride has sustained in the award of the arms, he sets out to murder the Greek chiefs, and the madness in which he is lost at the beginning of the play is a divine punishment for his violence.[31] That an act of what can be called moral madness—the attempted murder—should be punished by real madness, which turns the attempted crime into senseless slaughtering of animals, is not accidental of course. The punishment fits the crime not only by its external irony but as a perverted extension of Ajax's own violent nature; but we should not therefore, I think, suppose that the divine intervention is purely symbolic and the madness self-sprung from Ajax's violence of mind. Athena is objectively real. Much has been

---

[31] A problem is raised, concerning Ajax's punishment by Athena, by a passage in the messenger's report of Calchas' speech to Teucer. Calchas tells Teucer that "the anger of divine Athena drives [Ajax] for this one day" (756–757). These words permit the interpretation that Ajax is driven by Athena's anger for the *entire* day. Therefore not only his madness but his death too is caused by Athena. This is divine cruelty or something very like it. It seems almost certainly wrong, however, to press the letter of the passage so closely. For if all the events of the day are imposed by divine will, then the whole action of the play is so imposed, and the characterization of Ajax becomes meaningless. It seems certain that Sophocles had nothing of the sort in mind. What Calchas' words mean, surely, is simply that Ajax has been driven into madness by Athena. The succeeding events of the day follow from this situation, so that it is quite natural to speak of the "day," even though only the first event of the day, the madness, is specifically meant. For an interpretation that takes Calchas' words literally and supposes that Ajax is under the power of Athena and is mad throughout the action, see Vandvik, "Ajax the Insane," in *Serta Eitremiana*, 169–175; I do not find the argument convincing.

said of the cruelty of her display of Ajax's madness.[32] But she seems cruel only because Ajax's conduct makes her seem so, and Ajax, though mad, is still Ajax in his pride and self-confidence. Athena is just as ready to be cruel to her supposed favorite Odysseus, but his prudence and reverence give her no opening. To both men she is stern and impersonal. Ajax and his followers think that she is cruel to Ajax, but nothing else in the play suggests it. She is essentially the same as Heracles in *Philoctetes*, the voice of deity, neither cruel nor kind, but just. The two epiphanies have entirely different atmospheres, but the difference is not in the nature of deity so much as in the human attitude to deity. Heracles appears in answer to Philoctetes' nobility, Athena to Ajax's *hybris*.[33] The specific divine figure is in each case chosen by the playwright for its mythological fitness, not for its religious significance.

Antigone's suffering comes, not through divine will or purpose, but from Creon. Creon's conduct is wrong, and it is clear from the Teiresias scene that deity frowns on his wrongness and hence vindicates Antigone. We shall only doubt divine justice in *Antigone* if we hold that it is unjust of deity to permit undeserved human suffering—a dubious religious principle—or if we attribute to Sophocles the archaic concept of "a house shaken by deity" set forth by the chorus in the first system of Stasimon Two, a concept not suggested by the rest of the play.

Oedipus Tyrannus and *The Trachinian Women* are the only plays likely to give rise to the notion of cruel gods or gods who have no concern for human morality. Whitman, who regards the two plays as a pair, chronologically and in spirit, is

---

[32] Cf. Reinhardt, *Sophokles*, 22; against this view, see S. M. Adams, "The *Ajax* of Sophocles," *Phoenix*, 9 (1955), 97.

[33] Adams argues that Athena is the helper and vindicator of Ajax. There is undoubtedly a measure of truth in this view, for, as Adams points out, it is Athena who prepares Odysseus in the prologue for his later role as the champion of Ajax. But the fact that Athena's appearance is a consequence of Ajax's *hybris* is not challenged by this view.

impressed by "their constant sense of irrational and inescapable malignity." [34] In commenting on *OT*, he declares that "the gods cannot be just, if Oedipus is morally innocent." Scarcely anyone doubts that Oedipus is morally innocent, but it is more usual to lay the blame on "fate" than on the gods. Concerning fate in Sophocles something will be said below. But before blaming either gods or fate, it is well to recall that there is no suggestion in the play that either Apollo or the oracle was responsible for Oedipus' suffering.[35] Apollo no doubt *knew* what he would suffer ("Zeus and Apollo are wise, and know the affairs of men"), and the oracle announced it, but Sophocles alters the traditional oracle, as we saw above, in order *not* to have it say that Oedipus' fall was a divine punishment for paternal misdeeds. The oracle need mean no more than that Oedipus is such a man as must, because of his masterful and irrepressible spirit, not only bring great good to pass, but cause and submit to great suffering. In other words it may be a "character" oracle, interpreting not without profundity the nature of Oedipus.

But our immediate point is the relation of deity to Oedipus' suffering. I have said that the play does not suggest that it was divinely caused. It is true that Oedipus, in anguish, says so: Ἀπόλλων τάδ᾽ ἦν. But earlier he has supposed, rather, that it is Zeus who has planned suffering for him (738); and Teiresias

---

[34] *Sophocles*, 106.

[35] In lines 376–377 Teiresias says (if we accept, as all modern editors have, Brunck's emendation), "It is not your lot to fall at my hands; Apollo is enough, whose concern it is to bring these matters to pass." I do not think that these words are as crucial as they are often taken to be. Surely the fall of Oedipus to which Teiresias is referring is his expulsion from Thebes, which has been ordered by Apollo. There is no implication here that the sins of Oedipus, which necessitate his expulsion, were caused by Apollo.

I am not able to agree with Bernard M. W. Knox, *Oedipus at Thebes*, 7–8, that the reading of the MSS, whereby Teiresias says, "It is not my lot to fall at your hands, etc.," can be retained. The introduction here of the idea that Teiresias will fall at Apollo's hands seems quite out of place.

tells us that it is his intellectual skill that has destroyed him (442). When we find such varying ascriptions of cause, none of them canceled out, we cannot very well pick out any one of them as the truth. We must, instead, rely on what can be deduced from the circumstances; and no logical deductions from the events of *OT* can ascribe responsibility for Oedipus' suffering to Apollo or to "the gods." In this play deity is farther from the center of the action than in any of the others. The contrast with *Philoctetes* is striking: there it is several times indicated that Philoctetes' suffering is part of a divine plan that involves Philoctetes' heroism; here there is no mention of divine plan, only the mysterious conviction of Oedipus that he was born "for some strange evil," which is not fulfilled or in any further way prepared for in this play. The role of deity in *OT* is remote and largely neutral; only if we regard their failure to protect Oedipus as injustice can we ascribe injustice to the gods.

In *The Trachinian Women* divine presence is closer than in *OT* but hardly clearer. There is a reason for this obscurity. We have seen that the fate of Heracles after the end of the play is deliberately excluded from the plot, except for one slight hint which is introduced only to be dismissed at once in what seems a deliberate silence on the playwright's part (1206–1211). We are not intended to concentrate on any divine plan in this play, even though the thought that there is a divine plan concerning Heracles is suggested. Is deity negative here, as in *OT*, or can we find injustice in its action? So far as Deianeira is concerned, the agent of disaster is not deity but a chain of human or bestial (Nessus) deception and misunderstanding. We are incensed at Deianeira's suffering, as at that of Oedipus, and we cannot help feeling that there is cruelty from some quarter. But of divine malice or active injustice toward Deianeira there is no evidence. About Heracles surely no decision can be made because we do not have the evidence for a decision, not knowing for sure whether he is to end in wretched death or in apotheosis. There is a slight hint of apotheosis, enough to warn us away from interpreting the play as an outcry against divine cruelty, but that is all. As in *Oedipus*, then, the place of divinity in the plot is essentially negative.

There is, of course, the spirited outburst of Hyllus at the end. Hyllus certainly thinks that the gods have behaved basely, and, chiefly on the grounds of his complaint, it has been supposed that in this play Zeus is "something which prevents man's best from being of any worth" [36] and that "the injustice of the gods is bitterly accused." [37] We have already seen that it is dangerous to accept the statement made by any one character about deity, and caution is especially needed in judging the statement of a character in as bewildered an emotional state as Hyllus is at the end of this play. Furthermore, the final words, "There is none of these things that is not Zeus," are in a different tone from the foregoing complaints. It is probable that the closing four lines are spoken, not by Hyllus, but by the chorus. [38] The change of speaker and of tone modifies the harshness of Hyllus' preceding words. I cannot see how one can read or hear these closing words without recalling the whole mysterious activity at the end of the play—Heracles' precise knowledge of what he must do, his abrupt insistence on carrying out his plans, his mysterious reference to the "healing" of the funeral pyre on which he demands that he be burnt. Surely these things too are "Zeus." Even if the final words are spoken by Hyllus, the wider reference, not to suffering alone, is probable though less certain. Hyllus' anger, too, springs in part from his sorrow for his mother's misfortunes, which are not to be ascribed to divine malignity. All things considered, the statement of Hyllus is frail evidence from which to deduce that the playwright is inveighing against divine injustice.

Where do we stand now? In his two latest plays Sophocles

[36] Whitman, *Sophocles*, 120.
[37] *Ibid.*, 122. [38] Cf. above, Note 22.

presents divinity as actively interested in and beneficent to human moral values. The gods in these plays, though remote and impersonal, are undeniably just; their plans take account of human greatness. In *Electra* what evidence there is points in the same direction. In *Ajax* and *Antigone* human transgression meets with obvious divine disapproval, though in these plays there is no rewarding of human excellence. In *The Trachinian Women* and *Oedipus Tyrannus* there is no clear evidence either of divine injustice or of divine reward. All in all, then, divinity in the plays of Sophocles, when active in human affairs, is just. But it permits human suffering, and everywhere it is stern, impersonal, and, though linked to ultimate good, careless of individual human suffering. There is a difference between earlier and later plays: in the last two the poet's attitude is more positive than in the rest, and the power of deity manifests itself clearly on mankind's behalf. *Electra* offers no substantial evidence.

In the four earlier plays deity permits human suffering and there is no counterbalancing reward for human goodness, though in *Antigone* moral rectitude is implicitly vindicated. In two of the plays, *Ajax* and *Antigone*, wrongdoing is punished by deity; in the other two earlier plays the question of the punishment of transgressions does not arise. There is no real difference in outlook between the two pairs of plays; the situation differs, not deity. Indeed, even between *Philoctetes* and *Oedipus at Colonus* on one side and the earlier plays on the other, though there are differences in the relation of god and man, I doubt if these give evidence of a fundamental change in Sophocles' concept of the gods. Throughout, wherever positive evidence is to be found, the gods in Sophocles are in league with justice and hostile to violence and moral evil; and throughout they are impersonal, remote, and indifferent to human suffering. If we find this indifference unjust, then the gods of Sophocles are unjust. I venture to suggest that the most thoughtful view of deity does not involve complaint because deity permits man to suffer, and I do not believe that any such complaint was in Sophocles' attitude. Job rebels and declares God unjust; then he is vouchsafed a poetic vision of the majesty and scope of the divine, and he complains no more. So with Sophocles: his suffering characters complain of divine injustice, and we sympathize with them as with Job; but the poet, I think, has always before him a wider and calmer view. He can look on human suffering with intense sympathy and yet not become bitter against deity.[39]

The irony of circumstances that weighs upon Sophocles' tragic heroes is not, then, imposed by the will of the gods.[40]

---

[39] For a valuable study of the gods in Sophocles, see H. D. F. Kitto, "The Idea of God in Aeschylus and Sophocles," *La Notion du Divin* (Geneva, 1952), 169–189, especially 173–180. Kitto declares that the gods in Sophocles "symbolise Sophocles' conception of a framework of law which permeates life as it does the physical universe." There is no important point in Kitto's presentation with which the views expressed in the present chapter are in conflict.

Cf. also *Form and Meaning*, where the views of the above-mentioned article are expanded and form part of Kitto's concept of "religious drama." (See especially Ch. VIII, "Religious Drama and Its Interpretation.") While I cannot agree with Kitto that Sophocles' plays are religious drama in his understanding of the term ("a form of drama in which the real focus is not the Tragic Hero but the divine background"), I believe that his interpretation of Sophocles' religious outlook as a playwright is both sound and illuminating.

[40] I have not included references to fragments because, lacking as we generally do all knowledge of context, we cannot be certain of the tone or the application of statements. In general, the fragments with religious ideas are brief utterances on the power of deity and the need for piety, preserved by the gnomologists and others who had a strong taste for the sententious. For examples, see Pearson, Frs. 196, 228, 590, 646, 895, 961, 964. Two fragments are on the cruelty of the gods: 107, 680. There are none extolling the justice of the gods.

Extreme caution is necessary in ascribing to Sophocles the sentiments expressed in fragments. It is very easy to assume that these apparently self-contained, complete, and wise utterances are the poet's *sententiae*, but it is dangerous. Fr. 247 declares that "if deity bids you depart from

Before we go on with the question of its source, there is one more observation to be made concerning the gods in Sophoclean drama. It was remarked above that Athena and Heracles, the only deities who actually make an appearance, are chosen for their mythological appositeness, not because their particular selves have a specific religious point; religiously considered, they are simply the voice of deity, replaceable by any other of the Olympians.[41] Reference to any specific deity is more likely, in Sophocles, to be an artistic than a religious accuracy: when the plot of revenge is going into action in *Electra*, Hermes the god of stealth is invoked; at the end of *Philoctetes* the sea nymphs are called upon for a fair voyage; deity in *The Trachinian Women* is called Zeus because Zeus is mythologically correct. There is no consistent sense of a religiously felt personal deity or group of deities like the figure of Zeus in Aeschylean drama.[42] In Sophocles it scarcely matters, religiously, whether deity is invoked as one of the Olympians or simply as θεός, or θεοί, or δαίμονες. This absence of discrimination with regard to divine personality is in keeping with the remoteness, impersonality, and impassiveness that characterize the attitude of deity toward human affairs. It is easy, but incorrect, to think of deity

justice, it is right to make the journey; for nothing under divine guidance is base." This satanic concept is foreign to Sophocles' ideas as revealed in the extant plays, and it is really not reasonable, without other evidence, to ascribe it to Sophocles. Yet because it is a good round *sententia*, Pearson was led to comment that "Sophocles is serenely confident that no reconciliation of . . . claims is necessary; if morality seems to conflict with the will of the gods, so much the worse for it." No admirable character in Sophocles' plays would assent to this, except perhaps the morally neutral Orestes of the beginning of *Electra* and the barely respectable Odysseus of *Philoctetes*.

[41] In *Ajax* the characters are generally in agreement in ascribing Ajax's troubles to Athena; yet the chorus, in line 137, speak of the πληγὴ Διός falling on Ajax.

[42] It is true, as S. M. Adams emphasizes in *Sophocles the Playwright*, that Apollo has a place of special prominence in Sophocles' extant dramas. But even Apollo is an impersonal figure.

282   *A Study of Sophoclean Drama*

in Sophoclean plays as equivalent to absolutely impersonal fate or as representing "universal circumstance as it is."[43] Clearly this description will not fit deity in *Philoctetes* and *Oedipus at Colonus;* nor, I think, is it really applicable to deity anywhere in Sophocles, for Sophocles has another way of expressing the notion of that unpredictability of circumstances that can operate with such amoral and ironic cruelty.

Impersonal fate does not occupy a conspicuous place in Sophoclean drama. The common idea that *Oedipus Tyrannus* is a drama of fate certainly needs modification,[44] and in most plays of Sophocles there is little suggestion that "chance" (τύχη), or "necessity" (ἀνάγκη), or Moira, or the other representations of what is imposed on man or what falls to his lot (τὰ εἱμαρμένα, ἡ πεπρωμένη) are paramount.

Far the commonest of these expressions is *tyche*, but there are, in the seven plays, not many places where *tyche* rises beyond the religiously and morally insignificant meaning of "accident" or "event," and in several of these places *tyche* is ascribed to the gods (θεία τύχη, *Philoc.* 1326, *OC* 1585; τὰς ἐκ θεῶν τύχας, *Philoc.* 1317). In *OT* there are three passages in which τύχη is credited with independent power; but in two of these, as we have already seen, the power of τύχη is only illusory (977, 1080; see above, p. 134), and the third, if too far away from the other two to be confidently regarded as joined to them in a deliberate pattern of repetition, is at any rate to the same dramatic purpose: Oedipus avers that "*tyche* leapt upon the head" of Laius (263) without knowing that it was he himself who killed Laius. Twice there are references to "inevitable *tyche*"

J .T. Sheppard, in his edition of *OT*, p. xxxvi.
The case against taking *OT* to be a play of fate is well argued by Abby Leach, "Fate and Free Will in Greek Literature," in *The Greek Genius and Its Influence*, ed. by Lane Cooper (Ithaca, 1917, 1952). See also Knox, *Oedipus at Thebes*, Ch. i.

(ἀναγκαία τύχη), but in one place (*El.* 48) it is uncertain whether the phrase means more than "unavoidable accident," and in the other (*Aj.* 485), though it is used by Tecmessa most impressively ("Lord Ajax, in the life of man there is no greater ill than inevitable chance"), it loses its force as a statement of philosophic thought when it is promptly followed by Tecmessa's explanation that what she has suffered by inevitable chance was "decreed by the gods and by your right hand" (489–490). The statement of the guard in *Antigone* that "*tyche* will decide" whether the burier of Polyneices' body will be found (328) is a very casual kind of fatalism, and a statement at *OC* 1026 that "*tyche* has caught" Creon is scarcely more impressive as philosophy. A somewhat more solemn and thoughtful fatalism is enunciated by the messenger in *Antigone*, who declares that *tyche* "sets a man upright in prosperity and topples him in ruin" (1158). But the instances where *tyche* has a philosophically significant meaning are few in number.

"Moira" as the molder of a person's lot or fate (as opposed to mundane "share") occurs no oftener. Only four times is Moira clearly an active agent, and in one of these (*Philoc.* 1466) Moira is joined with Zeus as the creator of Philoctetes' fortunes. In *Antigone* 987 a lyrical reference to the Moirai is without great significance, and in *Electra* 1414, where the text is not altogether certain, Moira does not appear to be endowed with independent power. The one instance in which the power of Moira is clearly referred to as an independent thing is in Stasimon Four of *Antigone*, where the chorus declare that "the power of Moira is a terrible power" (951–952). Ἡ Εἱμαρμένη, ἡ πεπρωμένη, and ἀνάγκη are used only rarely.

Far more often than these impersonal terms Sophocles uses the word *daimon*. Precisely what *daimon* means to Sophocles it is difficult to know. Reinhardt, who in his book on Sophocles says much that is true and profound about the place of the *daimonisch* in Sophocles, does not, if I understand him, dis-

tinguish *daimon* from deity. Certainly the distinction is not
clear-cut. On the other hand, neither can the activity of a man's
daimon be altogether separated from character. There is in
Sophoclean thought some reflection (perhaps unconscious) of
the Heraclitean aphorism ἦθος ἀνθρώπῳ δαίμων.[45] In this realm
of the "daimonic" there lies an answer, of sorts, to our problem
of whence comes the ironic cruelty of circumstances to man.

The plural, δαίμονες, usually means simply "the gods," no
different from θεοί. The singular occasionally means θεός, or
even a specific deity; in *Philoctetes* 1468 it means Zeus. But the
singular usually, and the plural occasionally, cannot be interpreted as specifying deity. Nor is the reference quite the same
as "fate" or "luck," though μοῖρα or τύχη could often replace
δαίμων intelligibly enough. But there is a personal quality in
the meaning of δαίμων; it is conceived as an active, driving force.
Ajax is "sacrificed to a hateful *daimon*" (Aj. 1214–1215); a
daimon "puts to rest Antigone" (*Antig.* 833–834); Oedipus refers to the "cruel *daimon*" that brings suffering on him (*OT* 828–
829); in *OC*, Oedipus tells Polyneices that "the *daimon* looks
upon" him (1337); Antigone and Tecmessa are "driven" by a
daimon (*OC* 1750, *Aj.* 504).

Yet, though there is this personal force and the *daimon* is a
separate entity, the relationship between sufferer and *daimon*
can be almost that of identity. When Oedipus exclaims, "Oh,
daimon, what a leap you have made," he includes in this
"daimonic" action his own actions as well as the external power
that has, as the chorus have just said, leapt upon him (*OT* 1300–
1302). A man's *daimon* is not something external to him: it is a
driving force from without and within. Ajax speaks of "my
daimon" (*Aj.* 534); and the chorus tell Oedipus that never will
they regard anything as fortunate, having before them the
example of "your *daimon*" (*OT* 1194); in *OC* the stranger

[45] This point is made by J. C. Kamerbeek, "Sophocle et Héraclite,"
in *Studia Vollgraff* (Amsterdam, 1948), 84–98.

comments to Oedipus, "You are noble, if sight can tell, except in your *daimon*" (76); Electra speaks of the "unhappy *daimon*" of Orestes and herself (*El.* 1156–1157).

Daimon is luck with a personality. But it is more, too. It is attached to the individual man, an integral part of his life; it is a spirit with a purposefulness that luck cannot have. Most striking of all its qualities are its despotic power and its malignity. It is the driver, the guide, the fulfiller; and nearly always it brings to pass suffering and disaster. The "daimonic" seems to be Sophocles' customary way of expressing the dark and enigmatic agency by which disaster is flung suddenly upon unexpecting man. Neither wholly separate from deity nor identical with it, neither wholly external to man nor entirely a part of his own nature, neither an impersonal force nor a wholly definable spirit, the "daimonic" is as close to an answer as Sophocles gives to the question whence suffering comes to man.

The "daimonic" gives no moral or theological explanation of suffering or of the cruelty of circumstances. It means, as Reinhardt says, the inclusion in oneself of something foreign to oneself,[46] a drive against oneself from within, an inner fate that is personalized and to some degree externalized. It is the *daimon* that drives a man on his ignorant course, for only the gods have knowledge of *aletheia*. The "daimonic" is Sophocles' way of leaving an element of human experience in darkness; catastrophe descends unexpectedly and unavoidably from somewhere. But no moral reason is apparent for its descent, and neither divine nor human nature is the deliberate agent. It would be pedantic to insist on precision in a realm that Sophocles leaves vague; the "daimonic" represents no ordered philosophical concept in Sophoclean thought. When Ajax bitterly says, "That [to have killed Eurysaces] would have been in keeping with my *daimon*" (*Aj.* 534), he does not mean his character, nor yet his luck

[46] Reinhardt, *Sophokles*, 63.

(he does not usually associate his sufferings with luck), nor can he mean deity. It is something that touches on all three of these realms and is identical with none of them.

To suppose that Sophocles' use of the word *daimon* provides a key to full understanding of the playwright's views on suffering or that it altogether clarifies the deep "practical irony" of his plays would be rash. It is to be remembered that Sophocles does use, though less often, other terms, such as Moira and *tyche*, to express the source of what descends on man. Moreover, there is no complete distinction between *daimon* and deity.[47] Nevertheless, I think that the emphasis given to *daimon* in the preceding paragraphs is just, because the word, though it occupies no exclusive place in Sophocles' vocabulary, is Sophoclean in a way that none of the other terms applied to the same realm of experience is. It is personal, a living creature of the imagination, rather than an abstract philosophical concept; and it is involved with human character as much as with deity. It is therefore symbolic of both the "mythical thinking" and the concentration on character that we have found dominant throughout the plays.

Since the cruelty of circumstances is presented by Sophocles neither as the malignancy of the gods nor as the fruit of human guilt, the question why man suffers becomes less pressing. It is not central to the nature of deity or of human character in Sophocles. Suffering is a datum of human experience, accepted and embodied in the plays of Sophocles but not explained. It emphasizes the difference between divine *aletheia* and human *doxa*, and this is one legitimate way of viewing the meaning of human suffering in Sophocles. But the unforeseen catastrophes

[47] Sheppard, in his edition of *OT*, pp. xxxiv–xl, has some excellent comments on *daimon* in Sophocles, in which *daimon* and deity are regarded as different ways of expressing the same influence. On the interchangeable use of the terms *theos* and *daimon* in Homer, cf. Gerald F. Else, "God and Gods in Early Greek Thought," *TAPA*, 80 (1949), 24–36.

and sufferings of life serve also a further and more active purpose for Sophocles as dramatist, and one that is closely tied to his profound and detailed study of human character. Suffering exposes human nature. Man, with all his splendid powers, his intelligence, his bravery, his excellence of moral purpose, περιφραδὴς ἀνήρ, is vulnerable. Sophocles does not present man's suffering as primarily part of a learning process; [48] nor does he comfort us with the notion that those on whom catastrophe falls have morally earned their fate. And yet, for all the vulnerability of man and for all the pathos of human life, Sophocles is neither essentially a pessimist nor is his view of life purely ironic. For on the one hand Sophocles presents deity as being in harmony with ultimate justice; we are left with the feeling that the universe is not all chance and cruelty but that behind the enigmatic region of *doxa* there is an abiding and just moral order. And on the other hand Sophocles sees man, not as ruined and sunk in despair by his suffering, but as fulfilling his nature as a εὐγενὴς ἀνήρ by meeting with spiritual courage the challenge of his vulnerability.

We began this chapter by looking at irony as a technique of presentation in the plays. At its end we find ourselves drawn into questions that cannot be contained within the notion of technique. This is what must happen when one studies Sophoclean drama. Whether the starting point is the dramatic frame or the tragic essence, one comes to see, sooner or later, that the two are interdependent and indivisible.

[48] It is true that Sophoclean characters are sometimes represented as gaining in greatness through endurance. This is especially true of Oedipus in *OC* (cf. 7-8); it applies in some measure also to Philoctetes and Electra. (Cf. Whitman, *Sophocles*, 149-152, and elsewhere.) But learning through suffering has no such central and consistent importance in Sophocles' plays as in Aeschylus'.

On the Approximate Date of
The Trachinian Women

WITHOUT external evidence or such unequivocal internal evidence as a clear historical reference, no ancient play can be dated
with close accuracy. The difficulty is especially acute with the plays
of Aeschylus and Sophocles, because we have so small a fragment
of their dramatic output. Yet it is sometimes possible to feel confident that an undated play can be assigned to a certain general
period of an author's career. Thus it is with Sophocles' *Ajax*. We
do not know its date, but it is almost unanimously regarded by
scholars as an early play—early, that is, in relation to the other
extant plays. (We cannot say "unanimously," though only Perrotta
[*Sofocle*, 1935] among modern scholars would regard it as much
later than *Antigone*; Perrotta dates it to 431. In the old Müller-
Donaldson *History of the Literature of Ancient Greece* the following chronological order is assumed: *Antig.*, *El.*, *Trach.*, *OT*,
Aj., *Philoc.*, *OC.*) The grounds for regarding *Ajax* as an early play
are principally structural (stiffness in the unfolding of the plot,
a stationary quality in some of the scenes, a relative lifelessness in
some of the character depiction) and dictional (Aeschylean traits).
Not all scholars have exactly the same reasons for regarding the
play as early, but nearly all think that it is early.

The Trachinian Women, as we have seen repeatedly in the course

of this study, has many of the characteristics that have led scholars
to virtual agreement on an early date for *Ajax*. (We shall say more
of these characteristics in *Trach.* presently.) Yet, traditionally,
there has been no agreement that *Trach.* is early. During the first
half of this century, on the contrary, it was usual to regard it as
late, falling in the period about 420–410. Why is there this marked
difference in attitude toward these two plays? The answer lies
principally in the existence of three features of *Trach.* that have
been thought to have a Euripidean character: the prologue, the
figure of Deianeira, and the verbal similarities that exist, or can be
thought to exist, between this play and several plays of Euripides,
particularly *Heracles* and *Alcestis*.

That the prologue deserves to be called Euripidean is highly
questionable. It begins with a long speech, and so do nearly all
Euripides' prologues. At that superficial level, resemblance to most
of Euripides' prologues ends. But the feature that really distinguishes Euripides' prologues is that the introductory speech is a
monologue. Its detachment from what follows (either, as is usually
the case, another part of the prologue or the parodos) is an important characteristic; the mere question of length of the introductory speech is not a telling factor. Detachment and monologic
quality are most apparent when the speaker or speakers (for sometimes the play begins with a detached dialogue; the structural effect
is not altered) leave the orchestra after speaking, as do Apollo and
Thanatos in *Alcestis*, Dionysus in *The Bacchae*, Aphrodite in
Hippolytus, Iphigenia in *IT*, Hermes in *Ion*, Poseidon and Athena
in *Troades*. But even in plays where the first speaker does not retire,
Electra in *Electra* for example, the detachment is unmistakable. No
such detachment exists in *Trach.* The prologue is a unit, a scene.
There is no break between Deianeira's opening speech and the
nurse's following speech; the two are, in fact, in the closest relationship. Only one of Euripides' prologues is without the customary
detachment of the opening speech: in *Heracles* Amphitryon's opening words are spoken in the presence of Megara and the children
and are answered by Megara. The kind of prologue exemplified by
Heracles and *Trach.* might as well be called Sophoclean as Euripi-

dean. That the prologue of *Trach.* is in some respects unique among the prologues of extant plays of Sophocles is true, but this is explained by the nature of the play and need not be ascribed to the influence of Euripidean prologues which it does not in fact much resemble.

Deianeira has often been supposed to be modeled on Alcestis, and her use of poisoned garments has sometimes been supposed to suggest Sophocles' dependence on *Medea*. Since the motif of the poisoned garments (at least the crown) seems not to have originated with Euripides (cf. D. L. Page's edition of *Medea* [Oxford, 1938], pp. xxv–xxvi), this point of similarity cannot be taken as evidence of dependence. Concerning the fancied dependence of Deianeira on Alcestis, what there is to be said can be said briefly. In the first place, we need not look to Euripides for a model. There is an analogy closer than Alcestis to Deianeira's gentleness, humility, and conjugal devotion—Tecmessa in *Ajax*. The picture of Tecmessa is slighter, but the model for Deianeira, if we are looking for models, is there. In the second place, Deianeira is essentially *unlike* Alcestis and *like* other Sophoclean tragic heroes in that she has a distinct and emphasized idea of nobility and is guided, when faced by a crisis, by that idea. Her "nobility" is devotion to Heracles, and hence is a more mundane and less heroic-seeming matter than the nobility of Ajax and Antigone, but it is expressed and acted on in the same way as theirs.

Verbal similarities are ambiguous tools for comparative dating, since they regularly work equally well in either direction. The similarities which have been noticed between *Trach.* and the plays of Euripides, chiefly *Heracles* and *Alcestis*, are for the most part totally unconvincing. (For lists of these see Whitman, *Sophocles*, 257, 258, Notes 30 and 43, and the references given there.) Most of them are very general, arising from similarities of situation and personality: descriptions of Heracles and his career, descriptions of the grief and the devotion of Alcestis and Deianeira. There is precisely one striking verbal similarity (*Trach.* 1101 and *Heracles* 1353) in which the same words, μυρίων ἐγευσάμην end both trimeters; ἐγευσάμην is a striking usage. (But cf. *Antig.* 582, κακῶν ἄγευστος;

and this usage of γεύομαι is frequent in Pindar, e.g., *Pythian* 9.35, 10.7.) Here, and here alone, it is reasonable to suppose a borrowing. But the question of who borrowed is open, and there is no more need to assume that the similarity indicates proximity of date than to suppose that the obvious reminiscences of *The Choephoroe* in Euripides' *Electra* indicate proximity of date.

These points are slight evidence, if they are evidence at all, of Euripidean influence on *Trach.* Let us now turn to the indications of relatively early date.

Reinhardt's whole chapter on *Trach.* (*Sophokles*, 42–72), which gives close attention to matters of structure, is a valuable analysis of problems bearing on the date. I need only summarize here the principal points of structure that indicate an early date. The speeches of *Trach.*, like those of *Ajax*, have an immobile, detached quality that is not like the manner of *OT* and the later plays, where one speech leads to the next in an intimate and creative way. Compare, for instance, the dialogue between Deianeira and Lichas with the dialogues in *OT* between Oedipus and Teiresias and between Oedipus and Jocasta. (To some extent, but not entirely, the detachment of speeches in *Trach.* depends on the general build of the play.) Similarly, transitions from one incident to another have a disjointed quality; this has been commented on above in Chapter II. The development of the dramatic theme as a whole has also a stationary, monologic character; Deianeira and Heracles are in virtual isolation, whereas Antigone, Oedipus, Electra, and Philoctetes are not. In particular, as Reinhardt points out, plans and intentions do not "ripen" as part of the action but are formed off stage; even Deianeira's change from error to knowledge takes place off and is only reported by her. This characteristic is like *Ajax*, unlike *OT*.

Other details are adduced by Reinhardt, and we have seen above, particularly in Chapter II, reasons for agreeing with his opinion that the structure and movement of the play are much closer to *Ajax* than to any other play. The fact that the latter part of Episode Two is a more elaborate and finished scene than anything in *Ajax* is some slight suggestion that *Trach.* is later than *Ajax*. One further small point indicates the priority of *Trach.* to *Antig.* and *OT*:

the silent withdrawal of Deianeira (*Trach.* 813–820) is repeated, with slight variations, in these other two plays, when Eurydice and Jocasta leave in silence or virtual silence. In neither of these other cases is the incident quite so fitting and effective as in *Trach.*; and this suggests that they are repetitions of a device that conspicuously succeeded.

Further evidence for relative earliness is adduced by Earp, in *The Style of Sophocles*, especially pages 164–170. Earp's most convincing evidence has to do with diction. He finds that in *Trach.*, as in *Ajax*, there is a larger number of "strikingly heavy compounds and bold formations of other kinds" and that there is a strong tendency toward linguistic ornament. He also finds a good deal more periphrasis and amplification in *Trach.* and *Ajax* than in the other plays. His tables show an especially extensive use of periphrasis in *Trach.* Earp notices the monologic character of the speeches, as does Reinhardt, and finds that the dialogue is "more leisurely in movement" than in later plays. There is, too, an increase in the later plays in "lucidity and naturalness."

The new Budé text (1955) places *Trach.* chronologically first of the extant plays. Nothing is said in specific support of this extreme dating. For an early date generally, the same stylistic arguments as Earp gives are adduced, and evidence from the depiction of Heracles is added. The tendency of scholars in the first half of the twentieth century to find Euripidean influence is rejected as "une des erreurs les plus singulières de la critique moderne."

The evidence for early dating is not really strong. But it is more substantial and less subjective than the "Euripideanism" and other evidence found for a later date. Abstract considerations of interpretation must be left out of account, especially in view of the great differences that there are in the interpretation of this play. Questions of general "tone" and of the nature of the tragic theme are more likely to confuse than to solve the problem. I have refrained from introducing the diptych form of the play as an argument for its date, because, as is obvious, Sophocles may have written plays in this form at any time in his career. When, however, we find that other evidence suggests that this diptych belongs to the same period as the other two, we are given some reason for believing that at one period in his career Sophocles favored this form. So far as there is any real evidence for a date, a date after *Ajax* and before *Antig.* is indicated.

Some extensive considerations of the dating of the play, in addition to those of Reinhardt and Earp, with different points of view are found in: Gennaro Perrotta, *Sofocle,* 526–558, dating the play at the end of Sophocles' career; Pohlenz, *Die Griechische Tragödie,*[2] *Erläuterungen* 85–87, dating it after *Alcestis;* Whitman, *Sophocles,* 46–49 and Notes, also placing it after *Alcestis.* See also Kitto, "Sophocles, Statistics, and the *Trachiniae,*" *AJP,* 60 (1939), 178–193, arguing against the validity of metrical evidence for dating the play; Kitto's own choice is about 420.

Bibliographical Note

[This list is not in any way a bibliography of works on Sophocles or even of works referred to in this book. It consists solely of books referred to several times in the course of this book, chiefly in the Notes, by abbreviated titles. Three important books mentioned below appeared too late to be used by me as much as they deserve, though I have been able to avail myself of all three of them to some extent: *Sophocles the Playwright*, by S. M. Adams, *Form and Meaning in Drama*, by H. D. F. Kitto, and *Oedipus at Thebes*, by Bernard M. W. Knox. For a survey of works on Sophocles, especially in the period 1945–1956, the reader is referred to my article, "A Review of Recent Sophoclean Studies," *CW*, 50 (1957), 157–172.]

Adams, S. M. *Sophocles the Playwright*. Toronto, 1957. (*The Phoenix*, Supplementary Volume III.)

Bowra, C. M. *Sophoclean Tragedy*. Oxford, 1944.

Campbell, Lewis. *Sophocles, Plays and Fragments*. Vol. I,[2] Oxford, 1879. Vol. II, 1881.

Dodds, E. R. *The Greeks and the Irrational*. Berkeley, 1951. (Sather Classical Lectures, Vol. XXV.)

Earp, F. R. *The Style of Sophocles*. Cambridge, 1944.

Goheen, Robert F. *The Imagery of Sophocles' Antigone*. Princeton, 1951.

Jebb, R. C. *Sophocles*. Cambridge, 1883–1896. *Oedipus Tyrannus*,[3] 1893, *Oedipus at Colonus*,[3] 1900, *Antigone*,[3] 1900, *Philoctetes*,[2] 1898.

Kitto, H. D. F. *Form and Meaning in Drama*. London, 1956.

Kitto, H. D. F. *Greek Tragedy*. London, 1939. 2nd ed., 1950.

Knox, Bernard M. W. *Oedipus at Thebes*. New Haven, 1957.

Kranz, Walther. *Stasimon*. Berlin, 1933.

Letters, Francis J. H. *The Life and Works of Sophocles*. London, 1953.

Norwood, Gilbert. *Greek Tragedy*.⁴ London, 1948.

Opstelten, J. C. *Sophocles and Greek Pessimism*. English trans. by J. A. Ross. Amsterdam, 1952.

Pearson, A. C. *The Fragments of Sophocles*. 3 vols. Cambridge, 1917.

Pearson, A. C. *Sophoclis Fabulae*. Oxford, 1923.

Perrotta, Gennaro. *Sofocle*. Messina, Milan, 1935.

Pohlenz, Max. *Die Griechische Tragödie*. Leipzig, 1930. 2nd ed., Göttingen, 1954.

Reinhardt, Karl. *Sophokles*. Frankfurt-am-Main, 1933. 3rd ed., 1947.

Schadewaldt, Wolfgang. "Aias und Antigone," *Neue Wege zur Antike*, 8 (1929), 61–117.

Sheppard, J. T. *The Oedipus Tyrannus of Sophocles*. Cambridge, 1920.

Waldock, A. J. A. *Sophocles the Dramatist*. Cambridge, 1951.

Webster, T. B. L. *An Introduction to Sophocles*. Oxford, 1936.

Weinstock, Heinrich. *Sophokles*. Leipzig, 1931. 3rd ed., Wuppertal, 1948.

Whitman, Cedric H. *Sophocles, A Study in Heroic Humanism*. Cambridge, Mass., 1951.

Wilamowitz-Moellendorff, Tycho von. *Die Dramatische Technik des Sophokles*. Berlin, 1917. (Philologische Untersuchungen 22.)

Bibliographical Note
to the Paperback Edition

Listed below are some books devoted specifically to Sophocles which have appeared since 1958. On Greek tragedy in general, different critical approaches are presented in *Greek Tragedy*, by Albin Lesky, trans. H. A. Frankfort (London 1965), *La tragédie grecque*, by Jacqueline de Romilly (Paris 1970), *Towards Greek Tragedy*, by Brian Vickers (London 1973), and *Reading Greek Tragedy*, by Simon Goldhill (Cambridge 1986). A comprehensive critical bibliography, "Sophocles 1939–1959," by Holger Friis Johansen, was published in 1963 in *Lustrum*. No recent exhaustive bibliography exists, but Lesky's *Die Tragische Dichtung der Hellenen* (Göttingen 1972) provides substantial help up to its date of publication. Among the books listed below, those of Segal and Winnington-Ingram have extensive bibliographies of recent criticism.

In the Preface to this edition I mention the influence exerted by anthropological structuralism and the study of Greek religious rituals on recent criticism of Greek tragedy and express reservations about the value of these influences on the overall interpretation of Sophocles' plays. Conspicuous in the relevant critical literature are essays in the volume *Mythe et tragédie en Grèce ancienne*, ed. Jean-Pierre Vernant and Pierre Vidal-Naquet (published as *Myth and Tragedy in Ancient Greece*, trans. Janet Lloyd [New York 1990]), and two books by René Girard, *Violence and the Sacred*, trans. Patrick Gregory (Baltimore 1977) and *The Scapegoat*, trans. Yvonne Freccero (Baltimore 1986). For the criticism of Sophoclean drama the most influential of these is Vernant's essay in *Mythe et tragédie en Grèce ancienne*, "Ambiguité et renversement," an interpretation of *OT*. Although Vernant is correct (as are others) in finding traces of a scapegoat ritual in the play, his emphasis on the presence of this ritual in the play, in what is otherwise an admirable interpretation, apparently misleads him into a complete mistranslation of line 31. The priest, addressing Oedipus on behalf of the Thebans, says that the Thebans regard Oedipus as *ouk isoumenon theoisi* ("not an equal of the gods"); Vernant translates this as "the equal of the gods," and, apparently on the strength of this line, several times in the course of the essay refers to Oedipus as a "divine king," this being what Vernant wishes to find in the play to strengthen the *pharmakos* ("scapegoat") pattern. Girard, in *The Scapegoat*, asserts that "Oedipus limps," thus fulfilling, according to Girard, one of the "stereotypes" of the scapegoat pattern. Girard gives no textual reference for his assertion, which has been made (and rejected) before, but presumably it is made on the strength of lines 1031–1035, where the Corinthian says that Oedipus got his name from the damage to his feet or ankles when he was exposed as an infant. Although the damage is clearly a mark by which Oedipus can be recognized, there is no suggestion anywhere in the play that Oedipus limps. It seems incredible that this basic attribute of the scapegoat—according to Girard—should be ignored if we are meant to see it.

Perhaps the scapegoat pattern is simply too variable to have much specific reference. But it must surely be essential to any such pattern that the scapegoat be expelled from the community. Sophocles seems to leave the future of Oedipus in doubt: Oedipus may or may not be banished later, but so far as the immediate future is concerned, he goes back into the palace at the end of the play, his fate undecided. There are other features of the play that do not correspond in any way to the scapegoat ritual. Walter Burkert observes in a recently published lecture, "Oedipus, Oracles, and Meaning" (published as a pamphlet, Toronto 1991), that although the scapegoat pattern "apparently reveals essential aspects" of the play, "it is far from explaining the whole." Burkert characterizes the pattern as "an introductory device rather than a fundamental principle" of the drama. But since there is no way we can regard Sophocles' Oedipus as a "divine king," the scapegoat pattern, as described by Vernant and Girard, has shortcomings even as an introductory device.

The importance of characterization in Greek tragedy has long been contested, though very few critics deny its significance, especially in Sophoclean drama. A still influential study relevant to the question is John Jones's *On Aristotle and Greek Tragedy* (New York 1962). Jones's principal concern is to stress the primary importance Aristotle assigns in the *Poetics* to plot (*muthos*) and action (*praxis*), and to protest against the emphasis on the character of the "tragic hero" in modern criticism of Greek tragedy. Jones's insistence on the primacy of plot in Aristotle's essay is clearly right, but that does not in itself mean that characterization is unimportant or slight in the plays. Jones speaks of Aristotle's "reverence for dramatic action" (p. 160), and declares that it is wrong to speak of the "tragic hero" as an Aristotelian concept. Most critics interpret Chapter 13 of the *Poetics* as defining the best kind of tragic hero as well as the best kind of tragic action. Jones's objection to this interpretation is that since Aristotle usually refers in Chapter 13 to "men" rather than a single man, it is a misrepresentation of Aristotle's meaning to say that he speaks of the tragic hero's change of fortune rather than simply "the change of fortune" (Jones describes this as a "momentous" shift of meaning [p. 20]). It is true that several times in this passage Aristotle refers to "men," but in the very crucial sentence in which he speaks of the change of fortune he is clearly talking about the fortunes of a single man.

Hence it seems to me that Jones overstates his case, and that it is reasonable to speak of an Aristotelian "tragic hero" provided we understand that the term need not mean "hero" in the modern (and Homeric) sense, but only the principal person of a tragic action (see pp. 16–17, this volume). Jones himself puts the matter more fairly, in my opinion, when he writes, "He is saying that character is included for the sake of action; he is not saying, or he is saying only incidentally, that character is less important than action" (p. 31). The relationship between plot and character described in the *Poetics* is well set forth in the introduction to James Hutton's *Aristotle's Poetics, Translated with an Introduction and Notes* (New York 1982), especially pp. 13–16.

Entretiens sur l'Antiquité classique. Tome XXX; Sophocle. Geneva, 1962.

G. H. Gellie. *Sophocles: A Reading.* Melbourne, 1972.

Bernard M. W. Knox. *The Heroic Temper: Studies in Sophoclean Tragedy.* Berkeley, 1964.

Albert Machin. *Cohérence et continuité dans le théâtre de Sophocle.* Quebec, 1981.

Gilberte Ronnet. *Sophocle, poète tragique.* Paris, 1969.

Charles Segal. *Tragedy and Civilization: An Interpretation of Sophocles.* Cambridge, Mass., 1981.

R. P. Winnington-Ingram. *Sophocles: An Interpretation.* Cambridge, 1980.

Index

A. SOPHOCLEAN PASSAGES DISCUSSED

[Figures at the left of the columns refer to lines in the plays of Sophocles; those at the right, to pages of this volume.]

Ajax

Line	Page	Line	Page	Line	Page
78	255	522	106, 230	952-953	256
79	102	526	104	1036-1037	265, 270
91-93	102	528	218	1071-1088	107
98	72	534	284f.	1091-1092	107, 189n.
100	72	545-582	106	1109-1110	230
101-113	255	582	222	1125	107
113	102, 218	584	223	1125-1126	230
121-122	102	590	265, 266n.	1125-1129	227
121-126	48f.	596-645	182	1134	107, 231
125-126	109	612-613	204n.	1135-1136	72n.
132-133	32, 267	625-626	223n.	1163-1167	189n.
137	281n.	646-692	48, 86, 107, 158, 160	1185-1222	182, 198
148-150	187, 256	651	223	1196	204n.
172-178	264	651-652	104	1214-1215	284
201-256	191	656-659	161	1231	227
254	204n.	658	223, 229	1243-1244	72
293	104	666	161	1248	230
319-322	162	678-683	109	1257	227
348-429	103, 191	679-683	161	1272-1287	108
379-382	256	682-683	109, 231	1275	227
382	103	685-686	266	1282	230
383	103, 265	687-689	218	1334	108
386	103, 187	689-690	161	1334-1335	230
401-403	264	693	200	1335	231, 108
430-480	105	693-718	184n., 185, 194, 198f.	1342	230
441-449	72			1343-1344	108
455-456	264f.	756-757	274n.	1344-1345	230
479-480	105	779	266, 270	1345	231
485	283	784	104	1347	49, 231, 256
485-524	105	808	105, 230	1359	231, 109
489-490	283	815	223	1361-1363	109
504	284	815-865	266	1364-1366	108
506-507	223n.	879-960	191	1367	109
510	106	898-899	229	1395	109
				1400-1401	48

B. AUTHORS